Samuel Phillips

# A
# MEMOIR
OF
# HIS HONOR SAMUEL PHILLIPS, LL. D.

BY

REV. JOHN L. TAYLOR,
ANDOVER, MASS.

"FINIS ORIGINE PENDET."

BOSTON:
CONGREGATIONAL PUBLISHING SOCIETY,
CONGREGATIONAL HOUSE, BEACON ST.

# PREFACE.

THE effort to exhume from the past such relics as may serve to portray, with any degree of justice, the character of one whom his contemporaries rather admired than ventured to describe, is unique. It may seem presumptuous as well as arduous: yet with a fitting subject, it has some peculiar attractions. The antiquarian vein is struck; interesting historical reminiscences blend with it; incidents of the times will reflect their light upon the subject to be sketched in the foreground of the picture; facts worthy of note in topography interweave themselves with it; the causes of things are laid open in the light of their effects; the study of "endless genealogies" will beguile some passing hours; the writer and reader will stand amid the scenes, and inhale the air of ancestral virtues; the pure, the good, the true, will appear in its fine essence, divorced by time from the passions and prejudices to which it was wedded.

Yet, the expediency of such an undertaking must depend upon the urgency of the occasion for it, and the aims with which it is prosecuted. How far these considerations may justly be considered as weighing in the case of this work, the work itself must witness. It has been prepared under advantages of position and relation to the subject which it would be ungrateful not to recognize, while yet impeded by great embarrassments, from incessant interruption and frequent suspension, under the continual pressure of numerous other cares.

Much of the work has been of special delicacy, from its connection with the living as well as the dead. To the various members of the family of Judge Phillips's descendants, and to some others, many acknowledgments are due for their courtesy in furnishing the manuscripts which have been used.

It may be thought that some chapters in the Memoir are too full, and others too brief; or that in some other respect a due proportion has not been preserved between the different topics. It was, however, supposed that not only the proportion, but the order and sequence of the various points as they appear, would on the whole best subserve the chief ends of the volume. So great a departure from a strict chronological arrangement as will be here discovered, and such a grouping of widely scattered facts to illustrate in succession separate phases of the character and life, must be considered in itself undesirable; yet no other method seemed fitted to give such vividness as this, with its occasional repetitions, to one's impression of the extraordinary man to be described, in the great prominence and variety of his characteristics: and no other would allow such freedom as was desired in the occasional interweaving of collateral incidents, or in sketching contemporaneous and kindred personages, as well as events.

Had the book been written for any one class, large portions of it might have been omitted, but as now completed, what may seem a mere incumbrance to one, without interest and worthless, may possibly be of some value to another; there may be a local or a personal interest where it cannot be general. The utmost care has been taken to secure the copy from errors, yet it is not improbable that some will be detected.

In the letter press and embellishments of the work, including the portraits of Judge Phillips and of Lieutenant-Governor William Phillips, the writer has been anxious to give it a dress worthy of the subject, at whatever cost; and the Board of Publication, in their liberality and good taste, have left him nothing to desire, but that they may have their reward.

ANDOVER, September 1. 1856

# CONTENTS.

---

## CHAPTER I.

### ANCESTRY.



## CHAPTER II.

### BIRTH AND CHILDHOOD.



## CHAPTER III.

### ACADEMIC LIFE.



## CHAPTER IV.

### COLLEGE YEARS.

## CHAPTER V.

### MARRIAGE.



## CHAPTER VI.

### PATRIOTISM.



## CHAPTER VII.

### CIVIL SERVICE.

## CHAPTER VIII.

### BUSINESS.



## CHAPTER IX.

### HOME.



## CHAPTER X.

### EDUCATION.

## CHAPTER XI.

### RELIGION.



## CHAPTER XII.

### DECEASE.



---

## APPENDIX.

# MEMOIR.

---

## CHAPTER I.

### THE ANCESTRY OF LIEUTENANT-GOVERNOR SAMUEL PHILLIPS.

"The memory of the just is blessed:" whoever has personally known the late Lieutenant-Governor Samuel Phillips, or has had occasion to study his character and life with much care, must have often been impressed with the vigorous tenacity and freshness with which his name still lives. During his comparatively short but most active and useful life, he with so much individuality, consistency, and symmetry, exhibited the essential traits of an attractive and noble character, that at his death the most affecting and emphatic tributes were paid to him, in every variety of form, from men of all ranks and parties; and it is impossible now, after the lapse of more than half a century, to speak of him to a survivor of that generation, without exciting an outburst of enthusiasm in praise of his rare virtues.

We need not attempt to explain under what influences we have, at this remote day, been drawn into this deep current of interest in him as the study of our leisure hours for many years, growing only more eager as it has been protracted; nor how strongly we have come to feel that there is a manifest call of Divine Providence pressing upon us from without and from within, to undertake, amid all its difficulties, the work of preparing some suitable memorial of so extraördinary a man.

With no wish or design to add any lustre to his name from the circumstance of his honorable lineage, we find grouped prominently around him in the life-picture before us, the portraits of several of his ancestry, and of his contemporary kindred, whom any just view of his character and life would constrain us at intervals in the current of our narrative to sketch, and who are, in themselves, deserving of commemoration with him; yet, in the necessity of selection, while so many of the family name have distinguished themselves, we could properly mark only such for special notice, as, besides their own great merit, stand in the nearest connection with our chief aim, the delineation of his character.

SAMUEL PHILLIPS, the late Lieutenant-Governor, was the *fifth* Samuel in the line of descent from the young son, whom, with a daughter, the *Rev. George*

*Phillips* and his frail wife brought with them to this country on board the ship Arbella, in company with Governor Winthrop, Sir Richard Saltonstall, Rev. John Wilson, Isaac Johnson, Simon Bradstreet, and others, in 1630, landing at Salem on the 12th day of June. The mother of young Samuel, borne down by the hardships of the long voyage, died soon after, and was buried by the side of the Lady Arbella Johnson, in honor of whom their little ship had received its name when the company were setting sail.

In the annals of that early period of our history, no man is honored with more uniform and emphatic expressions of the high consideration in which he was held, than the Rev. George Phillips;[1] in many particulars he reminds us of his worthy descendant the Lieutenant-Governor. Educated at Cambridge, and admitted to holy orders in the Church of England, he was yet so strongly imbued with the spirit of nonconformity as to be ill at ease in his work; and, at the ripe age of thirty-seven, we find him enlisted, heart and hand, in the congenial enterprise of planting the Massachusetts colony. From the moment

[1] He appears to have come over at the expense as well as the solicitation of the company. Governor Winthrop, in rendering his account to the Court of Assistants, September 25, 1634, says, "I disbursed also for the transportacion of Mr. Phillips and his ffamily, which was to be borne by the Generall till hee should be chosen to some particular congregation." — *Records of Mass.*, Vol. I. p. 131.

when he stepped on board the Arbella with his heart's treasures by his side to the day of his death, he was a leader in the councils of the Church and the State. During the voyage he made arrangements for catechizing and preaching regularly, as the virtual pastor of the company; and at an early day after their arrival, notwithstanding his great bereavement in the death of his wife, he went forth with the boldest and hardiest to begin a new settlement at a place on Charles River which they named Watertown. Here, for fourteen years, he expended the wealth of his rare learning, wisdom, and zeal, for the welfare of the town and of the rising Commonwealth, until his sudden death in 1644, at the age of fifty-one.

It is implied in various contemporary notices of him, that in his views of church polity he was a pioneer, for a time far in advance of his brethren in the ministry; having by careful study of the Scriptures early been brought to adopt the main features of Congregationalism, in distinction from the two extremes of Prelacy and Independency. These convictions in regard to ecclesiastical polity made him also a zealous republican in civil affairs; in all the important deliberations and decisions of the colony, in which the well-adjusted fabric of our free government originated, his counsel was sought, and had great weight. Thus, by the force of his own independent and originating character, as well as under the influence of a great popular movement toward full civil and religious liberty, he not only became eminent in his own day, but lives still in the type which he gave to his wide spread and remarkable family, and in the whole civil and religious order of the State which he was so active in founding.[1] At his death, "he was much lamented by his church, who expressed their respect to his memory by educating his eldest son,"[2] *Samuel Phillips,* who was born in 1625, at Boxted, England, the place of his father's early labors in the ministry, and brought to this country when but five years old. He graduated at Harvard College in 1650; and in 1651, was settled in the ministry at Rowley, as colleague of Rev. Ezekiel Rogers, where he continued to labor with great acceptance and usefulness for a period of forty-five years, until his decease, at the age of seventy-one, in 1696.

In 1678, he preached the election sermon before the general court of the province. In 1687, his faithful reproof of iniquity involved him in a temporary persecution, and he was imprisoned "for calling Randolph a wicked man." His piety and talents are spoken of as being "of no common order." His widow, though they had been married from the very commencement of his ministry in 1651, survived him nearly eighteen

[1] See Appendix A.

[2] Allen's Biog. Dic. p. 476. This statement of Allen has been lately questioned. See Bond's Genealogies and History of Watertown, p 874.

years, so that their grandson, *Rev. Samuel Phillips* of Andover, preached her funeral sermon. The original manuscript of this discourse is now in our hands. Of his revered grandmother, the preacher says, "she was an early seeker of God, and spent much of her time daily in reading the word and in prayer. . . . *She took great care of her children's souls;* she could say that which one in ten of God's children could not, namely, *I know the time of my conversion.* She was always humble and penitent; and as she lived, so she died, depending on Christ for righteousness and salvation." This incidental mention of her special religious watchfulness and solicitude in her children's behalf, in connection with the ornament of her own meek and quiet spirit, shows with what unity of counsels and efforts these most estimable parents transmitted to their posterity the type of character to which they had themselves been so carefully trained; so that not only children, but children's children, were rising up and calling them blessed.[1]

Rev. Samuel Phillips, of Andover, their grandson, (in the line of descent from their elder son Samuel, who had settled in business at Salem, while a younger brother, George, devoted himself to study, and entered the ministry,) whom we thus meet at their grave, paying his tribute of affectionate homage to their virtues,

[1] See Appendix B.

here rises before us in character, and mien, and manner of life, which strongly impress us. In his individuality, simplicity, decision, energy, strength, and pristine hardiness of character, he abated nothing from the spirit of his worthy ancestors. He was, like them, also a model of industry, and frugality, and resolute self-restraint, and order, in all that he did. His portrait, which hangs before us, bespeaks a man of authority, born to command, and knowing his birthright; and such was he, in an eminent degree, a conscious and acknowledged leader wherever he was known. Born at Salem, February 17, 1689–90; and graduating at Harvard College in 1708, he was, at the early age of twenty-two, ordained the first pastor of the second church[1] in Andover, on the 17th of October, 1711, the church having been on that day organized in the South Precinct.[2] There is yet living a parishioner of his, hale and vigorous, in the ninety-first year of his good old age,[3] who distinctly remembers the venerable pastor's calls on horseback at his father's door, with madam on a pillion behind him, which was their usual mode of making parochial visits in company. It was his habit, in the regular services of the sabbath,

[1] The present Old South Church.

[2] See Appendix C.

[3] Mr. Moses Abbott, born November 30, 1765, and baptized by Rev. Mr. Phillips, the Lord's day following, December 1.

to preach to the full hour's end, measuring his discourse by the sands of the glass at his side. One tenth of his scanty income he regularly and religiously gave to the poor, or to other objects of charity; and out of his estate at his death he bequeathed one hundred pounds in trust for the benefit of the poor in the church of which he had been pastor, and one hundred pounds "for y$^e$ pious and charitable use of propagating Christian knowledge among the Indians of North America." His will, making bequests in detail to these charitable objects, and to his wife, children, and grandchildren, and executed when he was seventy-four years of age, is remarkably minute and exact in its specifications, closing with these characteristic words, expressive of the spirit which he had sought, and still wished, to breathe into his children: —

> "And now my desire and prayer is y$^t$ my s$^d$ three sons may continue to live in love, and y$^t$ they still behave respectfully and dutifully towards their aged tender and good mother, even unto the end; and y$^t$ they go on to shew kindness to y$^e$ motherless children of their beloved sister Lydia; and, in a word, that they make it their care to be found in Christ, and to serve their generation according to y$^e$ will of God, by doing good as they shall have opportunity unto all men, and especially to y$^e$ household of faith; as knowing y$^t$ it is more blessed to give than to receive."

This "aged tender and good mother," the "daughter of the worshipful John White, Esq., of Haverhill," survived him only about two years, expiring in the bosom of her son Samuel's family, January 7, 1773; the Rev. Mr. Phillips himself having deceased June 5, 1771, at the age of eighty-one, after a pastorate but little short of sixty years, and a ministry of nearly sixty-two years, with the same people, and without a colleague, retaining his vigor and his commanding hold upon the respect and affection of his people to the last. During the course of his ministry, he published numerous occasional sermons, which evince his ability and faithfulness. In accordance with his methodical exactness in every thing, his discourses, as preached to his people year after year, were all carefully numbered and filed away in successive volumes, large numbers of which are still preserved; his handwriting, even to the latest stroke of his pen, was remarkably neat and legible, though often in extremely small characters, never giving any indications of haste or of carelessness. In passing from the parsonage to the meeting-house for divine worship on the sabbath, as remembered now by eye-witnesses, flanked by his black body servant on the left, and by madam and her servant and the children on the right, his movements were precise and stately, as became his ideal of the ministerial office; and when he entered the sanctuary, it was in meet reverence for the man of God, as well as in compliance with the old custom of the day, that the whole congregation rose and stood before him until he had seated himself in the pulpit. So he lived and passed away; worthy to be esteemed by his people, as Mather tells us his ancestor at Watertown was, "the irrefragable doctor."[1]

The three sons mentioned in his will, as referred to above, *Samuel, John,* and *William,*[2] had already, even before his decease, by their own energy and sagacity, won for themselves a prominent place in society, and were now, in the prime of life, showing the far-reaching power of that exact yet liberal and high-toned discipline to which he had subjected them. The sketch which these will successively claim at our hands, is reserved for a later stage of our narrative; and we pass now to the chief subject of this memoir, the grandson of Rev. Samuel Phillips of Andover, (in the line of his eldest son Samuel, also of Andover,) *His Honor*, SAMUEL PHILLIPS, *the Lieutenant-Governor.*

[1] Magnalia, Book III. p. 84.

[2] See Appendix C.

# CHAPTER II.

## HIS BIRTH AND CHILDHOOD.

It will be seen from the preceding brief statements, that there descended upon his young spirit, at his birth, the richest legacy of ancestral virtues and memories. How far he was touched by the inspiration of such an influence, and how worthily he reflected and transmitted it, not only undiminished but in even fairer lustre, the story of his life will testify, though wanting the breadth and power of that life itself as it was everywhere impressed upon his times.

He was the son of Samuel and Elizabeth Phillips, of Andover, born February 5, 1752; the youngest but one of seven children, and the only one that lived to adult age.[1] It was at the beginning of this year that the change in our calendar was made by an Act of Parliament, from the Old Style to the New Style,[2] which may explain the discrepancies in different notices of the date of his birth. The house in which he was born is still in the family, occupied by the widow

[1] See Appendix D: —

[2] Holmes's Annals, Vol. II. p. 189.

and daughters of his elder son;[1] a spacious and venerable mansion, with few marks of the century of winters that have beaten upon it. At the birth of young Samuel this home had just been completed; the family having removed to it from their old house only two or three weeks before. It was in a portion of this edifice that his father continued his business as a merchant, adding, year after year, to the very considerable fortune which he had received with the hand of Miss Barnard[2] as his bride. At that time, this portion of Andover could scarcely be called a village, and the mansion and store of Mr. Phillips were the centre of resort for a wide spread agricultural community in the region which embraces much the richest lands of the ancient town. The native deer were then

[1] Several months after these pages were written, and when they were nearly ready for the press, Mrs. Phillips was called to her final rest. It had been one cherished hope with us, that we might contribute to her gratification, in this effort to commemorate those whom she so much revered and loved; but instead of this, her decease has reminded us, as we have gone with others down to the family tomb and gazed on the garnered dust of those whose names we seek to honor, how soon every one who could aid us, as she did by invaluable personal reminiscences, must be numbered with the dead. That the work we have undertaken was begun before the last relic of that generation was removed, is well; but we can never cease to regret that it was commenced so late.

[2] Elizabeth Barnard, daughter of Theodore Barnard, and granddaughter of Rev. Thomas Barnard.

roaming abundant in the forests of the town, and deer-reeves were annually appointed, as regularly as the selectmen, as they were elsewhere in the province. It was amid such rural quiet, industry, thrift, and beauty, with the variety and quickening stimulus of merchant life at home, under the eye and borne upon the chastened heart of the tenderest parental watchfulness, that the early days of young Phillips opened.

Yet in contrast with these daily home scenes, there was another current of influence pouring in upon his child-life, which, as subsequent events show, strongly impressed and tinged his character. The continued encroachments of the French were now precipitating a decisive rupture between them and England; and soon the old French war, as it is commonly termed, broke out. For ten years the excitement of this contest continued to agitate the country, the citizens of Massachusetts being ever foremost in zeal for the common liberty and safety. The summer of 1755, when Samuel was a child of three years, was the era of Braddock's defeat, of the capture of Nova Scotia by the Massachusetts forces, and the repulse of Baron Dieskau on the banks of Lake George,[1] so that the earliest and most exciting stories which fired his imagination were of war,—war, not in the spirit of con-

[1] Holmes's Annals, Vol. II. p. 204–217.

quest or military glory, but in the calm energy of patriotism, — war for the soil and the institutions of his country, — for hearth, home, liberty, and life itself. His father was every inch a patriot; a man to feel strongly but calmly every great bearing of such a struggle, and by word and deed to impart his spirit to the son of his hopes. As the strife wore on with varying fortunes through the whole period of his childhood, the name of Washington was continually heralded to him as the rising star of hope, to be cherished only with increasing veneration every succeeding year.

In these early but long continued impressions, we find the origin and explanation of traits in his character, and of enterprises in his life, which had well nigh made him simply a bold revolutionary statesman, or a brave military leader. Yet the ancestral bias in the family toward a literary life, together with his frail constitution, which seemed unsuited to physical hardship, would appear to have countervailed, in a good degree, all such attractions of the forum or the camp. The fact, too, that his parents had been called to bury all their other children, made him an object of special tenderness. While, therefore, by the whole force of their own simple, exact, frugal, busy life, they were training him up a gentle, amiable, active, winning boy, fond of business and of books, the plan of giving him a liberal education, as his most congenial line of life, was early matured.

To be an only child, intent on manly studies, in a family of the strictest method in all its life, could hardly fail to make one sedate, grave, orderly, and manlike beyond his years,—and least of all, a boy of his temperament. Had the glee of brothers and sisters rung often in his ears, to keep alive the freshness of boy nature; had the goodly home been more astir with childish chat and incident,—the parents looking ever gladly on the full circle, instead of meekly bowing to their desolate lot,—this darling son would, we cannot doubt, have been longer a child and later a man; he might also have been more robust, under the stimulus of sports and gambols that invigorate the frame, as well as of emotions that swell every nerve and muscle with the fire of their own life. But the good hand of Providence had not so ordered his path.

Growing up in comparative solitariness,—his companions not only in the main his elders, but his revered parents, who were now approaching the meridian of life, wearing the subdued expression of mourners, and proverbial for the strictness of their habits,—it would have been little less than a miracle, if he had not soon come to be spoken of as an uncommonly grave and considerate boy; a remarkably systematic, industrious, mature child, full of bright promise in kindred virtues for the future.

With such marked traits, early germinating, and as

rare in degree as in kind, he appears to have prepared the way in his very boyhood for that self-consistent ascendency, which, in his opening manhood, he had gained over his father and other relatives. He had not gone out from under the parental roof before the elements of his character, as afterwards perfected, were distinctly visible; and from what he was then, a boy of a dozen summers, he never departed an iota, except to add virtue to virtue.

From his father alone he might have received, in both constitution and education, his early habits of prudence and exactness, his deep sense of justice, his patriotic impulses, his tenacity of purpose, and his admirable self-government; but from his mother, it is said, he inherited the fire which glowed in all these virtues, the nervous restlessness, which not only impelled but in the end consumed him, the enterprise, the fertility of invention, the self-immolating spirit, and withal the serenity and suavity of manner with which he spent himself in the various plans of his life. From both he drew the strength of a calm, practical, devout, religious faith.

# CHAPTER III.

## HIS PREPARATION FOR COLLEGE.

At the age of thirteen, in the spring of 1765, he repaired to Dummer Academy, in Byfield, (which had been established in 1763, in accordance with the will of Lieutenant-Governor William Dummer, devising his estate for that purpose,)[1] and commenced fitting for college under the instruction of Samuel Moody, Esq. Here, one who had the best means of information respecting him says, "his proficiency, his manliness and sobriety and regular conduct, secured the esteem and confidence of his instructor and fellow-students."[2]

His health, however, was not firm; in a letter to his mother, dated June 25, 1765, he speaks of a complaint under which he had suffered as subsiding, and adds: —

[1] This Academy was not incorporated until October 3, 1782, two years later than Phillips Academy, at Andover, and more than a year after Phillips Exeter Academy.

[2] Mr. Abbot, in his History of Andover, p. 144.

"I have asked Mr. Moody about boarding with him, but he is so full at present that he is not determined; shall depend upon your coming this week, or at farthest the beginning of next week; the horse is orderly, I should have sent him by Jonathan Gage, but he came in a chair and could not lead him. I could have brought him home a Saturday, but you said, if Oliver did not come, I need not concern myself any thing about it; should be exceeding glad to see you as soon as possible. Mr. Moody gives his compliments to father, and thinks that it is very necessary that I should have a horse here, considering my health, and the heat of the season."

This letter, which is the earliest we have been able to obtain from his hand, is subscribed Samuel Phillips 3d, his aged grandfather having lived until a few weeks before he graduated from college. The handwriting is here unformed, but plain, and it is interesting to notice how by an occasional erasure or interlineation the diction is improved, showing at what an early period he began to pay special attention to his style.

While connected with the Academy his religious character, as well as his mental discipline, was maturing rapidly; so that, when admitted to college, it was with the best safeguard against its temptations, and an eager desire to profit by its advantages; although his public profession of religion was deferred until his Junior year in college, when he was admitted to the church of which his father was then deacon, in North Andover, February 3, 1770. When this step was taken, as it was the result of long deliberation, so as the record shows he did not shrink from standing *alone* in it, before all who had known him from his birth.

# CHAPTER IV.

## HIS COLLEGIATE LIFE.

FROM the Academy he was transferred directly to the University at Cambridge, when but fifteen years old, where his father, his uncle John, his grandfather Samuel, his great-great-uncle George, and his great-great-grandfather Samuel Phillips, had been educated before him. "He entered college," we are assured, as we should have predicted, "with a habit of application and order, and with a high sense of moral feeling and love of learning."[1]

When his class graduated in 1771, it was much the largest that had ever gone forth from the institution, and none so large left it again until 1810. It was also distinguished, then and afterwards, as a class, for talent as well as numbers. Hon. James Bowdoin, afterwards United States minister to Spain, David Parsons, David Tappan, Zedekiah Sanger, David Osgood, Jonathan French, all of whom became eminent as ministers of the gospel, Winthrop Sargent, subsequently governor of Mississippi, and John Warren, the first

[1] History of Andover, p. 144.

Hersey Professor of Anatomy and Surgery in the College, were among his class mates, and some of them his most intimate friends.

In those days the members of a class were arranged, at their exercises and on the catalogue, not alphabetically, nor according to their relative scholarship, but in conformity with the current family rank of the students. It is an honorable testimony to the consideration in which his father was held, that in a class of sixty-three the name of his son should stand, as it does, the seventh; evidence, too, of the weight which was then attached to the question of rank, as also of this father's tenacity in maintaining his rights, is given in the circumstance that the Faculty of the College who had at first made young Phillips's grade the eighth, were constrained by his father's energetic protest and appeal, to modify their decision by a formal vote, and place him one name higher![1] — a transaction so peculiar and alien to the then dawning republicanism of the times, as to have led to the disuse of this artificial system of designating rank, soon after he graduated, when a new President of the College had been inaugurated.

During the college life of young Phillips, there is abundant traditional and documentary testimony to his

[1] See Appendix E. Also Quincy's Hist. H. U. Vol. II. p. 157–158.

great diligence, and his eminent position as a scholar. It is reported to us, as the unanimous testimony of his school mates in early life, that he was naturally slow to learn, but incessant in his application, and of an exceedingly tenacious memory; so that his studiousness made ample amends for any want of native quickness of parts. The fragment of a brief journal, mainly religious, which he kept, covering more than two years of his collegiate course, is still preserved, in which there are frequent references to the value which he set upon his opportunities, but especially upon *time;* expressed, ordinarily, in the form of humble self-reproach, thus: —

"February 25, 1768. — I am confounded when I think of my misimprovement of my time."

"April 3, 1769. — Have improved my time better than sometimes, tho' have misspent a vast deal of it, especially evenings by sleeping; but with deeper concern I may inquire, how I have neglected my soul's concern. The children of Christ can be known only by their fruits; and what fruit have I brought forth? have I not great reason to fear that I am not a Christian, that I have nothing but a profession? Let me be fervent in my petitions for the Divine assistance, and diligent in my watchfulness to guard against sin."

"May 13, 1769. — Time once gone, is gone for ever. We take no notice of it, but by its loss; how short! and of what vast importance is a diligent improvement of it."

"November 25, 1769. — I am very thankful I went to Boston, for by that means, I escaped being in a great confusion in the hall; such revelling is most unfit for a day for offering the sacrifices of thankful hearts to the Great Benefactor.

"This week I have been more diligent than any other before since I came down, but have let slip many precious moments unimproved."

These reiterated and intense upbraidings, instead of being evidence of any special misimprovement of his time and opportunities, show us rather how keenly he had already learned to feel the loss of a single golden hour,—how resolutely he was holding himself to the best possible use of every moment,—and we shall see that this high sense of the worth of time grew ere long into a consuming passion with him.

When chastening his spirit and desponding under his sense of defect in this manner, a line from his gentle mother would sometimes come to calm him, by directing him to the true source of rest. She writes, March 7, 1768:—

"I hope your various employments won't take your mind from the things of the greatest moment; there is no compare between time and eternite, between the favour of God and the friendship of the world. You are in the midst of temptations, enemies within as well as enemies without. I commit you to the care of a kind Providence,—keep your mind easy, it will be much for your advantage upon all accounts; endeavour to conduct so as to lay no foundation for uneasiness.

"I remain your ever affectionate mother,

ELIZABETH PHILLIPS."

His intense jealousy of himself in regard to the use of time, although one of his most prominent characteristics at this period, was blended with a kindred self-scrutiny in regard to his manners, his morals, his interior religious life, his controlling aims and motives, which in one yet so young are very extraordinary. How much, for example, is indicated by the following brief paragraphs in his journal.

"August 28, 1768. — I am now beginning another week; may I be enabled to perform in the best manner (for a frail creature) my duty to God, my fellow-creatures, and myself."

"September 17, 1768. — The week past my father and mother were at Boston, and on Thursday I went to Boston, when my father bought for me several books; how thankful should I be for these favors! How ought my soul to expand with gratitude, and in what better manner can I demonstrate it than by a virtuous, studious life! How can I answer it, if I neglect these golden seasons; now is the time, and the only time, to gain those accomplishments, on which my future usefulness will in a great measure depend."

"December 10, 1768. — I have heard my grandfather this week was so indisposed that it was not supposed he would get about again; may I make it my business to be prepared for the agonies of dissolving nature."

"December 17, 1768. — This week I have seen my father; it refreshed my spirits. What an affection there is between father and son, which nothing but death can dissolve! but is my soul so attached to my Heavenly Father? My heart often expands with gratitude for his liberality, but do I meditate on my continual uninterrupted obligations to the Father of lights? It is to him I am indebted for the favors I receive from my earthly parents."

"February 25, 1769.—Have enjoyed less tranquillity of mind since I left home than any term before. My great foible is a readiness to open my soul; to-day my chum and I had some variance about his birthday, but I hope that maxim, in this instance, will prove true, 'the falling out of lovers is the renewing of love.'"

"March 11, 1769.—How cautious should we be of giving causes of offence to one another! Whereby can the children of God more distinguish themselves than by a meek, loving, forgiving temper towards each other?"

"March 25, 1769.—Last Monday evening was observed here as the anniversary of the repeal of the Stamp Act; but the fatigue that I experienced therefor is folly; I have misspent a vast deal of precious time."

"August 19, 1769.—I have spent this vacancy very differently from my purpose; made no addition to my little stock of knowledge, only gained a little farther knowledge of the world."

"December 9, 1769.—Many valuable thoughts are gone entirely, for want of proper care to lay them up or fix them in the noble repository of the soul."

What various and pithy utterances for a youth of seventeen years! But young and self-distrusting as he was, in that large class he held at this time an acknowledged ascendency. In a notice of him, written soon after his death, it is said[1] of his character and influence in college,—

[1] Eliot's Biog. Dic. p. 378, 379.

"His conduct was peculiarly correct and exemplary. He was much esteemed by his fellow-students, as well as by the officers of the society. Among the ingenuous youth of the University, were certain associations for practical improvement and usefulness. They consisted generally of good scholars, who combined good principles and pure morals, with an ambition to shine as sons of knowledge. At the head of these, and among the most active, was Phillips, whose name and character were often mentioned to stimulate others to adorn their own lives."

His intimate friend and class mate, Dr. Tappan, in his discourse at the funeral, says:—

"While a member of the University, he was a model and patron, not only of literary industry, dignified manners, and the purest morals, but of devout, ardent, yet rational piety. He there displayed that capacity and zeal for useful projects, which remarkably distinguished his future life. He was either a founder or leading member of three select associations, devoted to scientific or patriotic pursuits. He also earnestly promoted, and ably assisted in a society formed for religious and moral improvement. In the meetings of the society, he gave striking proofs of his proficiency in divine wisdom, especially in the gift and spirit of prayer." [1]

The end of such a diligent, exemplary, and useful collegiate course, could not well be unnoticed or unhonored. It was, as indeed the entire period of his University life had been, an era of alarm and agita-

[1] Page 10.

tion. The established round of college exercises had been often disturbed, and so far as can be learned, if, on taking his degree and in the previous years, he was specially honored in the exhibitions, there is no record of the appointments; yet, as in the case of his college journal, the fragment — evidently nearly the whole — of a salutatory oration in Latin is preserved, which he appears to have delivered on his Commencement day. The oration is carefully composed, and in its graceful references to President Holyoke, then deceased, but filially commemorated, to Professors Winthrop, Wigglesworth, and Sewall, and to his tutors and class mates, spoken after his manner, with a calm earnestness and sincerity, together with the hearty encomium which, both in his exordium and his peroration, he bestows upon the College itself, must have been warmly applauded.

In anticipation of his most honorable appearance in this part, as well as on other grounds connected with the custom of the day and with his social position, we find him, in the following letter, conferring with his father in reference to providing an entertainment for his friends upon the occasion. The highly deferential tone of the letter, on his part, is not less honorable to him, than the evidence it furnishes of his rank as a scholar, and of his father's unwillingness to determine the question, without first obtaining his own considerate views.

"CAMBRIDGE, May 27, 1771.

"HONORED SIR, — That period is just at hand which I have been looking for with trembling this long time, but its nearer approach raises a greater solicitude concerning the event. You, sir, at our last interview, seemed undetermined in what manner to conduct my Commencement, and repeatedly inquired my opinion. I found the same difficulty of proposing any thing that I feared would not be perfectly agreeable to my father, that I always did; indeed, in this case I could not offer so much violence to myself as to do it. But concluding it would give him pain not to know his son's inclination, I can't excuse myself, if I do n't acquaint him of it with some of my reasons, that he may have an opportunity, should he disapprove of my sentiments, to show the impropriety of them by the suggestion of those more weighty arguments, which his superior wisdom shall dictate. You asked me, sir, whether we could be accommodated in town? I would answer, there is no doubt of it; and further, it is generally (I do n't know but universally) imagined that there would be no difficulty from the government of the College; for instances of the kind were taken *no* notice of last year. And now, sir, if I could be persuaded this would be agreeable to my father, I would make no hesitation to inform him it would be agreeable to his son's wish.

"And, in the first place, I can't discern but there is a propriety in the nature of the thing, for in any joyful event there seems to be great fitness in calling in our friends to rejoice with us, as well as to desire their attendance when under the cloud, to impart the tear of sympathy; of this opinion have been the most venerable of our fathers, as they have evidenced in similar circumstances, and, indeed, in the very same; and among the many respectable characters that I might mention under this class, whom could I better place at the head, than the former worthy Judge Foxcroft, my uncle Phillips, Mr. Bromfield, and the like?

"That this is a time to rejoice I think I may venture to say; for (*thro' the goodness of God*) I do n't know how I could have made a more honorable egress, than I have a prospect of making, if we take into consideration the whole term of my residence. Many instances present themselves in Holy Writ, of eminent servants, who assembled their friends to partake with them in the happiness of any prosperity. Some of the other sex seem to be so connected, that it is hardly possible to avoid inviting them, but it is clear that they *cannot* be made comfortable in College; then if a place is provided in town on their accounts, others seem to expect it upon good grounds, and, indeed, will upon their own accounts; those, especially, who have so often and so handsomely repeated their invitations on the same occasion. (The bearer waits.)

Whether your circumstances don't raise such an expectation in the minds of all your connections? — especially, as this is the *only* opportunity you can have to show regard to friends on the same occasion: — I do n't mention the advantage to myself, just at entering the world. The cost, I know, will be great; but why is wealth given, but to be used in a lawful and proper way? After all, sir, with all the duty and veneration that a son can show, this subject is rested with that wisdom which is ever a rule to *him* who infallibly wishes to act agreeably to his kind father.

"Duty and love, sir, if you please.

"S. P."

We know not what response was made to this representation; but a discerning father could not fail to be pleased with such a letter from his only son, so filial in every line, expressed with so much carefulness and tact, and so winning in its modest tone, at an hour when the ardor of youth might without censure have written in a more eager, if not imperative, strain.

With such propitious auguries, he went forth from his literary home at the age of nineteen years, bearing with him not only the mental discipline of which he soon began to make such use in public, but impressions and impulses derived from the peculiar circumstances of his college life, as well as deep-seated traits of character, which at once gave direction to all his plans.

# CHAPTER V.

## HIS MARRIAGE.

BEFORE his sun had set in Cambridge one star shone out in the clear sky, which was to his eye evermore the brightest and best. It was here that, for term after term, he had met Miss Phœbe Foxcroft, the youngest daughter of Hon. Francis Foxcroft. Their Sabbath worship was at the same church, under the ministry of the venerable Dr. Appleton; they were soon personal friends, intimate friends; but who would have anticipated that they could have any interest in each other beyond this? She was nearly nine years his senior,[1] highly cultivated in mind and manners, the very centre of an attractive and courted circle, sprightly, ardent, sanguine: he was sedate, considerate, intent on preparation for full manhood, rather than conscious of his manliness, and must have deemed himself extremely youthful before her, notwithstanding her constitutional vivacity. Yet, in spite of this great disparity, their acquaintance ripened into a devoted and lasting mutual affection.

[1] She was born August 12, 1743.

It does honor to her sagacity, that she should have so soon seen in that frail youth, the type of rare manliness which she could respect and honor in him as her husband; and our confidence in his discernment, which falters at first when we see him thus early even so much as entertaining the question of such an alliance, is not abated but enhanced, as we find him calmly setting every adverse consideration aside, and reaching the conclusion that she was preëminently fitted to be his wife. For in truth the disparity was rather apparent than real. When he was but eighteen and she nearly twenty-seven, she was, in every thing but years, the younger of the two; and so she always appeared after their union; while, with much diversity in their distinguishing characteristics, they were eminently congenial spirits.

The knowledge of this attachment fell heavily upon the heart of his parents. They saw and felt keenly the objections, on the score of age, — and these were the only objections, — to such a connection, while he who had weighed them all and set them aside, was now hoping for an early marriage. A steady refusal to consent to the union, and even a demand that the connection should cease to be thought of, was all that he could obtain from his father; and he was too dutiful not to yield, however great the sacrifice.

It was with this bitter weight on his spirit, in other

respects so glad, that he left the college. For a time, he struggled against the deep current of his feelings and judgment, if so be he could possibly ere long forget her, and she him; but in health his spirits were depressed, and in sickness his wounded heart was his worst malady. It was in an hour of deep solicitude for him, when there were but faint hopes of his life, that his parents, who had not been sensible, till his physician then told them, how deeply he had suffered on account of their opposition, consented to yield; and after two years delay, the marriage was consummated, in 1773. The correspondence by which they gladdened or solaced each other during these years of trial, prior to their union, is still, to a large extent, preserved in the family, full, it is said, of the incident and the romance of their unique position, but so religiously kept, as it should be from all eyes, that we have not even asked to see it.

Without any more interior view of the case than is here given, it is easy to see that he was, in all this experience, drifting upon a strong current away from the life of study, which, as an educated, scholarly young man, we should say, now opened before him. He seems to us, as his words ring out upon the stage on that Commencement day, the very model of a candidate for the bench, if not the bar, or for the pulpit. He will surely, we think, be eminent, too, in his profession; and so he might have been, nay, probably would have been, notwithstanding any thing we have yet seen, had not other influences also here been pressing as strongly upon him, to throw him upon a widely different career.

# CHAPTER VI.

## HIS PART IN THE REVOLUTION.

DURING the whole period of his college life, Cambridge was the very focus of all patriotic sentiment and agitation in the country; as it had been indeed prior to this, and continued to be afterwards. Mr. Everett says:—

"If, in any other quarter of the globe it has been objected to seats of learning, that they nourish a spirit of dependence on power, such has never been the reproach of our Alma Mater. Owing much, at every period before the Revolution, to the munificence of individuals in the mother country, it never was indebted to the Crown for a dollar or a book. No court favor was ever bestowed, and no court lesson ever learned. Generation after generation went forth from her lecture-rooms, armed in all the panoply of truth, to wage the battles of principle, alike under the old charter and the new; and, when the fulness of time was come, and the great contest approached, the first note of preparation was sounded from Harvard Hall.

"Yes, before the Stamp-Act was passed; yes, before Committees of Correspondence were established throughout the colonies; before Otis had shaken the courts with his forensic thunders; before a breath of defiance had whispered along the arches of Faneuil Hall, a graduate of Harvard College announced in his Thesis, on Commencement day, the whole doctrine of the Revolution. Yes, in the very dawn of independence, while the lions of the land yet lay slumbering in the long shadows of the throne, an eaglet, bred in the delicate air of freedom which fanned the academic groves, had from his 'coigne of vantage' on yonder tower, drunk the first rosy sparkle of the sun of liberty into his calm, undazzled eye, and whetted his talons for the conflict.

"Within the short space of twenty-three years, there were graduated at Harvard College six men, who exercised an influence over the country's destinies, which no time shall outlive. Within that brief period, there went forth from yonder walls, James Otis, John Hancock, Joseph Warren, Josiah Quincy, besides Samuel and John Adams, '*geminos duo fulmina belli.*' Yes, fellow-students, if our college had done nothing else than educate Samuel Adams, who in 1743, on taking his second degree maintained the thesis, that it is lawful to resist the chief magistrate, if the State cannot otherwise be preserved; — or James Otis, who by his argument on Writs of Assistance, in the words of one[1] well authorized to express an opinion, 'first breathed the breath of life into the cause of American freedom;' — or John Hancock, the patriot merchant, who offered his fortune a sacrifice to the country, and placed his name first to the Declaration of her Independence; — or John Adams, 'the colossus who sustained the Declaration in debate;' — or Josiah Quincy, (your honored father, Mr. President,) who in 1774, wrote

[1] The elder President Adams.

to his countrymen from London, 'that they must seal their testimony with their blood;' — or Warren, who, on yonder sacred heights, made haste to obey that awful injunction; — had Harvard College done no more than train up any one of these great men to the country's service, what title could it need to the world's gratitude and admiration?"[1]

When the troops were paraded on the Common at Cambridge, on the evening of the 16th of June, 1775, prior to their marching to occupy Bunker Hill, President Langdon offered "a fervent and impressive prayer," invoking the Divine favor upon the momentous expedition. At the inauguration of President Willard in 1781, when the issue of the great contest was no longer doubtful, Governor Hancock in his speech, called the College "in some sense the parent and nurse of the late happy Revolution in this Commonwealth;"[2] and while the struggle was in progress, the entire college community, officers and students, became, in a remarkable degree, identified with it. We find this entry in the journal of Mr. Phillips, among other indications of the prevailing college spirit.

"October 2, 1768. — Last Tuesday night the Senior and Junior classes met, and voted to use no tea of foreign production, till they should see fit to recall the vote. On Wednes-

[1] Address to the Alumni, at the Centennial Celebration, 1836.

[2] Quincy's History of Harvard University, Vol. II. p. 244.

day night the Sophomores and Freshmen voted the same, though there were some in each class that dissented and were very resolute."

When the legislature, in 1769, could not longer, with due regard to its own dignity and freedom, sit in Boston, because of the presence of the king's troops, it was promptly adjourned to Cambridge, and held its sessions in the College Chapel.

In the journal of Mr. Phillips, who was then in the second year of his college course, repeated references are made to these sittings of the General Court.

"June 17, 1769. — Thursday, the General Court was adjourned to meet on Friday at Cambridge." — "July 1. — My father got to court some time before it sat, which was to have been at 9 or 10 o'clock. The Court received a message from His Excellency, specifying the business which he advised the House to proceed upon, that so their inactivity might not by any means be charged upon him; at the head of the particulars, the necessity that care should be taken for the administration of government; after long debates upon it, they voted unanimously (the speaker not excepted) not to grant his salary." — "July 8. — This week the Court have continued sitting; voted not to grant the governor his salary for the present, not to chuse an agent in America or Great Britain, — passed a number of spirited Resolves, etc."

It was at just this period, when the patriot legislature was here making its stand for freedom, that President Holyoke died, (of whose funeral Mr. Phillips gives a minute account,) and President Locke was chosen in his place, partly, if not mainly, because he was "a friend to liberty;" as we are assured that "at this period no individual, not known to be favorable to the popular cause, could have been elected President, whatever might have been his literary qualifications."[1] In fact the Provincial Congress had, in September, 1775, ordered a committee to bring in a resolve, recommending to the Corporation and Overseers of the College, "not to appoint any person as Governor or Instructor, but such whose political principles they can depend upon, and to inquire into the principles of such as are now in office, and dismiss those who are not friendly to the country;" and the Resolve passed.[2]

The year previous to this election, according to Mr. Quincy, (1768,) "when the patronage of American manufactures was the test of patriotism, the students of the senior class unanimously voted 'to take their degrees in the manufactures of the country.' This resolution was publicly applauded in the journals of the day, as reflecting the highest honor on the College; and at the ensuing Commencement, in July, the class came dressed accordingly, in American manufactures, and were permitted by the governors of the College

[1] Quincy's History Harvard University, Vol. II. p. 150, 151.

[2] See Journal of the Congress, p. 134.

to appear in them on the stage, when they took their degrees." A letter from Rev. Andrew Eliot to Thomas Hollis, gives the following account of the effects of the political excitements of the times on the students.

> "The removal of the General Court to Cambridge hinders the scholars in their studies. The young gentlemen are already taken up with politics. They have caught the spirit of the times. Their declamations and forensic disputes breathe the spirit of liberty. This has always been encouraged, but they have sometimes been wrought up to such a pitch of enthusiasm, that it has been difficult for their tutors to keep them within due bounds; but their tutors are fearful of giving too great a check to a disposition which may, hereafter, fill the country with patriots, and choose to leave it to age and experience to check their ardor." [1]

In 1770, also, as well as in 1769, the legislature sat in Cambridge, thus continuing to fan the patriotic flame with which it had fired the students; and through all this period, the insolence of British tyranny in Boston, which had driven the General Court to this dignified retreat, was kindling the spirit of indignation, as well as the spirit of liberty; every pulsation of which throbbed quick through the college artery, as it beat strong in the city heart.

In June, 1768, Governor Bernard had summarily dissolved the General Court because of its patriotic

[1] Quincy's History Harvard University, p. 163.

firmness in resisting the encroachments of the Crown; the selectmen of Boston instantly concerted measures to secure a convention of delegates from the several towns in the Commonwealth, "to deliberate on constitutional measures to obtain redress of their grievances;" in September this assembly, composed of "committees" from ninety-six towns and eight districts, met, and after disclaiming all legislative authority, "petitioned the governor; made loyal professions; expressed their aversion to standing armies, to tumults and disorders, their readiness to assist in suppressing riots and preserving the peace; recommended patience and good order; and, after a short session, dissolved."[1]

The father of Mr. Phillips was an active member of this convention, stimulating his son's zeal in the cause of liberty, not less than his own, by his participation in such counsels. It was on spirits already so excited and sensitive, that the news of an approaching British armament fell like an electric shock. The very next day after the convention rose, "two British regiments escorted by seven armed vessels, arrived at Boston from Halifax."[2] Dr. Holmes says: —

"The fleet having taken a station which commanded the town, the troops, under cover of the cannon of the ships,

[1] Holmes's Annals, Vol. II. p. 285.

[2] Works of John Adams, by his grandson, Charles Francis Adams, Vol. II. p. 213.

landed without molestation, and to the number of upward of seven hundred men, marched with muskets charged, bayonets fixed, martial music, and the usual military parade, into the Common. In the evening, the selectmen of Boston were required to quarter the two regiments in the town; but they absolutely refused. A temporary shelter, however, in Faneuil Hall, was permitted to one regiment, that was without its camp equipage. The next day, the State house, by order of the governor, was opened for the reception of the soldiers; and, after the quarters were settled, two field-pieces with the main guard were stationed just in front. Every thing was calculated to excite the indignation of the inhabitants. The lower floor of the State house, which had been used by gentlemen and merchants as an exchange, the representatives' chamber, the court house, Faneuil Hall, — places with which were intimately associated ideas of justice and freedom, as well as of convenience and utility, — were now filled with regular soldiers. Guards were placed at the doors of the State house, through which the council must pass in going to their own chamber. The Common was covered with tents. Soldiers were constantly marching and countermarching to relieve the guards. The sentinels challenged the inhabitants as they passed. The Lord's day was profaned, and the devotion of the sanctuary disturbed, by the sound of drums and other military music." [1]

Mr. Phillips's account of this exciting event, as entered in his journal, is: —

[1] Holmes's Annals, Vol. II. 285–86. Also, Memoir of Josiah Quincy, Jr., by his son, p. 17, 18.

"October 1, 1768. — This week two regiments came to Boston. The governor called the council together, that there might be provision made for the regiments in Boston; but the council told him it was in the face of an Act of Parliament, to make any provision for his majesty's troops before the barracks at the castle were full, and that they imagined the barracks sufficient to contain all that were coming; — which occasioned warm words, but the council would not yield. This day about one thousand men came ashore prepared in the best manner for a fight, after the men-of-war had surrounded the town, their great guns charged with chain-shot."

It will be seen, by comparing dates, that on the Tuesday and Wednesday following, the students passed their spirited votes already cited, not to use any more tea. Later in the month, Mr. Phillips says, "I saw the regiments and heard of their hardships;" so impossible was it for the royal governor to enforce his demands for their accommodation.

In November a portion of two other regiments arrived. The Legislature, as we have already seen, indignantly refusing to sit during the two succeeding years in the State house thus invaded, and in the vicinity of troops marshalled to overawe the people, had been convened at Cambridge; and with continual collision and exasperation, growing out of this high-handed step of quartering the soldiers in the city, the catastrophe of the massacre on the evening of

March 5, 1770, at last threw the town instantly into the greatest commotion; the drums beat to arms, the alarm-bells rang, thousands of the inhabitants thronged the streets. Early the next morning the citizens, by a unanimous vote, formally notified the Lieutenant-Governor and Council, who were deliberating upon the event, "that nothing can rationally be expected to restore the peace of the town, and prevent blood and carnage, but the immediate removal of the troops," which was at once stipulated. The funeral of the four men who had fallen in this tragedy, and were buried together, was a memorable spectacle in honor of them personally as martyrs, but still more of the cause in which they had died. The immense procession was formed in ranks six abreast, closed by a long train of carriages belonging to the principal persons in the town.

Yet, exasperated as the people were to the last degree, John Adams and Josiah Quincy — the very oracles of popular liberty — consented to act as counsel for Captain Preston and the soldiers when arraigned, lest it should be thought that in such a tumult they could not have a fair trial; and the jury, with equal courage and justice, calmly rendered their verdict according to the law.[1]

[1] Works of John Adams, by his grandson, Charles Francis Adams, Vol. II. p. 230, 231; also Memoir of Josiah Quincy, Jr., p. 31–64.

Who can wonder that "the removal of the General Court to Cambridge," in times like these, "disturbed the scholars in their studies;" or that "their declamations and forensic disputes breathed the spirit of liberty!" Their fathers and brothers were inaugurating a REVOLUTION, whose master-spirits had gone forth from those very halls. The crisis touched them *personally*, and not merely nationally. This was especially true of Mr. Phillips, so many of whose relatives were in Boston, sharing in these agitations and suffering from them. Josiah Quincy — "the Boston Cicero" — whose flashing eye and clarion voice everywhere meet us in this opening of the great drama, was his cousin by marriage; his uncle, Hon. William Phillips, and his cousin, the late Lieutenant-Governor William Phillips, whom he often visited, were conspicuous in the struggle then, and still more so afterwards; while his steadfast father, as a member of the General Court, and of the convention of "committees," was often forsaking his rural home to come down and share in the conflict. In a college theme on Liberty at this crisis, Mr. Phillips writes in the following strain: —

"Let this truth be indelibly engraved on our breasts, that we cannot be happy without we are free, and may it have a desirable effect. The cause requires our utmost vigilance; we should watch against every encroachment, and with all the fortitude of *calm, intrepid resolution* oppose them, lest the burden should become too great, or from length of time acquire such a force that the difficulty will become insurmountable. It is a matter of very great importance. The consequences will not only be great, but very lasting. Unborn generations will either bless us for our activity and magnanimity, or curse us for our sloth and pusillanimity. But let an Englishman forever keep silence (a reflection which I can 't forbear) when he can't pass the streets without seeing instances of the cruel usurpation of those rights and privileges, for the defence of which whole kingdoms are ready to sacrifice their lives and fortunes. Happy, thrice happy, would it be for us, if all, in their several spheres, would lend a helping hand for this grand enterprise, so that every man may sit down under his own vine and fig-tree."

It was not merely the natural influence of these Boston experiences on Cambridge, nor the influence of that spontaneous and universal enthusiasm in the cause of liberty which thrilled the College, that was impressing itself deeply on the young student. He had come to the University, the representative of a patriotic family, now more than ever aglow with a self-sustained enthusiasm in the popular cause; he could not remember a year in which wars and rumors of wars were any but the most familiar sounds in his ear. If the patriotic excitement of his childhood in the Old French War could have subsided in any degree, as he gave himself to study, the passing of the Stamp-

Act with kindred measures by Parliament, had served to keep it alive. War itself could not have agitated him, or the country, more.

The Act was passed in January, 1765, when he was about to enter the Academy at Byfield, to take effect on the first of November following. These months were a most eventful interim. The legislatures of several of the colonies, at their sessions, passed spirited resolves denying the right of Parliament thus to tax his majesty's loyal subjects; the General Court of Massachusetts, besides passing such resolutions of the strongest character, proposed a congress of deputies from all the colonies, which was held in October, at New York, composed of delegates from Massachusetts, Rhode Island, Connecticut, New York, New Jersey, Pennsylvania, Delaware, Maryland, and South Carolina, (the assemblies of Virginia, North Carolina, and Georgia being prevented by their governors from sending deputations,) and at which the most determined stand was made in defence of their rights.

Nor did the spirit of freedom take on these orderly forms alone. Riots and excesses broke out in spite of every restraint. At Boston, especially, there were repeated and alarming tumults, in one of which, the house of Lieutenant-Governor Hutchinson was sacked, —"the plate, family pictures, most of the furniture, the wearing apparel, about nine hundred pounds sterling in money, and the manuscripts and books which he had been thirty years collecting, besides many public papers in his custody, being either carried off or destroyed."[1]

With such exciting antecedents in every direction, the first of November drew near. The demonstrations of sorrow and scorn with which the day was greeted when it dawned, were of the most emphatic character.

At Philadelphia, when the vessels which brought the stamps came in, all the colors of the shipping in port were hung at half mast, and the bells of the city were muffled and tolled till sunset. In New York, there were no bounds to the violence of the mob, countenanced by thousands of the less reckless citizens; the Lieutenant-Governor, who had received the stamps and made extraordinary exertions to have them secure, was first hung and then burnt in effigy, his own coach having been dragged from his stable to bear the effigy in the mock procession, and at the close cast into the bonfire and consumed. Early in the morning, at Boston, there was a general tolling of the bells, and through the day many of the stores were shut, while effigies of such as favored the Act were paraded about the streets, and at last torn in pieces by the frantic populace.

[1] Holmes's Annals, Vol. II. p. 272.

In Portsmouth and several adjacent towns an unique pageant was concerted.

"All the bells," in the words of our annalist, "were tolled to denote the decease of Liberty; and, in the course of the day, notice was given to her friends to attend her funeral. A coffin, neatly ornamented, and inscribed with 'LIBERTY, aged CXLV years' was prepared for the funeral procession, which began from the State house, attended with two unbraced drums. Minute-guns were fired until the corpse arrived at the grave, when an oration was pronounced in honor of the deceased. Scarcely was the oration concluded, when, some remains of life having been discovered, the corpse was taken up. The inscription on the lid of the coffin was immediately altered to 'LIBERTY REVIVED;' the bells suddenly struck a cheerful sound, and joy appeared again in every countenance."[1]

Throughout the length and breadth of the country the stamp distributers were execrated, threatened, compelled to resign, and in every way made to feel the determination of the people not to tolerate the obnoxious Act. And when, after struggling in vain for a year to enforce the Act, Parliament repealed it, in March, 1766, the joy of the colonies was expressed as tumultuously as their indignation had been, by the ringing of bells, and by illuminations, festivals, and processions suited to the occasion. The anniversary

[1] Holmes's Annals, Vol. II. p. 273.

5

of this repeal was observed, it will be remembered, by the students at Cambridge, in 1769, three years afterwards, recalling to every mind, not only the Act itself, but the spirit with which it had been successfully resisted.

The revolutionary impulses received while in College merely, surrounded by ardent spirits like himself, might have died out of Mr. Phillips's heart when he went forth into the world, had they not been grafted upon these anterior and life-long excitements, in the same direction; — had not the calm, intelligent patriotism of principle been a part of his mental growth, as really as his ideas of virtue, or his estimate of time.

But when we trace this long and varied process, which had so well served to exercise his mind upon the great questions at issue, and when we consider that every month after he graduated was filling the country with increasing alarm, it no longer seems surprising that all plans for a professional career, if any had been matured, were at once abandoned. Indeed, it is very remarkable that he should, through all these disturbances, have been such a model as he was of successful application to study; clearly showing that no reasons but such as he deemed the most imperative, would have led him to relinquish so congenial a life. Yet in the question between study and action, equally fitted as he was for either, the scholar yielded to the patriot; and he threw himself with the utmost ardor into the Revolutionary struggle. "I never saw him," says one who knew him well, "I never saw him so much interested in any thing else, as he was in the Revolution, unless it was the Academy."

He had been out of College less than two years, when in the spring of 1773 — three months before his marriage — his fellow-citizens elected him town clerk and treasurer, in place of his father, who had filled these offices in the town continuously for fourteen years previous. At this period, as the records amply witness, every thing else in the frequent town meetings of Andover was secondary to its spirited action upon the state of the country. As early as October 21, 1765, the year of the Stamp-Act, the town had by a unanimous vote addressed the following "instructions" to their Representative, the elder Mr. Phillips: —

[To Samuel Phillips, Esq., Representative for the town of Andover in his Majesty's province of the Massachusetts Bay.]

"Sir, — We, the freeholders and other inhabitants of said town, legally assembled in town meeting on said day, to consider what may be proper on our part to be done at this critical conjuncture, being a time, we apprehend, that we and the rest of his majesty's subjects of this province, as well as those of the other provinces and colonies in British America, are by sundry acts of Parliament of Great Britain, especially by an act commonly called the Stamp-Act, in danger of being not only reduced to such indigent circumstances as will render us unable to manifest our loyalty to the Crown of Great Britain, as upon all occasions we have hitherto done, by cheerfully exhibiting our substance for the defence of the British dominions in this part of the world, but of being deprived of some of our most valuable privileges which by charter and loyalty we have always thought, and still think, ourselves justly entitled to;

"Therefore, we take it to be a duty justly due to ourselves and posterity to instruct you, that you do not give your assent to any act of Assembly that shall signify any willingness in your constituents to submit to any internal taxes that are under any color imposed, otherwise than by the General Court of this province, agreeable to the Constitution of this government; that you join in such dutiful remonstrances to the King and Parliament, and other becoming measures, as shall carry the greatest probability to obtain a repeal of the Stamp-Act, and an alleviation of the embarrassments the commercial affairs of this province labor under by the rigorous execution of the acts of Parliament respecting the same; and we also desire you to use your utmost endeavors that all extraordinary grants and expensive measures may upon all occasions, as much as possible, be avoided; and we would recommend, particularly, the strictest care and the utmost firmness to prevent all unconstitutional draughts upon the public treasury; that you would use your best endeavors, in conjunction with the other members of the General Court, to suppress all riotous unlawful assemblies, and to prevent all unlawful acts of violence upon the persons and substance of his majesty's subjects in this province."

In May, 1768, Mr. Phillips, senior, as chairman of a committee appointed by the town, had presented a report, which was adopted unanimously, in these words: —

"In order to securing to ourselves and transmitting to posterity those invaluable rights and privileges both civil and religious, which have been dearly purchased by our predecessors, the first settlers of this country, the loss of which is greatly threatened by the great and growing imprudences and immoralities among us, the committee are humbly of opinion, that it is absolutely necessary that the inhabitants of this town use their utmost endeavors, and that they enforce their endeavors by their example, for the suppressing of extravagance, idleness, and vice, and for the promoting of industry, economy, and good morals; and by all prudent means endeavor to discountenance the importation and use of foreign superfluities, and to promote and encourage manufactures in the town." [1]

[1] It is exceedingly interesting to notice how much prominence is given at this crisis, not only in the action of this town, but of various other bodies in the country, to this important point in political economy; nor were these views of self-support in so important a respect, the fruit of revolutionary tendencies merely. They had prevailed to a very considerable extent, twenty years earlier, the development of its internal resources being regarded of great moment to the prosperity and thrift of the country then, as it now was to its independence. Among the illustrations of this fact, which we have collected, we give the following. In 1753, "the anniversary of a society in Boston for encouraging industry and employing the poor, was celebrated with extraordinary attention. In the afternoon, about three hundred young female spinsters, decently dressed, appeared on the Common at their spinning-wheels. The wheels were placed regularly in three rows, and a female was seated at each wheel. The weavers also appeared, cleanly dressed, in garments of their own weaving. One of them, working at a loom on a stage, was carried

5*

Two years later, May 21, 1770, we find the following record: —

"The town, taking into consideration the distresses this province is laboring under by the operation of a late Act of Parliament imposing duties on tea, paper, glass, etc., made and passed for the express purpose of raising a revenue in the American colonies without their consent, which Act we apprehend is oppressive; repugnant to the natural and constitutional rights of the people; contrary both to the spirit and letter of the royal charter, granted by their majesties King William and Queen Mary to the inhabitants of this province, whereby are ordained and established the having and enjoying all liberties and immunities of free and natural born subjects; and subversive of the great and good designs of our most worthy ancestors, who crossed the ocean, willingly exposed themselves to every danger, parted with their blood and treasure, suffered hunger, cold, and nakedness, and every other hardship human nature is capable of, to purchase and defend a quiet habitation for themselves and posterity:

"Therefore, Voted, *nemine contradicente;* 1. That it is the duty of every friend to liberty and to the British constitution to use all legal measures to prevent, if possible, the ex-

on men's shoulders, attended with music. An immense number of spectators was present at this interesting spectacle."

"Rev. Dr. Cooper preached a discourse, and a collection was made for the benefit of the institution. A manufactory house, a large and handsome brick building, was erected about this time on Long-acre street; and an excise, laid by the General Court on carriages and other articles of luxury, was appropriated to it." — *Holmes's Annals,* Vol. II. p. 196.

ecution of said act; and would embrace this opportunity to express our warmest gratitude to the merchants and other gentlemen of Boston and other trading towns in this province, for the regular, constitutional, and spirited measures pursued by them, from principles truly noble and generous, for repelling tyranny and oppression, and establishing those rights for themselves and country which they are entitled to as men and as Englishmen.

"2. That we will by all legal and constitutional measures in our power, support and encourage the non-importation agreement of the merchants; and that we will have no commercial or social connections directly or indirectly with those persons, who, as enemies to the country, divested of every public virtue, and even of humanity itself, regardless of, and deaf to, the miseries and calamities which threaten this people, preferring their own private interest to the liberty and freedom of the community, are sordidly endeavoring to counteract such benevolent and salutary agreement.

"3. That we will encourage frugality, industry, and the manufactures of this country; and that we will not make use of any foreign tea, or suffer it to be used in our families (cases of sickness only excepted) until the Act imposing a duty on that article shall be repealed, and a general importation take place."

Such was the spirit of the town, when Mr. Phillips, Jr., began to take part in its deliberations, and to bear its offices; and here, with his honored father, he at once became conspicuous. Early in the year 1774, he was appointed, in town meeting, at the head of a committee to draft a series of resolutions expressive of the temper of the times; his report embodied, with slight modifications, the resolves which had then recently been passed at Philadelphia, as a declaration of principles, and added the following for practice: —

"Resolved, That no person in this town, who has heretofore been concerned in vending tea, or any other person, may on any pretence whatever, either sell himself or be in any way accessory to selling any tea of foreign importation, while it remains burdened with a duty, under penalty of incurring the town's displeasure."

At a subsequent meeting in June, he was one of a committee to report a covenant to be signed by the citizens, and on its adoption, was upon the committee to see that it was strictly enforced.

In December, his father, as chairman of a similar committee upon the resolves of the Provincial Congress, made a report to the town, which there is reason to believe the son had assisted in carefully drafting, from which we quote the following words: —

"Resolved, That it is the indispensable duty of this town strictly to conform and firmly adhere to the Association of the Grand American Continental Congress, and to the resolve of the Provincial Congress of the fifth of December, thereto relating; and, in order that this may be thoroughly effected, that the inhabitants of the town, of the age of twenty-one years and upwards, subscribe the following agreement, namely: We, the subscribers, having attentively considered the Association of the Grand American Continental Congress, respecting the non-importation, non-exportation, and non-consumption of goods, etc., signed by the delegates of this and the other colonies on the continent, and the resolve of the Provincial Congress of the fifth of December thereto relating, do heartily approve the same, and every part of them; and in order to make said association and resolve our own personal act, Do by these presents, under the sacred ties of virtue, honor, and love of our country, firmly agree and associate fully and completely to observe and keep all and every article and clause in said association and resolve contained, according to the true intent, meaning, and letter thereof, and will duly inform and give notice of every evasion, or contravention of either, as far as we are able; and we further covenant, that if any person or persons, of the age of twenty-one years and upwards, shall neglect or refuse to subscribe this agreement when tendered to him or them, we will withdraw all commerce, trade, or dealing from such, so long as they shall continue thus inimical to the public good, and that their names shall be entered on the records of this town, and published in the Essex Gazette as enemies to their country."

Upon the adoption of this report, — which made Andover a community of "Covenanters," — Mr. Phillips, senior, was made chairman of a large Committee of Safety, charged with the duty of executing the measure proposed; while the record of all these doings was kept by his son, who, in these and many kindred movements, was not less active. That oft summoned town meeting was a noble spectacle; a determined assembly of sturdy freemen, who knew their rights so well, voting again and again without one dissenting voice, while the young scholar, just from his college groves, was their clerk, and his tried father their moderator, — for during this entire period, the elder Mr. Phillips was almost invariably called to the chair, — both helping to clothe all their resolute doings in the convincing words of truth and soberness.

It was thus that the town, when the war at last broke out, directed a portion of its militia to enlist in the army, at the same time voting their pay and supplies; established its night-watch as a precaution against fires, and the regulars, upon which all the citizens from sixteen to sixty years of age were liable to serve at forty-eight hours' notice; organized, in addition to the Committee of Safety, its Committees of Correspondence and of Inspection; engaged to supply the families of those who were serving in the army with the necessaries of life; and took measures to forestall disturbances of the peace, and to enforce the laws among such as seemed inclined to be lawless. Nor did these citizens hesitate when the progress of the war had brought on the issue of separation from the mother country.

At a meeting June 12, 1776, three weeks before the ever memorable 4th of July, the records inform us that, —

"The question being put, whether should the Honorable Congress, for the safety of the colonies, declare them independent of the kingdom of Great Britain, you will solemnly engage with your lives and fortunes to support them in the measure, — it passed in the affirmative, *unanimously*."[1]

[1] All of these resolves of the citizens of Andover in the great contest, were amply seconded by both means and men devoted to the war. In February, two companies were raised under the command of Capt. Benjamin Farnham, and Capt. Benjamin Ames. — "On the 19th of April, 1775, the alarm drew these companies into the field, and they were stationed at Cambridge. They were detached to take possession of the heights of Charlestown on the 16th of June, and were in the battle of the next day. There were fifty-eight belonging to Capt. Ames's company, more than fifty of whom, belonging to the South Parish, were in the battle of Bunker Hill. Three were killed and seven wounded. Two in another company, under command of Capt. Furbush, were killed. Capt. Farnham was wounded, and some of his company." "The day following the battle, the Lord's day," says Rev. Mr. French, "our houses of worship were generally shut up. It was the case here. When the news of the battle reached us, the anxiety and distress of wives and children, of parents, of brothers, sisters, and friends, were great. It was not known who were among the slain or the living, the wounded or the well. It was thought justifiable for us, who could, to repair to the camp, to know the circumstances, to join in the defence of the country, and prevent the enemy from pushing the advantages they had gained; and to afford comfort and relief to our suffering brethren and friends." In the siege of Boston following this, another company of more than fifty men, under Capt. Lovejoy, served, being stationed, at different times, on Prospect Hill, at Cambridge, and at Roxbury. — See *Abbot's History of Andover*, p. 174, 175, etc.

It was to represent such a town, in this critical era, that our Mr. Phillips, the younger, was elected, with great unanimity, to the Provincial Congress, which met at Watertown in 1775, at the age of only twenty-three years! Whether this reflects most honor upon him or upon his fellow-citizens, we need not inquire. They certainly were not men to be blinded by the young patriot's ardor in the cause merely. It required something besides zeal for liberty to speak and act for them in that assembly; yet without this enthusiasm in the contest, neither he nor any other deputy could have truly represented them. Young as he was, and the more because of his youth, this election intimates to us their confidence in his judgment, his probity, and his firmness, not less than in his courage and devotion.

The Congress to which he was thus sent, convened in sight of his venerable ancestor's grave, was near the head-quarters of the army at Cambridge,[1] acting

[1] The very aspect of Cambridge and its vicinity at this time, must have added to the zeal of the patriot scholar: "Thousands," writes Rev. Mr. Emerson, a chaplain in the army, "are at work every day, from four till eleven o'clock in the morning. It is surprising how much work has been done. The lines are extended almost from Cambridge to Mystic River, so that very soon it will be morally impossible for the enemy to get between the works, except in one place, which is supposed to be left purposely unfortified, to entice the enemy out of their fortresses. Who would have thought, twelve months past, that all Cambridge and Charlestown would be covered over

in daily concert with it, and animated by its spirit. There was no longer a "Great and General Court" elected in the king's name, and legislating under the eye of the king's governor; but in its place this Revolutionary Legislature, in which, beyond all other subjects, the Revolution itself was the great theme. General Warren said of a similar body in November, 1774.

"About two hundred and sixty members were present. You would have thought yourself in an assembly of Spartans or ancient Romans, had you been a witness to the ardor which inspired those who spoke upon the important business they were transacting."[1]

In this and each succeeding legislature during the war to which Mr. Phillips was elected, he took a very active part. He soon came to be regarded as one of the best speakers in the House, and to the various important measures proposed in aid of the common cause, he brought the most effective support. For mere rhetorical declamation, he had no aptness and no taste. His was the practical and solid oratory

with American camps, and cut up into forts and intrenchments, and all the lands, fields, orchards, laid common, — horses and cattle feeding on the choicest mowing land, whole fields of corn eaten down to the ground, and large parks of well-regulated locusts cut down for firewood and other public uses?" — *Frothingham's History of the Siege of Boston*, p. 221.

[1] Frothingham's History of the Siege of Boston, p. 42.

6

of a calm, far-seeing mind, deeply moved, yet never swayed by simple emotion. Knapp, in his fiction of "Marshal Soult's Journal," says of him in this respect, "he was in the first grade of eminence; his speeches were clear, concise, logical, direct, and nervous; but he made no effort to amuse the fancy, and never sacrificed any thing to mere rhetoric."[1]

And the qualities which made him so convincing in debate, gave a corresponding weight to his suggestions, and his action, on the various important committees of the House upon which he was placed. In whatever pertained to the war, or to the important questions of state connected with the war, a large amount of this committee service was assigned to him year after year; and in it all he distinguished himself, not only by his zeal, but by his sagacity and despatch, and by his untiring industry. It is seldom that such capacity for the dry minutiæ of business is united with such ability in persuasive speaking in our legislative halls.

We have taken pains to examine the journals of these successive legislatures with some care, to obtain a view of Mr. Phillips's labors, and have been surprised at the number and variety of his committee services. The Provincial Congress at Watertown, assembled in the meeting-house July 19, 1775. The proscribed patriots, Samuel Adams and John Hancock, were both

[1] Pages 103, 104.

members, and with them many others who had already distinguished themselves in the great contest. This memorable Congress held four protracted sessions before it was finally dissolved on the 10th of May, 1776. During this period, Mr. Phillips was twice on a committee to confer with General Washington upon points connected with the war; he was also in rapid succession upon committees to countersign the colony notes emitted by the Continental Congress, and the notes of the Receiver-General; to direct the mustering and paying of one militia company, and to muster and pay another; to procure a suitable person to attend the Muster-Master-General, and obtain a return of the Massachusetts forces; to superintend the delivery of powder to the several towns, and to the Commissary-General; to view the defences of Boston harbor, and report their condition, etc.

In subsequent legislatures, he was appointed on committees, upon the petition of certain persons taken by one of the cruisers; to bring in a bill to punish deserters; to see what should be done with men "who enlist or are drafted into the army, but have not marched;" to report upon the remonstrances of a large number of towns against Bills of Credit, and to revise the Address of the House to the inhabitants of the State, setting forth the reasons for the Act for calling in these bills; to confer with the Faculty of Harvard College respecting grants to the officers; to consider a Resolution of Congress respecting the administration of justice; to bring in a bill for encouraging the manufacture of steel; to draft a letter to Congress upon the subject of the embargo, etc. In many of these appointments, he was made chairman of the committee raised; in numerous instances the persons appointed by the House were a joint committee, with such as the honorable Council might designate to the same duty. All of these legislatures, like the Congress at Watertown, held repeated sessions, usually three or four, varying from one to two and sometimes three months in length, relieved by intervals of adjournment.

But while exerting himself thus in the legislature for the liberties of his country, his interest in the Revolution stimulated him to serve the cause in other modes. There were junctures when he made efforts to procure loans from his friends for the government, becoming himself, to the extent of his ability, not only the negotiator, but the surety, with the parties. His daily conversation, too, with all classes, and in all circles, was perpetually touching upon the great theme, eliciting, by well-timed questions, the views of others, and breathing out the convictions of his own full heart. He is remembered to this day by some, with remarkable distinctness in this respect, as conversing everywhere upon the war, full of questions and of comments, both in a style peculiar to himself. And his deeds were in unison with his words.

In the winter of 1775–76, while serving in the

Congress at Watertown, and intent still upon practically aiding in the struggle, he erected, at great expense, a powder-mill, commencing and prosecuting the enterprise in a manner most characteristic of himself.

The exigency which prompted him to this enterprise was great. By a proclamation of the king, the year prior to the rupture with the Colonies, the exportation of all military stores from Great Britain had been prohibited;[1] and early in the contest, the efforts of the British troops had been specially directed to the seizure or destruction of all kinds of ordnance and ammunition. For this purpose, a detachment had marched to Salem and Danvers in February, 1775;[2] and this was the chief object of the expedition to Concord, which brought on the battle at Lexington on the 19th of April. The battle of Bunker Hill might have been still more disastrous to the British, had not the Americans been compelled to retreat in the very hottest of the conflict for want of cartridges.[3] So early did the scanty supply of powder especially begin to embarrass the patriot forces.

When General Washington took the command of the army on the 3d of July at Cambridge, his first care,

[1] Holmes's Annals, Vol. II. p. 316.

[2] Ibid. p. 324. See also Frothingham's History of the Siege of Boston, p. 48.

[3] Ibid. p. 147, 148, 153.

after a rapid survey of his own and the enemy's works, was to ascertain the amount of the various military stores at his service for the campaign. The returns showed that more than three hundred barrels of powder had been collected by the Province, but did not state how much had been expended. Without a suspicion of any important deficiency, therefore, the Commander-in-Chief at once arranged to complete the investment of Boston, and press the siege vigorously, hoping before winter to dislodge or capture the British, and return to Virginia.

On the issue of an order, however, in August, for a new supply of cartridges, the startling fact came to light, that there were not more than about thirty barrels of powder in the whole camp, barely enough to furnish nine or ten rounds to each man! Letters were instantly despatched by Washington to Rhode Island, the Jerseys, Ticonderoga, and elsewhere, urging immediate supplies of both powder and lead; he suggested, also, the expedient of fitting out an armed vessel to sieze if possible upon a magazine in Bermuda; and for a fortnight the army remained in this critical state, apprehending an attack every hour, when at length a partial supply was received from the Jerseys; but even with this, there was not ammunition enough to serve for more than a single day in a general action.[1]

[1] Irving's Life of Washington, Vol. II. p. 25–27; also Frothingham's History of the Siege of Boston, p. 232, 233, 255.

Even as late as December, after every effort to increase the stores, Washington spoke of the stock as "fearfully small;"[1] and in January, General Putnam, who had just constructed a new battery on Lechmere Point, was still roughly praying for powder. "The bay is open," writes Colonel Moylan, in allusion to the mildness of the season, "every thing thaws here except Old Put. He is still hard as ever, crying out for powder — powder — powder, — Ye Gods, give us powder!"[2] Yet with this appalling defect, month after month, to check him, Washington began to be thought too cautious in his movements. "Why does he not bombard the town and drive the enemy out?" it was asked. "Why is the army kept fortifying or parading and not fighting?"

The General-in-Chief was himself mortified and chafed beyond measure by this necessity for apparent inaction, when some great and decisive blow was expected, and when, to explain the real cause, would be to insure disaster. January 14th, he wrote: —

> "Few people know the predicament we are in, on a thousand accounts; fewer still will believe, if any disaster happens to these lines, from what cause it flows. I have often thought how much happier I should have been if, instead of accepting of a command under such circumstances, I had

[1] Irving's Life of Washington, Vol. II. p. 35.

[2] Ibid. p. 117.

taken my musket upon my shoulder, and entered the ranks; or, if I could have justified the measure to posterity and my own conscience, had retired to the back country, and lived in a wigwam.

"If I shall be able to rise superior to these, and many other difficulties which might be enumerated, I shall most religiously believe that the finger of Providence is in it."

On the 9th of February, he stated: —

"That two thousand of his men were without firelocks, and that he was obliged to conceal the state of his army even from his own officers."

On the 10th, he wrote: —

"I know that much is expected of me. I know that without men, without arms, without ammunition, without any thing fit for the accommodation of a soldier, little is to be done."

February 18th, he again wrote: —

"To have the eyes of a whole continent fixed with anxious expectation of hearing some great event, and to be restrained in every military operation for want of the necessary means to carry it on, is not very pleasing; especially as the means used to conceal my weakness from the enemy, conceal it also from our friends, and add to their wonder." [1]

He waited, therefore, in hope; but it was hope deferred; and it was not until March, 1776, eight months

[1] Frothingham's History of the Siege of Boston, p. 286, 290, 292.

after his arrival at Cambridge, that he felt justified in acting more summarily. On the night of the 2d, 3d, and especially the 4th of that month, the town was bombarded in good earnest, mainly with a view of covering his occupancy of Dorchester Heights that evening, where, as on Bunker Hill in the preceding June, the labor of a night threw up a redoubt, which the next morning filled the enemy with amazement. That evening, Mrs. John Adams, writing of the cannonade to her husband, said, "I hope to give you joy of Boston, even if it is in ruins, before I send this away." [1] A few days now sufficed to drive the British to their shipping. Early in the morning of Sunday the 17th, they evacuated the town; and a siege which might have been ended in eleven weeks as well as in eleven months, had there been no want of ammunition, terminated in a complete triumph.[2]

In reverting to their struggles for this great victory,

[1] Frothingham's History of the Siege of Boston, p. 305, 306.

[2] Holmes's Annals, Vol. II. p. 348. While Washington was in the midst of his embarrassments here, Dr. Franklin, Mr. Lynch, and Colonel Harrison came on as a committee from Congress, "to settle the plan for continuing and supporting the army;" and Dr. Franklin, who had recently returned from Europe, at this time paid over to a committee of the Provincial Congress at Watertown, £100, which had been sent to him, as a charitable donation from persons in England, for the relief of those who had been wounded in the battle of Lexington, and of the widows and orphans of those who had been slain. — See Sparks's Washington, Vol. III. p. 133, 134.

Washington writes to Congress: "It is not in the pages of history, perhaps, to furnish a case like ours. To maintain a post within musket shot of the enemy for six months together *without ammunition*, and at the same time to disband one army and recruit another within that distance of twenty odd British regiments, is more, probably, than was ever attempted."[1] The army had not been alone, however, in efforts to meet the exigency. The Congress at Watertown exerted itself strenuously for the same object. At first all the towns in the Province, where powder even in the smallest quantity was stored, were called upon to send it to the Commissary with the utmost despatch; and the amount which each town should endeavor to send in was specified. Andover was to send fifty pounds, which were promptly forwarded; so Haverhill, Danvers, Rowley, were to send fifty pounds each, and other towns in proportion.

But this was a temporary expedient; something must be done to insure a more permanent supply. On the 12th of December, 1775, a Resolve was therefore passed for the erection of two powder-mills, one in Sutton, and the other on the site of an old mill in Stoughton. On the 23d, however, a committee was appointed to visit Stoughton and Andover, and see in which of these towns the manufacture could best be commenced; and, on the 3d of January, Mr. Phillips made a proposal

[1] See Appendix F.

to the House, to erect a mill in Andover with their concurrence and coöperation. A Resolve was accordingly passed, with the sanction of the Council, on the 9th, encouraging him to proceed with all convenient despatch; engaging to supply his mill for a year with saltpetre and sulphur for the manufacture, and to pay him a bounty of eight pence per pound for all the good powder he should deliver to the Commissary; with the express stipulation that he was to sell only to the Government, or to such other parties as they should approve for the public use; and that he should maintain a night guard at his mill, "to prevent any wicked and designing person from destroying the same."[1] On the 13th of February, a bounty of £50 was offered also by the Congress to the person who should first erect a powder-mill capable of manufacturing fifty pounds per day; and £30 for the second mill of the same capacity. The mills at Stoughton and Andover being already begun, were not included in this offer.

It was with these preliminaries to stimulate him, and under the influence of such a general feeling in the body to which he belonged, that Mr. Phillips, who not only shared in the feeling, but had done much to increase it, hastened home in January, 1776, and set on foot his enterprise.

[1] See Journal of the Provincial Congress, 1775.

Having purchased his mill-seat, where a canal was needed for some distance, he called together his neighbors in considerable numbers, and spread before them the project. "Now," said he, "I want your help, and will engage to pay you, if the business pays; but if it fails, you must consent to lose your labor; the powder is needed for the common cause, and we must work together." At once his appeal was responded to with enthusiasm, and in that inclement season, ground was immediately broken by the spirited citizens, and the mill-race dug as a volunteer work; Mr. Phillips himself, in his farmer's frock, working from morning till night with the company, and superintending their labors. It has been said that this was the first powder-mill erected in the country, which appears to be an error, as the mill at Stoughton was to be an old one repaired; but certainly this was a most timely enterprise; for as early as the 10th of May, 1776, Mr. Phillips began to deliver from his mill to the several towns the quotas of powder which they had furnished according to the directions of the Provincial Congress; and in the summer and autumn, large supplies were drawn from it for the use of the army, and of the vessels engaged in cruising.

Mr. Phillips, as we have stated, had entered into an arrangement with the Government of the Commonwealth, to sell powder only as they should consent, and for the public service. Accordingly, we find an order of the Council, then sitting in Watertown, August 31, 1776, permitting the sale of one thousand six hundred pounds to three several parties at six shillings per pound, the Commissary-General of the State being responsible for the payment; September 6th, an order for one thousand five hundred pounds more; September 24th, for five hundred pounds; October 4th, for four tons; October 9th, for four thousand pounds,[1] etc. From the amount and frequency of these drafts, it will be seen that the mill was doing a great work. At this time, the Hon. William Phillips of Boston was a member of the Council, and his son, the late Lieutenant-Governor William Phillips, was part owner of one of the schooners which drew its stores of powder from this manufactory of their kinsman. While thus supplying munitions of war, Mr. Phillips, as chairman of a committee of the Legislature, was writing to the towns in the vicinity, to send in their supplies of wood and other necessaries to the army.[2] A letter of his to the selectmen of Concord is preserved, in which he states that they are recommended by the Legislature to send three cords of wood daily, and urges the importance of their doing it promptly.

Before the close of this year, powder-mills had been built, partly with the aid of the State, at Stoughton,

[1] American Archives, 5th Series, Vols. II. and III.

[2] Frothingham's History of the Siege of Boston, p. 275.

at Sutton, and at Springfield; but for a considerable period the mill at Andover was the leading manufactory. Before it had been half a year in operation a Resolve was passed in the Legislature, to pay Mr. Phillips £2,800 to meet his purchases of saltpetre merely.[1] The scarcity of this article was his principal difficulty in the enterprise; and at first, in the urgency of the demand, floors were, in many cases, taken up from kitchens and sheds in the vicinity, to obtain the earth beneath, and extract the saltpetre which it contained. The business, thus begun, proved sufficiently remunerative, notwithstanding an explosion in 1778, which destroyed a portion of the establishment, with the loss of three lives; and was continued until 1796, when a similar catastrophe brought it to a close, as, at that time, Mr. Phillips had a variety of other less hazardous business on his hands.

When the war, which he had been so zealous to sustain, was nearly terminated, the claims of the suffering army upon the country enlisted his warmest sympathy. "This is the day," he writes, to Mrs. Phillips, from Boston, under date of March 4th, 1780, "when I usually enjoyed the satisfaction of setting my face homeward; but duty forbids my enjoyment of that pleasure to-day; the importunity of hundreds of

[1] American Archives, Vols. II. and III.

poor soldiers who have been suffering much and hazarding life for my defence, and who are asking only for that which they were assured they should have received the first of last January, requires me to put on self-denial."

As the Revolutionary drama unfolded, too, in all its magnitude, the great problem of reconstructing the fabric of civil government in new forms, and with new doctrines underlying the whole, began to occupy his mind; thus launching him upon a career of varied civil service, which it is now time for us to trace.

# CHAPTER VII.

## HIS AGENCY IN THE ORGANIZATION AND ADMINISTRATION OF THE STATE GOVERNMENT.

WITH their early partiality which had chosen him to honorable offices in the town, and for several successive years elected him as their Representative to the Legislature, his fellow-citizens cast their united suffrages for him as one of the four delegates from Andover to the Constitutional Convention which commenced its sessions in Cambridge, September 1, 1779.

The independence of the Colonies had been solemnly declared; the tide of war, though not yet spent, was rolling away westward and southward, and all looked for its speedy and triumphant termination; it was time to enter upon the work of inaugurating a Republican Government, upon the basis of the great Republican Revolution. Indeed, one effort had already been made, by the citizens of Massachusetts, in this direction, but without success; the new constitution proposed by the Legislature of 1777–78, acting as a convention, not being approved by a majority of the people. It might have been inferred from this circumstance, that the patriotism of the times was better fitted to break down than to build up; more radical than progressive. It was the more important, therefore, that the second effort should be the best work of our best men. At the opening of the Convention in Cambridge, in the meeting-house of the first society, three hundred delegates presented their credentials, among whom stand the names of John Adams, Samuel Adams, John Hancock, James Bowdoin, Levi Lincoln, John Lowell, Theophilus Parsons, John Pickering, Robert Treat Paine, Caleb Strong, and scores of others who had distinguished themselves in the struggle for liberty.

In two days after it had assembled, the Convention was organized, and passed, as properly preliminary to its work, the following Resolutions: —

> "*Resolved*, unanimously, That the Government, to be framed by this Convention, shall be a FREE REPUBLIC.
>
> "*Resolved*, That it is of the essence of a free Republic, that the people be governed by FIXED LAWS OF THEIR OWN MAKING."

Proceeding upon this platform, a committee of thirty-one members, carefully selected and chosen by ballot, was then appointed to prepare "a Frame of a Constitution and Declaration of Rights," to be reported to the Convention; upon which committee, Mr. Phillips was placed as one of three from his county, being associated in this important service with both the Adamses, Mr. Bowdoin, Mr. Parsons, Mr. Paine, and other names of the highest distinction.

After six continuous weeks of arduous labor in scanning, and accepting or rejecting, the report of this committee, sentence by sentence, the Convention adjourned for a recess until January, during which interval, John Adams sailed for Europe, leaving to his associates the task of finishing what he and they had so well begun. The journal of the Convention in its first sitting shows that the discussions were often protracted; questions are spoken of as "largely debated," as having been decided after "an extensive debate," or after "a long debate;" on some topics the first draught of the committee was finally recommitted, and an entirely new one presented, so that much the largest part of their important work yet remained to be done when they adjourned.

The attempt to reassemble in January failed at first, the severity of the ever memorable hard winter of 1780 rendering it nearly impossible for the country members to get to Boston, where they now proposed to meet; and the smallpox having broken out in the city, so that there was great unwillingness to convene there; but after a week's delay, the new session began in the Representatives' Chamber, with the galleries opened to spectators. In February, after several weeks of close application to the details of their work, a motion was passed, "that a committee be appointed to form a declaration, or test, wherein every person, before he takes his seat as a representative, senator, or governor, or enters upon the execution of any important office or trust in the Commonwealth, shall renounce every principle, (whether it be Roman Catholic, Mahometan, Deistical, or Infidel,) which has any the least tendency to subvert the civil or religious rights established by this Constitution." Mr. Phillips was placed among the first on this committee, in connection with Mr. Pickering and Samuel Adams.[1]

[1] The test, reported by this committee, as finally incorporated into the Constitution, is as follows: — "Every person chosen to either of the places or offices aforesaid, as also any person appointed or commissioned to any judicial, executive, military, or other office under the government, shall, before he enters on the discharge of the business of his place or office, take and subscribe the following declaration, and oaths or affirmations, namely, —

"I, A. B., do truly and sincerely acknowledge, profess, testify, and declare, that the Commonwealth of Massachusetts is, and of right ought to be, a free, sovereign, and independent State; and I do swear that I will bear true faith and allegiance to the said Commonwealth, and that I will defend the same against traitorous conspiracies, and all hostile attempts whatsoever; and that I do renounce and abjure all allegiance, subjection, and obedience to the King, Queen, or government of Great Britain, (as the case may be,) and every other foreign power whatsoever; and that no foreign prince, person, prelate, state, or potentate, hath, or ought to have, any jurisdiction, superiority, pre-

By the 2d of March, the Convention had so far matured the proposed Constitution, as to adjourn again, meanwhile submitting their work to the suffrages of the people.

During these two months, the debates are represented as "very full," and the care with which every paragraph and phrase was adjusted, step by step, is exceedingly interesting to notice. At the third and very brief session, which was held in the Brattle Street Church in June, it appeared from the returns, that the Constitution had been adopted by the votes of more than two thirds of the people, and the Convention formally declared it to be "the Constitution of Government established by and for the inhabitants of the State of Massachusetts Bay."[1]

In all this work, of nearly four months in the aggre-

eminence, authority, dispensing or other power, in any matter, civil, ecclesiastical, or spiritual, within this Commonwealth; except the authority and power which is or may be vested by their constituents in the Congress of the United States: And I do further testify and declare that no man or body of men hath or can have any right to absolve or discharge me from the obligation of this oath, declaration, or affirmation; and that I do make this acknowledgment, profession, testimony, declaration, denial, renunciation, and abjuration, heartily and truly, according to the common meaning and acceptation of the foregoing words, without any equivocation, mental evasion, or secret reservation whatsoever. So help me God."

[1] See Journal of the Convention, p. 1–225.

gate, Mr. Phillips, though not entitled by age and experience to hold so eminent a place as some of the master-spirits of the Convention, is represented as having labored effectively, both in the committee rooms and in the House, supporting earnestly and often in the public discussions the matured propositions of his own and other committees, which were finally adopted. It is to be here remembered, that no such Republican Constitution had ever before been written; these men were to construct, not copy; and their position made them continually learners, while they were so acting as to be also the teachers of the land, in the science of government.

When they had so well done the work committed to them, therefore, they had acquired the best possible fitness to serve their fellow-citizens in the various civil offices which the Constitution established; and we accordingly find the prominent men of this Convention called at once, by the people, to the chief posts in the government which they had adopted. Mr. Hancock was the first Governor, succeeded in a few years by Mr. Bowdoin, and then in turn succeeding him. Mr. Samuel Adams was the first President of the Senate, and afterwards Lieutenant-Governor, and Governor. Messrs. Lowell, Lincoln, Pickering, Greenleaf, Holton, and others were called to the bench as judges in the various courts; yet others of the Convention became conspicous as members of the Governor's Council, or as leaders in the House of Representatives and the Senate.

At the very first popular election under the new Constitution in September, 1780, Mr. Phillips was chosen a member of the Senate, which became thenceforth his home as a legislator. In this canvass, his father also was upon the same ticket for councillors and senators with himself; but the son received, in his native place, treble the number of votes thrown for the father.

Early in the succeeding year, although not professionally versed in the law, and not yet thirty years of age, he was also appointed by Governor Hancock and his Council one of the justices of the Court of Common Pleas for the county of Essex, which office was the occasion of his being from this time conveniently distinguished from others of the family name, as *Judge* Phillips. It will best serve our purpose to speak of him briefly first as judge rather than as a senator, since his long judicial service, running parallel with his career in the Senate, was the more brief of the two.

He entered upon his duties as judge, not without careful preparation, we are assured, at a court holden in Newburyport, September 25, 1781, being associated in the office with his friends, the Hon. Benjamin Greenleaf, Samuel Holton, Esq., and John Pickering, Esq., all of whom had been with him in the Constitutional Convention, and subsequently in the General Court.

The uniform arrangement, for many years, was for this County Court to hold four terms annually; the September term in Newburyport, the December and July terms in Salem, and the April term in Ipswich; but in 1790, a change was made to three terms, September, April, and July. At the April term in Ipswich, 1782, about one hundred and fifty cases were tried; in July, there were one hundred and thirty cases at Salem; in September, one hundred and seventy-five at Newburyport; and the records for this year alone, cover nearly two hundred and forty folio pages.

It will be seen from this, that the business of the court in this large county was exceedingly onerous, consuming from three to four months yearly, and involving every variety of experience in the justices. Mr. Pickering served as one of the justices only two or three years; but Judge Greenleaf was in the office till 1796, and Judge Holton still longer. Judge Phillips held his office until 1798, appearing upon the bench for the last time in April of that year; and never having been absent, except in two cases, when serving the public in other duties, during the whole period of more than sixteen years! When he resigned, only Judge Holton was his senior in office. The high character of all these justices, and their long continuance in office, made this a model court for the times.

Of Judge Phillips, one who knew him well has said, "his wisdom, justice, and patriotism, were for a long time exercised in one of our judiciary departments; in which his ability and integrity, his patient, candid, and diligent attention, were universally approved."[1]

From a copy of one his addresses to the grand-jury at one of the terms, which is preserved in his handwriting, we quote the following, as an illustration of his judicial tone: —

"You having been chosen grand-jurors for the body of this county, and having taken the oath which has been administered, it is incumbent on the Court, to specify several parts of your duty in this capacity; — and as some of you have served the public in this office before, and most, if not all of you, must have been acquainted with the nature of it, it is hardly necessary to inform you, that it is your duty not only to receive complaints which may be made to you, when together or apart, of the offences against divers laws of the Commonwealth which are cognizable by this court, (some of which will be particularly enumerated,) but to make observations yourselves of those offences when they shall fall within your notice; and when convened at any term of the court, to communicate to each other any such observations as you may have made, and the informations you may have received, as well as the evidence to support them, — and also to judge of all such communications, whether made by any of your own number, or by any other person; in the first place to consider whether the complaints before you are cognizable by this court, and proper to be noticed by them, if found to be fact; in the second place, whether the evidence

[1] Dr. Tappan, Funeral Discourse, p. 9.

produced to support the complaint be sufficient for that purpose: — Thus you may be considered as the eye and the ear of the public, which the law has provided, to notice those offences that come within your knowledge, and which the public welfare requires should be corrected and suppressed.

" The laws which demand your attention, are those which require towns to provide and maintain schools within their limits, to keep their highways and bridges in repair, etc.; all these laws are important in their nature, and the execution of them necessary to the well-being of the community; but unless those who constitute the inquest of the County, are diligent and faithful in the discharge of their office, the labor and pains of the Legislature are worse than lost, and the people are deprived of that benefit which they have a right to expect, and which we, so far as the duties of our several stations extend, are solemnly bound to confer; for it ought to be remembered that every law, unexecuted, is a standing monument of the imbecility of government, and tends to bring its authority into disrepute and contempt. It may not, however, be amiss to caution you against the influence of prejudice and passion, as well as every undue bias whatever in all your inquiries and determinations, — wherever there is just reason to suspect that private animosities are promotive of public complaints, in such cases, you will exercise double vigilance."

" There is one object to which we would point your particular notice, I mean the laws which provide for the maintenance of grammar schools in our several towns. These laws are upon a subject which our venerable ancestors and fathers viewed to be of vast consequence to the welfare of their country; and to their views of it, under the smiles of Heaven, is in a great measure owing that degree of success, which has attended their posterity. To their salutary regulations of this kind may be ascribed, in a great measure, the improvements of various kinds which have been made in our country; and the effect of them has been remarkably conspicuous in the late surprising Revolution, from its commencement through the various stages of its progress, and especially in the very advantageous termination of it.

"These effects have been no less manifest in the formation and adoption of those excellent Constitutions of Government under which we live; but the harvest of benefits which are now opening to our view, and for which so high a price has been paid, will hardly be realized, or if realized, will be of but short continuance, *without an unremitted care to instruct the youth of the community generally*, in useful knowledge; to inculcate just principles, and form good habits, at that period of life which, *if not the only one, is incomparably the most favorable for those purposes.*

"In some instances, it may be found the law I am speaking of has been disregarded in all its parts; in others, where respect has been paid to the number of schools required to be kept, and to the periods for supporting them, another provision, which prescribes the qualifications of the instructors, and the judges of those qualifications, it is to be feared, has been greatly neglected; and this, perhaps, for the sake of obtaining *cheap instructors;* a parsimony this that is pitiable indeed; for, after all our pains, if we could leave posterity possessed of the wealth of the Indies, without virtuous principles and good habits, the habits of industry and economy particularly, the possession would not be very lasting;

and while it might continue, would not produce any considerable degree of rational enjoyment. Those who will undertake to cultivate and regulate the minds of youth, and are qualified for the undertaking, do well deserve an honorable reward; and by employing others, upon any terms whatever, we deceive ourselves, and do our children an injury which, in most instances, will never be repaired.

"I doubt not, gentlemen, you will discharge the duties of this office in such a manner as to afford satisfaction to your own minds, in reflection, and promote the peace, good order, and respectability of the county in which we have the happiness to live."

Admirably as such sentiments, clothed in so lucid a style, show him to have been fitted for this station, and congenial as it was to his natural tastes and habits of mind, his other multiplied public cares, together with frequent illness, compelled him at length to resign the office. We turn, therefore, to view him now in other civic toils and trusts.

After his first election from his district to the Senate of the Commonwealth, in 1780, he continued to be annually returned to that body during nearly the whole period of his remaining life. For the first five years, Mr. Samuel Adams was President, as already stated, and Judge Phillips was prominent only as his talents, weight of character, admirable business habits, and ripe experience in legislation, gave him influence. But when Mr. Adams "was persuaded to resign the chair," Judge Phillips succeeded him at once as President of the Senate, in which office he became more widely known, and is perhaps better remembered, than in any other that he ever filled. Once raised to this chair, it seemed thenceforth to be his by a sort of inalienable right, though he was too humble so to regard it, and at times, as we learn from letters to Madam Phillips, was disposed to decline it.

For fifteen years he was the choice of all parties, being elected President usually by a unanimous vote. Dr. Tappan, in the funeral discourse, already referred to, delineates him as a presiding officer, in the following words:—"In this high and delicate situation, he equally honored himself and benefited the Commonwealth, by his punctuality and assiduity, by his correctness and despatch, by his mild, impartial, and dignified conduct." In other notices of his senatorial life which appeared in the papers at the same period, special mention is made of "his singular and unremitted attention to business, and his facility in transacting it," and of his "known independence and integrity of character;" and Governor Strong, in a message to the Legislature, bears testimony to "his distinguished merit," characterizing him as "one of the best and ablest" men in the Commonwealth, who had long presided over the deliberations of the Senate "with candor and dignity." Indeed, though there were every year much older men than he on that floor, he was for many years officially the senior member, and was regarded as the father of the Senate, having more personal consideration by far than any other, in addition to the authority of his position.

By this long continued activity in the legislation of the Commonwealth, under such advantages of office and experience, he contributed largely to the dignity, as well as the stability, of the new civil order which his hand had helped to originate.

"The late surprising Revolution," as he terms it, had, however, left behind it some deep-rooted discontents, as in its origin and progress it had been marred by some excesses. There were men, in all these years, who sought not so much well-regulated liberty, as unrestrained license. The final, and much the most general, as well as dangerous exhibition of this lawless spirit, was the memorable Shays' Rebellion.

With many previous local disturbances, this wide spread concert to resist the Government of the Commonwealth, had become alarming in the summer of 1786, especially throughout the counties of Berkshire, Hampshire, Worcester, Middlesex, and Bristol. The administration of justice in the courts had been obstructed by the insurgents at Northampton, at Springfield, at Worcester, at Concord, at Taunton. A body of the conspirators, fifteen hundred strong, were under arms in the vicinity of Northampton, and smaller parties elsewhere, committing numberless outrages upon the supporters of the government. The same riotous spirit in New Hampshire, menaced the Legislature in session at Exeter, and was only quelled by the prompt rallying of the citizens. Contiguous portions of Vermont and of New York, were becoming in like manner disaffected. The collection of taxes was especially resisted, and loud demands for a redress of alleged grievances were made in every quarter.[1]

The General Court of Massachusetts had exerted itself to avert the impending storm, by conciliatory and temperate legislation; but its lenity was mistaken for timidity. The more it sought to win the turbulent populace, the more infuriated and insolent they became. The military were, therefore, at last called out in strong force, and civil war began in earnest. The chief command of the troops was committed by Governor Bowdoin to General Benjamin Lincoln, "whose reputation and mildness of temper rendered him doubly capacitated for so delicate and important a trust." About three quarters of the whole force were to be raised in the counties most disturbed, and the remainder in Suffolk and Essex.

A brief, but arduous winter campaign of two or

[1] Holmes's Annals, Vol. II. p. 471–477. Also Minot's History of the Insurrection.

three months, in 1787, sufficed. Such forces as Shays and his confederates could muster, in different localities, as at Springfield, Pittsfield, and their vicinities, were soon dispersed. There was little actual fighting, but much severe marching, the insurrectionists everywhere fleeing, and the troops pressing hard upon them in pursuit.

While the army were thus summarily dispersing the rebels, Governor Bowdoin issued his Proclamation, dated February 9th, setting a price of £150 upon the head of Shays and of £100 upon each of the other three leaders, Wheeler, Parsons, and Day. On the 16th of the same month, the Legislature passed an Act, defining the terms upon which pardon and indemnity might be extended to all who had borne arms against the State, excepting these; and, on the 10th of March, pursuant to this Act, a Resolve was passed, appointing a special commission to treat with the disaffected, and receive their submission, as there was now evidence that large numbers were anxious to be reconciled to the government.

The Commissioners were General Lincoln, the commander of the troops called out, Judge Phillips, President of the Senate, and Samuel Allyne Otis, Speaker of the House of Representatives, who immediately addressed themselves to their responsible work. Repairing first to Berkshire, and then to Hampshire, and other counties in succession, they in the brief space of a month, succeeded in effectually extinguishing the last hope of the conspirators. Scattering everywhere freely printed copies of the Act and Resolve, under which they were deputed, they invited applications for the offered amnesty.

All applicants were required, by them, to bring a certificate, signed by two persons of known attachment to the government, that they were believed to be really penitent; and were also obliged to subscribe a confession that they had been concerned in the rebellion, that they were sincerely penitent and wished to return to their allegiance to the State; and to engage that they would defend the government and comply with the laws as faithful citizens, and exert themselves to induce others to do the same.[1] As an illustration of the solicitude and gloom which now prevailed, as well as of the self-sacrificing devotion with which Judge Phillips participated in this commission, we cite here an extract from a letter of Madam Phillips to him while he was at Northampton.

After referring to two or three previous letters which she had written, without asking or expecting him to reply while so absorbed with cares, she says: —

"April 3, 1787. — I feel exceedingly for you, judging you must be anxious, very anxious, on account of the aspect of public affairs, which is truly alarming! — but I trust you will

[1] See Journal of General Court, 1787. Also Acts and Resolves.

not suffer your thoughts to make long visits to your family. I wish you to exert every faculty for the public good. I sincerely wish the Divine blessing may attend your consultations. I am very willing to make any sacrifice, might tranquillity be restored to our deluded States; — Heaven only knows where it will end!"

It was not long, however, that such forebodings continued. Moving, as the troops had done, with great celerity from point to point, the Commissioners had the address to conciliate and win the disaffected in great numbers. In their report to the government, dated April 27, they stated that seven hundred and ninety persons had returned to their allegiance; and that on the most careful inquiry into the various causes of the insurrection, they had found the chief cause to be "private debts," and "an undue use of articles of foreign growth and manufacture, the principal cause of these debts."

Meanwhile, many who had been involved in the insurrection quietly withdrew from the contest with the government, before the crisis came, and the leaders fled from the State. It was in consequence of Judge Phillips's service in this high commission, that in the State election for this year, 1787, he was not one of the senatorial candidates, and in the organization of the Senate Mr. Adams was again chosen President; but the next year Mr. Phillips was reinstated in the chair, while General Lincoln was chosen Lieutenant-

Governor; both, with their associate, having won golden opinions in the Commonwealth for their great success in this trust.

Year after year now glided away with no marked change in his position; he was still the indefatigable judge, as well as the eminent senator, and many were beginning to cast their suffrages for him for yet higher offices. At the very next election, after his mission to the western counties during the insurrection, he received several votes in his native town for Governor; and from this time, his friends, in increasing numbers, continued to vote for him either as Governor or Lieutenant-Governor annually, while invariably giving him a full vote for senator also. Indeed, for several successive years, his name was upon their ticket, at the same time, for all three of these offices; and in the year 1796, he had more votes in the town for Governor than any other candidate.

Yet, instead of desiring promotion, or even continuance, in the public service, except as a public duty, he sometimes intimates, during these years, his settled distaste for many of the scenes through which he is called to pass. "If our son John," he writes, March 2, 1795, "could be a witness to what has fallen within my notice in the four last weeks, public life, or rather General Court life, would be the last object of his wish;" — his allusion here is, to the protracted delay of business in the Legislature, in consequence of the tampering of interested parties with the committees, and "an uncommon degree of manœuvring by certain gentlemen."

While his fellow-citizens were thus, not without some reluctance on his part, holding him to his fitting station in the Senate, until he seemed a fixture there, and were intimating their wish to raise him to other dignities, the Commonwealth had borne its full part in the great work of consolidating the national government; the Constitution of the United States had taken the place of the old Articles of Confederation; party spirit had run high — and nowhere higher than in Andover, hitherto so united — in the debates connected with the adoption of this great Republican form of government.[1]

[1] The vote in the Massachusetts Convention upon the question of adopting the Federal Constitution stood, Yeas 187, Nays 168. In the other States there was a similar conflict of judgment, and of party feeling, so that as State after State finally adopted the great instrument the rejoicing of its advocates was enthusiastic.

The decisive vote in Massachusetts was taken February 6, 1788, and the Chronicle of the next day, in communicating the event to the public, introduces it with this exulting caption: —

"Hail the DAY, and MARK it well,  
Then old ANARCH'S kingdom fell,  
Then our dawning GLORY shone,  
Mark it, FREEMEN, 't is our own."

For this instrument itself, and for the great men who had devised it, Judge Phillips entertained the highest veneration; and when in 1797–8–9, our amicable relations with France were interrupted, and intrigues of every description were disaffecting many towards the government, he was not content to remain silent. Under his influence, a town meeting of the old type was held; the earnestness and unanimity of Revolutionary days again appeared, notwithstanding the federal and anti-federal lines had been so distinctly drawn. In the church where he now statedly worshipped,[1] before a very full assembly of the citizens, specially convened for the occasion, on the 14th of May, he as chairman of the committee, reported, and they unanimously adopted the following address:—

[To the President of the United States.]

"SIR,—We, the freeholders and other inhabitants of the town of Andover, in the Commonwealth of Massachusetts, beg leave to join the multitude of our fellow-citizens, in pre-

Arrangements were promptly made by the citizens of Boston for a splendid pageant, which, in a few days, was celebrated with every sign of joy;—and when, a short time after, the news came that New Hampshire had also adopted the Constitution, this being the *ninth* State, the number required to consummate the national Act, the whole town was thrown into a fever of excitement, and the bells rang for hours, as they had done when the Stamp-Act was repealed.

[1] The present Old South Church.

senting you our warmest gratitude, for that wisdom, vigilance, integrity, and patriotism which have marked your administration; and in particular, for your persevering solicitude to preserve to these States the blessings of peace and neutrality, upon such terms as would consist with the preservation of our essential rights and interests.

"Although repeated attempts to accommodate subsisting differences with the French Republic have not produced the effect which might have been reasonably expected, they may prove essential means of our political salvation, by unfolding the designs and enormous demands of that government, which we have been unwilling to conclude our enemy. This disclosure must produce universal conviction, that no hope of safety is left for us without our own united virtuous exertion.

"We therefore again thank you, sir, for your solemn and repeated calls on the proper departments to make the most speedy and effectual provision against the worst events; — for your firm resolution that you will never surrender the independence or essential interests of the country; — and for summoning the people to unite with you in supplicating the direction and blessing of that Almighty Being, under whose patronage, if not criminal ourselves, we have nothing to fear from any power on earth. In the same resolution, we hold it to be our duty, with that of every American, cordially to concur.

"Every attempt to detach us from our government, which is the work of our own hands, and from whence we have already derived blessings far surpassing the highest expectations of its warmest admirers, we repel with indignation. To abandon such a government, and the invaluable privileges, civil and religious, enjoyed under it, from any consideration whatever, would be acting a part unworthy the descendants of our renowned ancestors, bring indelible infamy on ourselves, be an act of treachery to our posterity, and betray the basest ingratitude to, and distrust of, that Supreme Being, who gave us these blessings.

" With an humble reliance therefore on this Being, whom we do, and ever will, acknowledge as the Arbiter of nations; and confiding in the wisdom, patriotism, and firmness of the constituted authorities of our country, we are determined, at every hazard, to support those measures which they shall prescribe for the defence of these blessings."

The cordial and very complimentary reply of the President to this letter,— which breathes alike the spirit of patriotism and of religion,— is interesting not only as showing his gratification in being thus addressed, but his large indebtedness to the diction of the address, for the very language of his answer. We copy it, as entered at large upon the town records.

[To the Freeholders and other inhabitants of the town of Andover, in the State of Massachusetts.]

" GENTLEMEN,— Your address, unanimously adopted at a legal and very full meeting, has been presented to me by your Representative in Congress, Mr. Bartlett, and received with great pleasure. When you acknowledge in my administration wisdom, vigilance, integrity, patriotism, and persevering solicitude to preserve to these States the blessings of peace and neutrality, upon such terms as would consist with the preservation of our essential rights and interests, you command my sincere gratitude.

"The unfriendly designs and unreasonable demands of that government, whom we have been unwilling to conclude our enemy, have been long suspected by many, upon very probable grounds; but never so clearly avowed and demonstrated as of late. May the discovery prove the essential means of our political salvation.

"The conviction appears now to be nearly universal, that no hope of safety is left for us, without our own virtuous exertions.

"The indignation with which you repel every attempt to detach you from that government, which is the work of your own hands, and from whence you have derived blessings far surpassing the highest expectations of its warmest admirers; and, in short, all the sentiments of this excellent address, do you great honor.

"JOHN ADAMS.

"PHILADELPHIA, May 25th, 1798."

At the very time of the date of this letter, the aspect of affairs had become so threatening, that Congress authorized the President to raise a provisional army without delay, and a few weeks later, General Washington was appointed Lieutenant-General and Commander-in-Chief. The old Revolutionary fire was kindled in all hearts. A letter from Judge Phillips to his son, at this time, shows that even he, the life-long civilian, had determined to serve personally in the army, and to encourage his only son to volunteer also, if the exigency should require it; so deeply did he feel the peril of his country. "No time," he writes August 3d, 1798, "ought to be lost in providing yourself and me with arms and accoutrements complete; the prospect of our needing them increases; it would not be very surprising to me, if we should be called on to use them much sooner than is generally expected." It was not a mere profession of patriotism in words, which he addressed to the Executive, but the sober language of one who meant to act as well as to speak.

The son, too, was animated by the same spirit. We cannot forbear to quote a few paragraphs from an oration delivered by him in Charlestown at this period: —

"Americans! The present is a momentous crisis! To the present actors on the stage is assigned the arduous and honorable task to determine whether man is capable of a Republican Government, or must ever be the passive subject of arbitrary power. . . . After sustaining *aggressions and depredations* unprecedented, with a forbearance and longsuffering which have encouraged the enemy to add insult to rapine; after *reiterated attempts at explanation* and accommodation, with a condescension and patience that have wellnigh excited their contempt; every question about the justice of our cause is solved, and the only alternative is *submission or resistance.*

"Are not a *commerce*, the source of our wealth and glory;

a *liberty*, purchased in fields of blood; a *constitution*, the fortress of our safety, worthy to be defended? Shall we behold freedom, humanity, virtue, public faith, morality, and religion trampled in the dust, and by our silence and inaction, become accessories to the crime? Rather let us sprinkle the mountains, and crimson the waves with our most precious blood!

"We have before our eyes those statesmen and warriors, who have acted a conspicuous part in conducting us through the Revolution, whose heads are silvered in their country's service, who anxiously mark what estimate their SONS place on the inheritance purchased for them, and are ready to lead them once more to victory or death. At the head of a host of experienced heroes, stands the man acknowledged by the oldest general in Europe to be the greatest general in the world; the beloved, the revered, the illustrious WASHINGTON still lives; and, at his country's call, has again unfurled the banners of freedom; has already, as with electric fire, inspired with redoubled ardor every American breast; and will confound with dismay the hearts of our enemies. Under such a leader, no American will refuse to become a soldier, and no soldier will dare to be a coward."

The crisis, however, was a bloodless one. This universal determination to maintain our neutrality at all hazards, convinced the French authorities of their mistake, if not of their injustice; and negotiation, after repeated failures, finally terminated in a treaty of peace.

9*

In Judge Phillips's career as a civilian, only one other point now remains to be noticed. It has already been stated, that for many years his friends had, in considerable numbers, voted for him as Governor or Lieutenant-Governor in the canvass for State officers.

At the election in April, 1801, his name was, by general consent, placed upon the ticket of the Federalists for Lieutenant-Governor, with that of Caleb Strong for Governor; and, although the contest between the two parties was spirited, these candidates were elected by a large vote. In Andover, Judge Phillips polled a larger vote by far than had been thrown for any previous candidate, and much larger than was cast for the able and popular Governor.

We have chanced to obtain a copy of a private letter inclosing a confidential circular, prepared with a view to secure his election, which incidentally discloses his own feeling and that of his friends at the time. "It is well understood," they say, "that Mr. Phillips will not decline, though he is incapable of soliciting the office;" and they now recount, in glowing terms, his many public services, together with the traits of character which he had exhibited in them all, as presenting the strongest possible plea for his election. "Those who were witnesses to his conduct," in the Revolution, they urge, "can testify, whether any honest exertions in his power were ever spared by night or by day, for attaining the object of that conflict;" then glancing at his career in the Constitutional Convention and in the General Court, they say of him as President of the Senate, "the members of that Honorable Board can testify with what punctuality, assiduity, fidelity, impartiality, and despatch, he has discharged the duties of that office;" and in conclusion, they add, "that his uniform practice has been to make his private concerns give place to his public duties."

Coming to this honorable station with these gratifying antecedents, and associated in the executive department now with a Governor and Council of distinguished ability, he adorned the office which thenceforth became associated with his name.

But though so long engaged in the public service, under such a variety of civic cares, which occupied his time and tasked his energies, he was not wholly a public man; and we must now return, to follow him through other less conspicuous, but not less useful scenes, that may give us a nearer and more full insight into his character.

# CHAPTER VIII.

## HIS ENTERPRISES AND PURSUITS AS A MAN OF BUSINESS.

WHEN his admiring friends tell us "that his uniform practice has been to make his private concerns give place to his public duties," they state the exact truth; for no man was more ready than he to forego all personal advantage in order to benefit the community, and none was ever apparently less ambitious than he of public distinction. Yet, to infer from this, or from any thing which has been said of his eager and manifold devotion to the general good, that his private affairs suffered disastrously in consequence, or that he had no careful oversight of them, and no marked interest in them, would be a great mistake. It is true that very few men, with such constant public engagements, would have found time to prosecute important private enterprises systematically; but in just this respect he was an uncommon man. "In every pursuit," says Knapp,[1] "he was distinguished for promptness, punctuality, and practical good-sense; and his short life, by order, exactness, and method, was filled

[1] Marshal Soult's Journal, p. 103.

with incredible attentions to business." There was not, in fact, a year of all his crowded civil labors, much as they demanded of his time and strength in preparing for them and performing them, in which he had less private engagements on his hands than most men of mere business.

It would be of little interest for us, of this generation, to trace out the details of his different enterprises, but enough may be seen at a glance to verify this statement. In addition to his effective coöperation with his father, in various affairs, soon after leaving College, he became at an early period the purchaser of several estates on his own account, which made him an extensive farmer; and the tradition is, that there was not in all the region a better farmer than he. His lands were constantly improving under his hand, and yet in a high degree, not only productive, but remunerative, although cultivated entirely by hired labor.

He was hardly settled in life, too, it will be remembered, when in the public crisis, he with so much tact and energy undertook the manufacture of powder in large quantities, not relinquishing the business till it had well repaid him, and the occasion for it had passed away, and not in the least impeded by it in his agricultural pursuits. In connection with his powder-mill, a grist-mill also was for a considerable period run by him, and a saw-mill, and finally a paper-mill; over all of which he exercised such supervision, as to know their condition accurately, and obtain a revenue from them. The paper-mill, especially, became, for a time, a leading branch of his business.

At the same time he owned and superintended two stores, one near his residence in Andover, and another in Methuen; and those who served him in them felt that, while he was not unreasonably distrustful or inquisitive, his practised eye was upon every part of the business, and his scores of questions ever and anon must be satisfactorily answered.

By various negotiations, too, at different periods, he obtained possession of large tracts of wild land in Maine and New Hampshire, amounting in all to about three thousand acres, which frequently required his care; while upon his various estates in Andover, he superintended the erection or repair of numerous buildings, including his own mansion-house, — the materials for which were drawn chiefly from his timber lands in New Hampshire.

In consequence of these numerous engagements in business, which centred in Andover, while his duties as judge and senator kept him very much from home, he was in the habit of making frequent journeys, especially from Boston to Andover, and usually in the night, on horseback, from which, neither his frail health, nor the urgency of his friends, could dissuade him. Sometimes in the darkness he missed his way, and did not reach home till nearly morning. Often, through weariness, he slept in his saddle, and was awakened only by the sudden stopping or starting of his horse.

Late in the winter of 1794, in one of these night excursions, he fell from his horse and fractured his leg; but fortunately, he had a riding companion, and was near the residence of his friend, Mr. Brooks, in Medford, where he was immediately carried.

The instant his accident was known to Mr. Brooks's family, their negro servant hastily dressed himself, hurried off with a sleigh to the spot, lifted Judge Phillips into the conveyance, and when they reached the house, took him in his arms and bore him carefully in, showing, in every motion, the greatest alacrity and tenderness. "What makes you so eager to help the Judge?" he was asked. "Help him!" was the reply, "I'd like to do any thing *for him;* he *always touches his hat to me when he goes by here.*"

This disaster, convinced him at last of his mistake in so exposing himself. The fracture did not prove to be a severe one. A few weeks of confinement, in which Madam Phillips and his cousin, Miss Sally Phillips,[1] were alternately with him, ensued; and then, long

[1] Married afterwards to Deacon Mark Newman.

before he could lay aside his crutches, he was busy at his work again in the Senate and at home. But another and more disastrous consequence of his ill-timed journeys, was already becoming apparent. His friends saw with deep pain, that his exposures were hastening toward a crisis the general debility under which he labored, and especially a chronic asthma, which had now become exceedingly distressing to him. In fact, many supposed that the foundation of this disease was laid in these very imprudences. When it was too late, therefore, he yielded to their entreaties, and spared himself; but through his whole life, his aptitude for business of every kind, and his interest in it, were such as to insure the full success of any enterprise in which he engaged, however remote apparently from all his usual tastes and toils it might be.

Much of all that he did, in carrying on his various private enterprises, was effected by correspondence chiefly. His letters to his son and others on business, of which we have examined large numbers, evince great sagacity and forecast, with the minutest attention to details, and a habit of applying principles of taste, or science, or political economy, or patriotism, or Christian morality, to one and another branch of his affairs, which any man might safely imitate.

The fruit of so much tact and effort was an ample estate, accumulated by his own hands, besides the liberal patrimony which he finally inherited from his father, and the ample fortune of Madam Phillips in her own right;[1] and with such a family as his, who had both witnessed and shared his successful efforts in so many branches of business, his property added largely to the attractions and enjoyments of his honored mansion, as the scene of his own domestic life, and of his fitting hospitalities toward others, to which we will now pass.

[1] Exclusive of the portion of Madam Phillips, the estate of Judge Phillips, as inventoried by the appraisers and administrator, amounted, at his decease, to nearly $150,000; a large proportion of the property being valuable real estate, in Andover and elsewhere.

# CHAPTER IX.

## HIS DOMESTIC AND SOCIAL LIFE.

We have already alluded to the embarrassments connected with his early marriage. It was a somewhat inauspicious commencement of his household history; for though *consent* to his marriage was fully given, several years elapsed before it was heartily *approved* by his parents. But the brilliant and yet solid virtues of their new daughter, blended with the mild but commanding demeanor of their son, "like apples of gold in pictures of silver," gradually won them over to the heartiest satisfaction. For nearly four years the two families lived virtually as one, in contiguous dwellings, and for a portion of the period under the same roof, in daily contact and sympathy, and engaged, much of the time, in joint labors.

But the plans of the son soon led him to remove from the old homestead, with the entire concurrence of his father. He was already, as we have seen, serving his native place as town clerk and treasurer. His fellow-citizens had elected him to the Provincial Congress. He had snatched an interval in which he could be absent without blame, to hurry homeward in mid-winter, and set on foot the powder-mill enterprise, which could be most advantageously located in the south village of the town; another long cherished scheme, too, the founding of an Academy, was fast maturing now in his mind, and, after some unavailing efforts to perfect this satisfactorily in his native village, the prospect of greater success in the South Parish invited him to change his residence. Indeed, it was this latter cause which mainly influenced him, as we shall presently see.

The precise date of his removal to the South Parish, it has not been found possible accurately to determine, but it is supposed to have been in the spring of 1777, about six months subsequent to the birth of his son John; such is the tradition in the family. In April, 1778, there is positive evidence, that he was already located here, in the occupancy of a house which has since then been invested with more historic interest than any other in the village; namely, the old dwelling on the estate of George Abbott, then recently purchased with the view of here founding the Academy. To some interesting reminiscences connected with this house, there will be occasion to refer more particularly hereafter. As connected merely with the home life of Mr. Phillips, we need only say of it, that the period of his residence here was eminently the type of all his subsequent career, both public and private.

It was here that Madam Phillips began to be left, in her self-relying dignity and energy, to act as sole head of the family, in his frequent and long absences, as she was obliged to do in all subsequent years. Here, his own and her cheerful self-denials and sacrifices, to accomplish great objects on which their hearts were set, first became a part of their daily experience. The house could furnish no elegances, or even conveniences, such as both of them had always enjoyed; yet they chose it, and gave it at once dignity and attractiveness. Tradition still points us to the western window in the attic, at which she loved to sit, in his absence, and gaze upon the extended landscape before her, and lift up her heart to the Heavenly One for strength according to her day. Taste and piety were here cultivated together.

It was most fortunate for him, that in her he had found one so willing to bear the great family cares and responsibilities thrown upon her in consequence of his many absences and absorbing engagements. This she appears to have cheerfully done, not only from the strength of her regard for him, but from her deep interest in the objects to which he was devoted. We have already seen how ready she was "to make any sacrifice," if she could thereby aid him in serving the public; with the same high appreciation of his other endeavors, she was daily not only encouraging him but coöperating with him.

While he was digging with his men in the trenches for his powder-mill, she was sitting up, sometimes till midnight, to prepare lint and bandages for the wounded soldiers in the army. When he could not personally be at hand to inspect the work which he had planned on the farm or elsewhere, she received his suggestions by letter, and saw that they were carefully followed. If any repairs of the house, or changes of furniture, were to be made, what he could not be present to superintend she procured to be done promptly; just as before their removal to the South Parish, she had with her own hand kept the records for him as town clerk; and done not a little of his business for him as town treasurer! We have carefully examined the town records, covering the period for which he was clerk, and find every page written by her; the marginal notes, or indices, only, being entered by his pen, although this was the period in which the town was so often acting upon revolutionary questions, and the records cover a very large space.

The manner of life, thus begun, in this their first residence here, was continued in the same spirit, when after a few years, this house was relinquished to the principal of the newly founded Academy, and they removed to another, still more retired and less commodious.

In this dwelling, now occupied after some material improvements by Mr. Moses Abbott, the admiring friend

10 *

of Judge Phillips, and long his confidential clerk, the family remained until at last their new and spacious mansion-house was erected. The aged mother of Madam Phillips, Mrs. Judge Foxcroft, was now a member of the family, and died here, and here the second son, Samuel, was born. The earliest recollections of the family by some now living, are of their residence in this secluded home, of which Judge Phillips obtained possession by purchasing the thirds of the widow of David Chandler, the interest of the heirs not being included. It was necessarily, and intentionally, doubtless, a temporary expedient, as we find from deeds of various lots purchased by him, that in April, 1782, he was already preparing to erect a mansion, suited to his taste and position.

With a numerous group of relatives, drawn toward them by no common attachments; with a wide and rapidly increasing circle of intimate friends, and general acquaintances in his public stations, to all of whom they wished to extend a generous hospitality, it had been hardly possible for them, in any good degree, thus far to realize their ideal of social life. They could willingly, year after year, incommode themselves, and move from place to place as if dwelling in tents; but to be habitually unable to entertain, in due style, their many valued friends, was a constant occasion of regret.

The building of the mansion-house was an era in the

village, not less than in their family history. Planned on a scale beyond any thing then known in the town, the massive timbers and much of the lumber coming from his New Hampshire lands, it was framed to be raised in sections in a manner entirely novel to the citizens, and requiring all the force that could be assembled; and the raising was a memorable occasion. "The whole town was present," says one who was there. When all the preparations for raising the first section had been made, the pastor, Rev. Mr. French, offered a solemn prayer; and then the strong arms grasped the ropes and pikes, and all was reared without accident. In due time the stately edifice was completed; the grounds were laid out; the elms, in front, were planted, Judge Phillips setting most of them with his own hand; and every thing about the premises was arranged, as the structure and furnishing of the house itself had been, upon a most liberal scale. It was not till the autumn of 1785 that the house was entirely finished, although it was so far done, that the family moved into it in the latter part of the year 1782.

From this date, their natural style of life at home commenced, — the style to which they had been born, and for which they were specially fitted, not more by culture than by their native tastes. The characteristic spirit of each is now associated with them, as seen in this house rather than from any other point of view. The scholars, who recall him, think of him as he used to meet them at the south door and impress some timely hint upon their minds. The people of the town describe him as they saw him in one or another room. Madam Phillips and the children are, in like manner, associated in their minds, and in the memory of guests, with this or that apartment, and with their place at the table, or their seat in the family group.

The period through which Judge Phillips had now passed, since his marriage in 1773, had been in the highest degree exciting. The incessant demands which it had made upon him for the sacrifice of his home society and enjoyments, together with his repeated removals from house to house, had not only been a severe self-denial to him, but a great perplexity to her. In addition to the double responsibility thrown upon her, by his engagements and absences, she could not be free from anxiety for him. He was continually overtasking himself. At times he was in the immediate vicinity of the seat of war. In June, 1775, the Provincial Congress had directed the removal of the college library and apparatus from Cambridge to Andover, under his supervision.[1] In a letter, without date, written while he was engaged in this work, he says: —

"Half a moment only is indulged to a heart that is too

[1] Quincy's Hist. H. U. Vol. II. p. 164–166.

full to open itself in a short period. . . . . Amid all the terrors of battle I was so busily engaged in Harvard Library that I never even heard of the engagement, (I mean the siege,) till it was completed. . . . . We have got near the conclusion of that arduous, and I hope useful service. Matters of so great importance are constantly urging, that I find myself impelled to control a very urgent desire of seeing my best self this night."

To this she replies, late in the evening of the next day:—

"I am now pleasing myself with the prospect of spending a little time *immediately* with my best friend. I wrote you to-day, 't is true, but *what* I wrote I am uncertain, as I was in the utmost agitation,—may you be preserved from every unhappy circumstance, exclusive of absence from your sincere friend."

The British were finally compelled to evacuate Boston, in March, 1776; and after this, there was little ground for any such anxieties respecting him.

In June, 1778, he narrowly escaped being blown up with his powder-mill, when it exploded, and three persons were killed. It was his intention to go down to the mill from his house that morning, early, and give some directions, prior to his leaving in the afternoon for Boston; but a gentleman unexpectedly called on business at his house, and detained him for an hour or two, and in this interval the explosion took place.

With deep gratitude, both he and his friends marked this as a signal interposition of Providence to shield him.[1]

It was a part of Madam Phillips's womanly nature to be in a high degree sensitive to every thing which affected his public character; she was gratified — who would not have been — when he was promoted or eulogized; she shrank from the very thought of his being censured. A life-long solicitude thus pressed upon her spirit, in connection with the elections, the parties, the acrimonies of the times, linked as his cherished name was with them all at some point continually.

Yet with all these checks, their home was to both the central attraction. To him it was the more gladdening, because of his many exiles from it. To her it shone in a new lustre, whenever he could return to it. The compensatory law of life, which brings blessing out of trial, if the trial be borne aright, intensified and elevated their enjoyments. The very reasons which parted them so much were stimulating in their power. It gave a richer tone to the character of each,

[1] In October, the General Court by a Resolve, requested Mr. Phillips to repair his mill without loss of time, and made him a grant of £400 in consideration of his losses, besides increasing for a time the bounty upon all powder manufactured by him, and engaging to bear half the loss should a similar disaster be again incurred.

to be thus enduring and acting for others' interests, at the cost of temporarily sacrificing their own.

Their correspondence became, for long periods, a substitute for conversation, both wielding a ready and accurate pen. Notwithstanding her remarkable conversational powers, she preferred to write rather than to speak. Her "beloved pen," as one of her admirers has called it, could best express her feelings. Her fondness for writing was a strong passion, whether it were her own or others' thoughts, which would grace the manuscript. His letters and other papers were prepared with much less facility. With her it was an exercise of spontaneous taste and tact; with him, it was careful labor. One of the peculiarities of all his manuscripts, not excepting his most familiar and confidential letters, is the careful revision which he bestowed on them, as shown in erasures and changes without number. Of the scores of letters written by them to each other, to which we have had access, there is scarcely one from either which will not illustrate these characteristics of their style; and from the first line to the last in them all on both sides, we have been surprised and gratified beyond expression, not to find a word that has detracted from our respect or our admiration for them.

Their letters are not in the style of books to be printed, it is true; if they were, they would not be letters. But while, in a thousand ways, they let us into the secret of their daily spirit, familiarly and freely, the individuality of each is preserved with remarkable distinctness; whether the subject of their letters for the time be conjugal sentiment mainly, or business, or the transient news of the hour, or the aspect of public affairs, or some religious theme.

Still, in such family communications, incidents and facts of every description always find a place, which no one would be expected to make public; even though their omission may be expedient, on no other ground. We must be content with mere extracts.

Recalling them now as installed in their new mansion, emerging from a long period of anxious self-denial, let us listen to them for a few moments, as they move along their prosperous and honored career. The following extracts are taken from letters written by him at Boston, and from her replies: —

"February 9, 1785. — I will write one line to my dear friend, if it be only to thank her for the kind favor indulged me by Mrs. B——; I was rejoiced to find that you did not hesitate to say that you was *well*, with an emphasis. . . . I am sorry you take so much pains to excuse the delay of copying the constitution.[1] . . . I hope my mother is still with you, and that she will protract her visit as long as she can. Do give my duty to her, and tell her I think much of her advice; I wish I may make nearer approaches daily to

[1] The Constitution of Phillips Academy.

her wishes, and that I shall have the advantage of that most powerful argument to induce a serious attention to my health; namely, the *example* of those for whose society I should be most desirous of a continuance here. This I hope will be noted by my best friend. . . . *Do be religiously attentive to your eyes, if you love me.*

"With the tenderest attachment,

"S. P. Jr."

"February 18, 1785. — Between twelve and one o'clock, the Governor took his leave of the General Court *in form;* the ceremony was in the Representatives' room; but after a message had gone to acquaint his Excellency that the Legislature were ready to receive him, a flutter ensued, which well nigh brought us into a disagreeable situation indeed. After the above-mentioned joint message, the House sent one to the Senate, informing that the body of seats in the south-west part of their chamber would be assigned to the Senate; (now the seats they had usually taken were the front seats, on the right and left of the chair). The Senate, after two or three propositions being made and rejected in *a hurry*, returned an answer to the House, that they *did not agree to the proposal of the House* respecting seats, but would *take those which had been usually assigned them, or would accommodate themselves.*

"Another message was soon returned, informing that the House had previously reconsidered their proposition before made, and voted to assign the usual seats; the two Houses then met. The Governor soon appeared, preceded by the sheriff, supported under one arm by the Messenger of the Governor and Council, and succeeded by his Council and a number of spectators, and was introduced by the President and Speaker to the Chair; then all sat down; after remaining seated a few minutes and the Governor had refreshed himself with some reviving drops, he arose, and, addressing the President and Senate, the Speaker and House of Representatives, told them the design of that meeting; thanked them and the people whom they 'so worthily govern,' for all their kindness; that however unfortunate he had been in the execution of the various important offices to which he had been elected, he was conscious that he had been uniformly actuated by the sincerest intentions to serve them; that his health made it his indispensable duty to retire for the present, but if he should ever be able to render them further service, he should be ready to afford it; then, after addressing himself to the Lieutenant-Governor, whom the Constitution assigned to the chair as his successor, and wishing his administration might be easy to himself and happy to the people, he addressed the executive and legislative branches, with the heads of each separately; and wished them the smiles of Heaven here, and that they might be introduced 'to characters of honor' hereafter."

"June 28, 1785. . . . After this week, I hope to take some burden from your shoulders; the court are determined to meet at eight in the morning, and last night they sat till after eight in the evening; you will, therefore, send a horse on Friday to Swan's on the neck, for your affectionate husband,

"S. PHILLIPS, JR."

"October 28, 1785. — Not a word more about the new professorship, saving some conversation that took place at club, at Cambridge, last Sabbath evening; our brother offered to pledge himself that neither my father or I would *ask* him to tarry, if he should choose to remove. . . . I hope my father tarries with you night as well as day; travelling back and forth morning and evening, must be considerable addition to his toil, and he is wanted as much at those seasons as any. I hope the little sons are well, and that they do n't haunt their mamma as sometimes; give my love to them, with a kiss for the younger, and tell him, if he intends to have one from his papa when he comes home, he must let me hear a good account of him."

"October 28, 1785. — . . . I can't content myself without catching a moment in the hurry of Senate to acknowledge your kind favor by Thornton, though it is pretty plain from the appearance of your letter, that you are too much pressed with care and business for your *health*, *comfort*, and *usefulness*, all of which we are bound to consult by the duty we owe to God, our country, our family, our neighbors, and ourselves; . . . hope to see you to-morrow, and to try the effect of *personal* solicitations for a visit to Boston."

"November 18, 1785. — I am very happy that things go on so smoothly with the new neighbors; may every agreeable circumstance continue, and every bright scene grow brighter and brighter. . . . . Love to our children, and duty to parents. No farther light yet from any quarter respecting the newly elected Professor; I rejoice exceedingly that your mind is in so agreeable a state relating to that matter."

"March 2, 1786. — Mr. Bingham had better attend the Academy only as health will permit, though it should be but half the time, than to overdo and render himself unable to attend at all.

"Your parting with Mr. Pearson will be, or has been, a

grievous one, but perhaps the parting will not be a final one, and that all your good days are not over. . . . . When you can without too much inconvenience, do let me hear from you. Adieu, your most affectionate

"S. P. Jr."

"March 23, 1786. — I thank my dear friend for her favor by our good neighbor; it must be something very extraordinary to prevent my being at home on Saturday. Your account of the smoke and cold[1] with which our friends have been visited, is very gloomy; such an evil *must* be remedied by some means or other, — I should propose one, if I did not expect to be at home before any alteration would probably be made. — Cousin John I have not seen this week, and shall be happy to deliver your message; advice from you will have great weight with him, though by no means so great as it would if received immediately from your own pen or lips; often have I wished that an epistolary intercourse was to take place between you and some of our most promising young gentlemen, after they have left us. I firmly believe such a measure would, in many cases, be a happy security from vice, and would be the means of *very useful improvements;* and this, not only from the letters themselves, but those letters and that correspondence would be a powerful incentive to improvements in knowledge, solid and ornamental; for I am very confident that a desire of appearing to advantage with the other sex will oftentimes influence minds, that are unmoved by other considerations; but I must run, after I have assured you of the ardent affection of your unworthy husband. S. P. Jr."

[1] In the Academy.

"June 2, 1786. — Mr. Wardwell is so kind as to give me an opportunity to convey a line to you, which will not be unacceptable, if it only serves to evidence that my attention is employed upon an object whose distance does not remove the power of attraction. . . . . Have you employed Dinah yet, and will you do it? by your conduct in this instance, I shall judge of your regard for my enjoyment, for as you lately said, *actions* speak louder than words. Please to tender duty, love, regards, etc., as due, and believe me to be in sincerity yours in the bonds of genuine affection.

"S. P. Jr."

Such expressions of his watchful solicitude for her happiness in the arrangements at their home, are constantly occurring in his letters, while she as uniformly manifested a deep interest in the great public exigencies which occupied his thoughts. Often her replies, in the correspondence, adverted to some such topic, more than to incidents of family or personal interest; so that while involved in his manifold public cares, he was never oppressed with the feeling that she would have him leave them for her sake.

Indeed, the predominant tone of her letters has seemed to us, in this respect, not less remarkable than his. He writes little of the times, or of measures to meet them, or even of his own part in public affairs, — but more of the kindnesses shown him by his friends, and of the pains he has taken to find some rare article to send her, and of some uneasiness which he feels, lest she should suffer from inadequate servants or excess of company. She touches upon all such matters lightly, and pours out the fear, the hope, the prayer of her generous heart for the suffering, distracted country, and for his welfare in its service.

Among her letters, we find one without date, which appears to have been written in the autumn of 1786, from which we copy a few paragraphs:—

"I find Mr. Holbrook is going to Boston in the morning, and as you mentioned my writing, (which looks as if it gave you pleasure to hear from me in this way,) I throw aside my tatterdemalions a few minutes to enjoy myself; believe me 't is the greatest pleasure I can have when absent from you; but here a gloom strikes my mind! I almost wonder that you can advert to me, at such a time of public trouble. I think it a pleasing proof of your affection, such a proof as I feel myself most sensibly affected by. . . . . Trouble still at the westward! What will become of us? from present appearances, I fear little ought we dare to hope for better times. . . . . Surely, we have no right to expect the interposition of Heaven in our behalf, till we can act from better motives. You seem to have some faith that we *shall* see better times. Heaven grant that we may; that virtue may be the pursuit of every mind; that every one may study and be convinced that the chief end and happiness of man is to glorify God and enjoy him forever. . . . . Accept my best wishes, and ask Mrs. Phillips's acceptance of affectionate inquiries after her health; love to the family,—pray don't ride late in the evening, if you love your best friend. Mr. Pemberton's respects to Judge Phillips. PHŒBE."

Subsequently she writes to encourage, and yet restrain him: —

"Do not suffer your mind to be unduly engrossed by *any thing;* soon it will be said of us, that we are gone! Let this consideration weigh with us, to incline us to *enjoy* what we *can* in the line of duty, without distressing ourselves as to the accomplishment of future scenes. By endeavoring to accomplish too much, experience teaches us, we often fall far short of a mark we might reach, if our wishes were not extravagant. I most ardently wish, my dear friend, that you may be so happy as to obtain such direction, assistance, and support, as shall finally set you above the reach of all trouble. Do not suffer yourself to be anxious about coming home; should you, you may lay a foundation for illness, which may prove fatal, for a time, to your active powers. I know there is much business to attend to here, but it will answer no purpose to hurry and distress yourself to get home; do enjoy what you can, and take as good care of yourself as possible. All happiness attend you.

"Yours, P. P."

A few months after this, in reply to a similar letter, he writes: —

"May 31, 1792. — I thank you kindly for your acceptable favor by Mr. Pemberton. I am bound to gratify you if I can in return.

"As to the transactions of yesterday, the paper will show you the elections. What you said and *looked*, determined me before I came from home to accept the office I had held, if offered again, unless something unexpected should turn up to prevent; but had it not been for this determination, the unanimity and cordiality of my brethren would have had great weight. The sermon was excellent as well as the prayer. The Governor gave me an invitation to dine, which I accepted, and was treated very politely.

"As the weather is so exhausting and the family larger than it was, let me entreat you to procure some other female help, — Moses' sister, Happy, or anybody, rather than none. Will you be so good as to desire with freedom the attendance of Betsy Whitwell? If you will gratify me in these matters, you will lay me under additional obligations to gratify you in your requests respecting my health.

"Your affectionate friend, S. P."

Toward the close of the succeeding General Court, under date of "February 13, 1794," he says: —

"I was much obliged by your favor by Mr. Abbott, and for the opportunity you gave me of presenting your acknowledgments to my aunt. I presume my uncle has been made acquainted with and gratified by the contents, as he has been more than commonly cheerful and pleasant since their receipt; although he preserves so uniform an appearance of good-humor that I have not seen the resemblance of a frown since I first came down. I was also pleased with our little son's remembrance of my aunt, and with the handsome manner in which he expressed his acknowledgments. He must have had the aid of some good friend, and such he will never want while he retains the disposition which he now discovers. Knowing how much you enjoy in Miss Sally, you will hardly thank me for dispossessing you of her on Saturday eve. . . . As she sometimes inquires for news, when people go from below, I hardly know what to say — unless that the Prince went to Cambridge to-day with Mr. Russell to visit the College, — that he *did not* go to the theatre on Monday night, though the public papers announced to us that he would be there — that the *House* have voted to impeach William Hunt, Esq., in which case a solemn trial will be had before the Senate — that Mr. Kirkland has united a pair in the bonds of matrimony, though he remains single and disengaged — and that, now 'Governor Hancock is dead,' and Lieut. Gov. Adams has made a speech, the two Houses cannot agree on an answer to it. A detail of General Court proceedings would not, it is presumed, afford much gratification.

"Please to present the book, herewith sent, to Miss Sally.

"Yours, in sincerity,

"S. PHILLIPS."

A few weeks later the Judge writes from his confinement in Medford, of which we have spoken in the preceding chapter: —

"April 16, 1794. — Mr. Abbott has been waiting while I have been writing on necessary business, and left me only time to tell you that I am as well in health as usual, (I was going to say, for Miss Sally and Moses have got into so high a gale, that I hardly know what I write,) — it is more doubtful what particular day I shall go up than it was yesterday; not that my leg is worse, but we receive many cautions about going too early. We are greatly pleased with the idea of seeing you to-morrow, and hope you will have a comfortable ride. . . . Pray make my love to the children, and suitables to all inquiring friends.

"Yours sincerely and affectionately, S. P."

Although disabled by this casualty and but partially recovered, he does not fail, notwithstanding the anxiety of friends, to appear upon the bench at the spring session of the County Court. In a letter dated Ipswich, May 19, 1794, he says: —

"On the presumption that my best friend will be willing to hear from me, one line is offered to inform her that my kind uncle conveyed and drove for me in his phaeton to Major Perley's, — then I took the chair, and arrived about six o'clock. The limb which has given you so much trouble was not worried so as to occasion me any uneasiness that is worth mentioning; — had not worry of mind prevented, my ride would have been pleasant; — the expression of your countenance at our parting gave me concern. I hope you have not suffered so much since as I have, and that you will always enjoy as much superior happiness as you are more deserving. Very affectionately yours,

"Samuel Phillips."

From his duties as judge, though still by no means strong again, he hurries to his post in the Senate, from which he sends the following: —

"June 18, 1794. — I am much indebted to my dear friend for her favor by Esquire Abbott, and am sorry you had such a puzzle in hunting for papers, especially as you met with so poor success; however, I don't wish you to give yourself further trouble on this head. As to the limb, it is gaining; — the crutches are still found very convenient, if not necessary. I believe I could walk with a cane, but a fear of meeting with the disaster which befell neighbor Town deters me. You will conjecture that I have doubts about seeing Andover this week: — it is true, I have; for the court will probably rise next week, and business crowds at this time, as usual, when the session is approaching a close.

"Yours, with sincere affection,

"S. PHILLIPS."

"June 26, 1794. — Mr. Abbott having hinted that there is some probability he shall leave town to-day, I must steal a moment in the hurry that attends the close of the session, to thank you for your last favor, which I do very sincerely; and to tell you that I hope on Saturday once more to revisit my best friend; for, unless something unforeseen prevents, the court will terminate their session to-morrow, if not this day. I still feel much concerned on the subject of help, but hope Mrs. Mack's arrival will afford you some relief. I am not a little rejoiced with the comfort you have in Mr. Newman.

"Yours, with sincere affection,

"S. PHILLIPS."

From this time the letters of Judge Phillips make frequent mention of his shattered health. The more sensible he became of his own infirmities, the greater was his solicitude to relieve her in every possible way; and her letters were prized more highly than ever, as he could not so often visit her. Thus he writes from Boston: —

"February 7, 1795. — The good things you sent me demand my gratitude. . . . Your advice to defer going to Andover, comports with that of all my friends here, though it seems very strange indeed to tarry within twenty-three miles of my best friend, a whole session, without seeing her; but you can hardly realize the difference of my feelings in regard to journeying, especially in the winter and on frozen ground, even between last winter and this. When the court will be up is quite uncertain; I fancy at least that the effect of the theatre may be discerned, in an increased disinclination to labor and close application to business. . . . Pray thank Mr. Newman, presenting my regards, — will endeavor to write him as soon as I can.

"Yours, with sincere affection,

"S. PHILLIPS."

"February 10, 1795. — Very unexpectedly this morning, when I stepped into Mrs. Phillips's, was told that Mr. N. was in the other room; finding that he brought a letter from your hand and had delivered it to Mr. Cooper, I went immediately in pursuit of it, and received a pleasure in the perusal of it, which amply rewarded me for leaving the company of good friends very abruptly. . . . Sammy will be obliged to lose his class if he attends French now: — English, Latin, and Greek, etc., seem enough for a child of his years to attend to at once: — but of this Mr. N. will say more to you.

"Mrs. M. Phillips says it will be very agreeable to go up

with me at Thanksgiving, if court, health, weather, and travelling should favor.

"Your affectionate husband, S. P."

"February 7, 1797. — One line written during the debate of Senate, will be acceptable to my dear friend, if it only informs her that we arrived *safe*. . . . Just before the Senate rose, Mr. Harding sent in your favor of this day, which was very grateful to me. . . . To-day Mr. March gave me a letter for Miss Greenleaf; — as to her going to Haverhill in the stage, it must not be; whenever she chooses to go over, Mr. Moses or Cassius will wait on her. Some small token of remembrance I wish you could give her: would Doddridge's Rise and Progress be acceptable? I hope you will be able to write a line by her to her mamma, expressive of the pleasure and comfort she has given us.

"By the next opportunity you will write to Mrs. Phillips, if you can; she feels so deeply interested in your happiness, I wish she may receive all the attention from you which you can find it convenient to give. Wishing you every support and comfort, which can result from the daily cultivation of all the Christian virtues, I am, with sincere affection, your unworthy S. PHILLIPS."

"February 13, 1797. — The sight of your letter this afternoon gave me much pleasure, and the perusal still more. I am glad to hear that Miss Greenleaf had so agreeable a conveyance to Haverhill — hope you gave the honest girl a letter for her mamma, expressive of our sense of her benevolence, and our gratification by her visit. The idea would be highly pleasing to her parents, and conveyed in *your manner* would be *a feast to them.* If you could not write when she left you, won't you let a letter overtake her at Haverhill? I had rather pay ten postages, than that our good friends should miss of the pleasure. As to Miss French I am quite willing she should be noticed, and wish you to inclose ten, fifteen, or twenty dollars to her father, with our regards; subjoining those wishes which your pen will dictate better than I can prescribe."

"February 17, 1797.—I thank you for your kind favor of the 13th, and am much gratified by the information that you have honest Timothy again with you. His fidelity is remarkable; indeed I don't recollect that I ever hired any person, on the farm or in the house, in whose fidelity I placed more confidence.

"I had some conversation to-day with our son respecting his situation. It must be considered unfavorable to the object intended; our intention was that he should be under the instruction of a gentleman most eminent in his profession. Mr. Dexter was thought to be such an one; but instead of having the advantage of Mr. Dexter's instruction, he is at Philadelphia. . . . On considering all circumstances he seemed convinced it was best to remove, and if so, the sooner the better. Your opinion, however, on this point is essential, for if it meets with your disapprobation I can't be willing to take measures to effect the change. If the proposition should appear to you as it does to us, the next question is, what place is most advantageous?—and here Mr. Reeve comes into view again. Mr. Bacon still speaks of him, and that frequently, as a man under whom more advantage is to be obtained than any other that he knows of. This is undeniable: that a man who makes the business of instruction his object, and gives his attention wholly to that, is much to be preferred to one of the same abilities and acquirements whose attention is employed other ways, or divided among a variety of pursuits. . . . In this case, as in all others, we have need to ask direction from the Fountain of wisdom, and may He graciously impart it unto us.

"Thus prays your affectionate,

"S. PHILLIPS."

"March 26, 1798.—I arrived at Page's about a quarter before seven. The travelling was much better than I had any idea of. Our son came in about three quarters of an hour after I arrived, and we have spent as agreeable an evening as the melancholy tidings he brought me would admit of.

"Upon inquiry after our friends, he soon informed me that Mrs. Quincy was no more![1] Last night, she departed this transitory scene. She had been considered by her physician, some days past, to be in a critical situation; on Saturday was pronounced by Dr. Danforth to be much better, and her friends were greatly encouraged; but soon, alas! was the prospect changed, and in a few hours was her account closed. What an affecting lesson of the uncertainty of this world and all that it contains!—of the delusive nature of the brightest prospects! Just arrived or arriving at the highest point of enjoyment, which she could ever expect or rationally desire, in the present life, and the irrevocable sentence is pronounced, 'time' (with you) 'shall be no longer!' How solemnly is the sacred admonition enforced by such events, 'to rejoice as though we rejoiced not!' How much brighter has been her prospect for continuance in life than mine has been these several years! And she is

[1] Mother of Hon. Josiah Quincy.

suddenly separated from the dearest connections, and from one in whom she lately promised herself a large increase of enjoyment, and with as much reason, too, as the uncertainty of sublunary joys would admit of; — while I am still spared, a wonder to myself, and a monument of the Divine forbearance and benignity! What an obligation to greater purity and fruitfulness than in time past I have exhibited! What a warning this to cease from depending on any thing on this side of the grave!

"My uncle must be deeply affected with this shock. The rest of the family will feel it very deeply; but his age and infirmities will render him more susceptible of the anguish. I think this is an hour to express sensibility for and sympathy with him. Is it too much to ask you to come down and join in paying our last respect to the memory of our friend, and expressing our condolence with the afflicted family? I can't forget her attention, on similar occasions, when we were bereaved of father and mother.

"Perhaps there is no occasion on which the attention of friends is more sensibly felt; and few, very few indeed, are the friends to whom we are under so great obligations as to my uncle and aunt. I have, also, at this moment, fresh in my mind the uncommon sensibility my uncle expressed for the notice, when I attended the funeral of his consort. But, although I should be uncommonly gratified by your presence, *if it can be granted consistently with your welfare, I shall be as much grieved, if you indulge me at the expense of that.* . . . . Yours, sincerely,

"S. Phillips."

To all such communications, year after year, Madam

Phillips, as we gather from his frequent acknowledgments, and from specimens of her letters which have been preserved, sent replies worthy of herself and of him; and with these delightful interchanges of thought, sentiment, plans, and incidents, they relieved the tedium of their separations; revealing more and more to each other in all the process, the rare virtues which composed their character.

We have chosen to give these copious extracts, continuously, for the purpose of showing, in their own words, the tone of their domestic life, as it affected each in their circumstances. That two persons could well have shown more mutual respect or confidence, or have felt a more fresh and gladdening attachment to each other, will not, we are sure, be imagined by any one. And when we think of him as consuming his life so fast, amid his many cares, it is a relief to turn and see how by word and deed she unfailingly cheered him.

It will be noticed that in all this correspondence, so free and frequent, there is a certain air of dignity, (of stateliness, we might be tempted to say, especially on his part,) which seems to check that familiarity for which we naturally look. He addresses her uniformly as his best "friend," or his invaluable "partner," not as his "wife." He subscribes himself, ordinarily, her sincere, affectionate, devoted friend, but seldom her husband. His suggestions and requests are, usually, in diffident and guarded terms; and often there is a tone of modesty, bordering upon despondency, pervading his letters, which contrasts strongly with her exuberant vivacity and hopefulness; a result doubtless of his jaded and diseased state, rather than of any trait in his character.

These guarded courtesies and deferences between them, however, serve to show us the type of their family in a strong light. It was eminently a family of refined manners, — refined even to punctiliousness in forms, as well as in its inner spirit. The children were trained to address them as their "*honored papa*," and "*honored mamma*." Scholars, who were inmates of the family, could never enter or leave the room, in their presence, without a respectful recognition; a rule which she enforced as habitually in his absence as when he was at home.

Yet they were the farthest possible from that affectation of gentility which shuns labor and vaunts itself in a ceremonious display. A simplicity that was almost severe, a steadfast frugality, and a diligence that scarcely spared time enough for necessary rest or relaxation, marked their life; and yet a most generous hospitality, and an open-handed charity to the poor, which shows that their frugality was not parsimony.

Indeed, no house in all the region was more frequently resorted to than theirs by the needy, and none were more anxious than they, not only to supply the wants thus made known to them, but to search out and befriend the poor who were too modest or sensitive to ask for aid. Habits of quiet beneficence which reached to many a family around them, at various seasons in the year, are still remembered with blessings on their name. One of the most common features in their correspondence is the suggestion, on the part of one or the other, of some such kindness to be shown to those in whom they had become interested; a book or a garment to be given, a sum of money to be sent, a quantity of wood, or flour, or vegetables to be left; and the *manner* of doing the favor is studied as carefully as the deed itself. In these numberless little ways, their just ideas with regard to the use of property were constantly illustrated, as we shall hereafter see they were in other modes on a more extended scale.

We cannot persuade ourselves to pass now to the notice of his domestic and social life in other aspects, without pausing to add a few words here to what has already been said of the character of Madam Phillips. In every relation, she more than justified his early and sagacious judgment of her rare worth. The virtues which had won his devoted regard, in spite of the disparity in their years, failed not, as we have seen, to win also his reluctant parents to her heart. Her children loved and revered her with a boundless homage. The admiring terms in which all who were ever members of her family, whether before or after her husband's decease, speak of her as a queen among the sex, testify to her commanding influence. The heartiness and intelligent appreciation with which she fostered the interests of learning, especially in connection with the plans of Judge Phillips for the Academy, or in continuation of them by founding the Theological Seminary, have served to give a wide spread distinction to her name which is most richly deserved.

The religious zeal which, as years glided away and trials multiplied, she increasingly evinced, became in the end her prominent characteristic, and endeared her to the good of every name. Much of her time, for the last ten years of her life, was spent in private devotional exercises, with a zest peculiar to herself. One little work, entitled "A Choice Drop of Honey from the Rock Christ," she carried daily in her pocket through this whole period, and when a moment of leisure occurred, she quickened her meditations by some line from it. The Contemplations and Letters of Dorney were so prized by her, that a large part of the entire volume was copied by her hand and sent to one and another of her friends. Whenever she met a striking sentence or paragraph from any religious work, she was in the habit of thus copying it, either to be retained for her own use, or to be sent to others. With these habits of religious reading and reflection, she cultivated, in a remarkable degree, also, the spirit of prayer; until communion with God, and cordial submission in all things, however dark, to his will, seemed to be as habitual as her breath.

Yet every sensibility of her ardent nature remained keenly alive to the last. It was not callousness nor stoicism, but piety, which reconciled her to the sharp and varied discipline of life. In tears she would often say, with a radiant smile, "*Ah, this trial is one of the all things which shall work together for good!*"

At her death, when the lips of her admiring friends were unsealed, and the heart spoke freely, the language of eulogy was exhausted in commemoration of so rare a combination of virtues; the strain of every encomium reminding us of Robert Hall's remark to William Jay respecting a friend: "Sir, she has the manners of a court, and the piety of a convent."

"Formed," said Professor Pearson,[1] "by the dignity of her person, and the virtues of her mind, to move in the higher walks of life, and destined by Providence for extensive usefulness, she commanded the esteem and affections of the man, whom, while memory lasts, we who knew him shall delight to honor. . . . Gratitude to Heaven, and justice to her, oblige us to say, that a very rare assemblage of virtuous qualities, improved by reading, matured by reflection, sanc-

[1] Funeral Discourse, p. 11.

tified by grace, tried and brightened by afflictions, constituted her character. . . . Nearly fifty years a professed disciple of Christ, she was a constant, punctual, and devout attendant on the public institutions and ordinances of the Gospel. On the Sabbath, also, to all within it, her house was converted into a sanctuary. . . . To her honor, it will be long said by strangers as well as by friends, that her house continued to be the same mansion of hospitality which it ever had been during the life of her noble consort. Of them both it may be said, that their hearts were not more united by mutual esteem and affection, than by acts of charity and munificence."

One of the many public notices of her in the papers, embodying recollections of her some years subsequent to her death, gives the following portraiture: —

"To her intimate acquaintance with the Faculty of Harvard University from childhood, may, in some measure, be attributed her elegant style of conversation, which surpassed that of any one male or female in this country. She saw the subject under consideration in all its bearings, and clothed it in the most felicitous language. There was no redundancy, no stint, no singularity except that of superior refinement; nothing to excite surprise in her conversation, but the most learned listened with profound admiration at her taste and skill in language. She was fond of her pen, and took delight in keeping up an extensive correspondence with literary and religious persons. She wrote with great ease and rapidity, in a chirography at once plain as a printed page, and whose beauty was only exceeded by the thought it contained.

"She was married to Samuel Phillips of Andover, a young man at that period most zealously engaged in the cause of his country, anxious for its political prosperity, and for its advancement in learning, and he found a most admirable coadjutor in his wife. During the dark period of the Revolution, she sat up until midnight with the females of her household, to make garments for poor, destitute soldiers, and in scraping lint and cutting bandages for the hospitals. The sick in her neighborhood of all classes were inquired after, and every thing that could administer to their comfort was sent from her hospitable mansion. The Academy, founded by her husband's father and uncle, was in the immediate vicinity of her residence, and every pupil's health was the subject of her attention; and to those who had come from a distance, and had no natural guardian near, she acted the part of a parent at all times.

"Devoted to religion with more than a 'cloistered maiden's zeal,' she had not a particle of bigotry in her disposition, and one might have lived with her for years without knowing her sentiments upon any particular point in divinity. . . . Her person was striking; tall above most women, her mien was majestic without awkwardness from her height, her features were prominent, but softened by a mild expression, and her large blue eye was full of sweetness of temper, while it beamed with genius."

As we read such enthusiastic eulogies, we are ready with Milton to exclaim: —

> "O! when meet now
> Such pairs, in love and mutual honor joined?
> With goddess-like demeanor forth she went,

Not unattended; for on her, as Queen,
A pomp of winning Graces waited still,
And from about her shot darts of desire
Into all eyes, to wish her still in sight." [1]

Favored by Providence with such a wife, as the chief light of his home, Judge Phillips needs to be seen with her now in his relations to their children.

The early training of the elder son, in the troubled era of the Revolution, was the earnest care of both the parents, their skill making the best possible amends for the disadvantages of the times, and of their own unsettled state as a family moving from house to house.

This child was physically and mentally in the especial likeness of his honored mother, and every year, with every form of culture under her hand, only added to the striking resemblance in manners, person, temperament, and aims. Both in childhood and later years, that ardor of spirit which characterized her, carried him along in his course with eager enthusiasm, which it was their study to check, as the chief source of danger to the character and prospects of a young man. Every thing was done by him heartily, generously.

After a careful preparation in the Academy for the University, he entered Harvard College in the autumn of 1791, pursued his studies with great assiduity

[1] *Paradise Lost,* Book VIII. 57–63.

through the course, and graduated in 1795 with distinguished honor; the salutatory oration in Latin being assigned to him, as it had been to his father before him. Many of the family letters while he was in College and afterwards, are worthy of being here cited, (omitting only such portions as relate to unimportant or strictly private matters,) although we shall reserve a part of the correspondence between the father and son for another chapter in our narrative. We quote, nearly entire, first a letter of Judge Phillips, dated,—

"ANDOVER, Sabbath Evening, August 19, 1792.

"MY DEAR SON,—I have received yours of the 16th, and hope you got down safe and found all well, as you did not inform us to the contrary. The vacation has expired before I had performed that duty to you which I intended, and probably before you had executed what you had purposed,—a specimen this of what will be the case with most if not all future periods of your life.

"Your term at College will expire before you are aware of it, and you will probably then find that you have not acquired all you designed,—life itself will soon be closed, while many of its schemes and plans will remain unaccomplished, but dreadful beyond expression will it be for us, if we shall have neglected the great business of life—that of making our peace with God. At every stage of our existence here, this is too little thought of; at your time of life and in such a situation as you are, there is great danger that it will be criminally neglected, though in all probability a more favorable opportunity will never afterward offer for attending to it. It will be of great use to inquire of ourselves at the close of every day, how our improvement of that day will appear at the great closing scene. . . . .

"After giving a due attention, in the first place, to this greatest of all duties, you will, I trust, give all the diligence that is consistent with health to the acquirement of useful knowledge. Your collegiate exercises will grow more numerous, or trying, or both, as you advance, and the ease with which you will go through those which are before you will depend much on the manner in which you perform present duty; — any deficiency in the foundation will affect every part of the superstructure; — besides, one neglect or omission will lessen your reluctance to another, and a third will not be so painful as the second, till presently a habit may be formed which will not only bring you out a lean scholar, but prove an effectual bar to your usefulness and happiness in life. *Obsta principiis*, be your motto, whenever feeling a propensity to neglect a duty or perform an action, or even when entering on a train of thinking, which, if formed into a habit, would injure your peace or reputation as a Christian, a scholar, or a gentleman.

"I mentioned your health as necessary to be consulted; — this may be preserved with very close application, if due regard be paid to exercise and temperance. The example of your friend Peele, gives full proof of this truth; as to exercise, I used to practise it by walking in my chamber, especially when I had any thing to commit to memory. Sitting or standing in an *erect* posture, when at your desk or table, is of great importance; — probably more scholars have injured their health by bending over a table or desk than in any other way. Walking, too, will be a favorable situation, while recollecting what you have read or learned, and the business of *recollecting* or reviewing will be of great use to you, especially at the hour of scrutiny at those serious examinations. I was much pleased with the account given of your performance at the last trial; — I hope it will be your ambition, at least to maintain your ground, and to advance forward as far as you can; — to acquit yourself with honor before so respectable a committee of the Board of Overseers and Corporation, and to be thus reported by them to the whole board, is not a small object; but to be recorded in the library, there to stand for the inspection of the numerous gentlemen and ladies who visit that place, and are disposed to inform themselves on that subject, must be a powerful stimulus to exertion.

"Mr. Pearson's exercises will be of great use to you; — for in every sentence that you speak and write the knowledge of grammar is concerned, and to be able to write and speak with propriety, correctness, and elegance, is of great and daily use, and a rich accomplishment. Connected with this branch is that of mathematics, as it will assist you in thinking clearly and methodically, both which are essentially necessary to good composition; for you must have pertinent, clear, and connected ideas, before you will have any use for clothing for them. . . . Adieu, my son; be wise and be happy.

"So prays your affectionate parent,

"SAMUEL PHILLIPS."

A letter from Madam Phillips, dated "February 18, 1793," contains the following: —

"Your letter, my dear son, afforded me much pleasure. You say you are alone; I am pleased to find you can *enjoy* yourself without a chum; but, can you forbid the dissipated to enter your apartment with so good a grace as if you had a companion? — excuse the hint, my dear; be assured every caution I give you I mean should promote your happiness; while in the world we are *all liable* to be led astray, and need be constantly upon the watch lest our feet slip. I would have given much for so kind friends as you have to point out the dangers of the road I travelled; — at your time of life I had a thousand difficulties to encounter which you know nothing of. I hope, my dear son, heaven will assist you to keep your heart with all diligence, since out of it are the issues of life, — yea, *everlasting* life.

"I am much pleased with your present taste for reading; . . . believe me, every good maxim you store your mind with in youth will yield you satisfaction hereafter. May you be directed to the happiest mode of acquiring that learning which shall make you useful here, and be enabled to adopt and practise those virtues which shall secure you an interest in that blissful region where nothing is admitted which can cause a sigh."

In June, of the same year, she writes: —

"I am happy, my dear son, that it is in my power to spend a few moments with you this evening, and pleased at having so good an opportunity to forward some necessaries to you.

"I hope, my dear son, if it be in the Divine plan for you to continue on earth, till and after you arrive at manhood, you will be steadily employing the interim for enriching your mind with the most valuable stores which will be of use to you, and indeed *constitute* the happiness of your life. O! never forget what your dear papa has a thousand times repeated, that '*youth* is the *seed-time* of life!' . . . I cannot express to you the pleasure it gives me to find you are desirous of walking in the right path. May the good Spirit lead your mind ever to make the wisest choice, strengthen you in the performance of your virtuous determinations, and continually effect the most pleasing emotions; surely I can have no higher delight than your happiness would bring. 'To be *good* is to be *happy; angels* are happier than mankind *because* they are *better*.'"

At the College Exhibition, in September of this year, an English colloquy was assigned to young Phillips with two others of his class; and Judge Phillips, in a letter soon after, dated September 9, 1793, writes: —

"Yours of the 2d instant I received on the 7th, and was much pleased with the contents generally. I am much gratified, my dear child, by finding the honor which is done you in the late assignment for exhibition; — I hope you will spare no reasonable pains to acquit yourself with honor to your instructors, your parents, and yourself. Don't delay your preparations. To be ready in season will afford your mind great ease, and will give you opportunity to correct errors and make improvements.

"You will have excellent friends in Messrs. Tappan, Pearson, and Kirkland, to advise and assist you, though it is doubtful whether they will do more than correct; and nothing will tend so much to free you from embarrassment in the delivery, as a confidence that you are master of your subject.

Do n't forget to guard against *precipitancy;* due moderation is very graceful. As to entertaining your class I shall not hesitate at the expense, if it can be conducted in such a manner as won't give offence to the government. You will be careful not to exceed what has been customary, only handsomely to conform to general practice. Those who come after may be fond of imitating your example.

"The subject of your forensic is excellent, and you have the best side of the question; I hope you will do it justice. You will naturally remark on the labor and risk of acquiring an estate, — the care in preserving and the anxiety about losing it, — the evil effects that affluence often produces on the mind, in nourishing pride and ambition, accompanied with insolence toward, and contempt of, the lower classes of society, — the shafts of envy that are often levelled against the possessor, though his character may be irreproachable. Further; is not a state of mediocrity or competency the lot of the great bulk of mankind, — and has not the Father of the great family, who is unerring in wisdom and infinite in goodness, assigned to the largest class of them, that condition which is most friendly to their happiness? It is true, where affluence is improved to communicate happiness to others, it affords the highest enjoyment; but a disposition for this improvement of wealth rarely accompanies the possessor of it, and where it does, to determine on the proper objects of liberality, and to decide the *quantum* requisite, and the best mode of granting it, is a work of care and labor to him who wishes to acquit himself with fidelity in his stewardship.

"Where great wealth is accompanied with great corruption of heart, which it often produces and still oftener increases, how melancholy are the effects to the possessor, —

how distressing to those within its influence:—a striking instance we have in the famous, or rather infamous, Duke of Orleans, said to be the richest prince in Europe, and if the crimes laid to his charge are well founded, distinguished no less for his vices than he is for his wealth; had this miserable man been blessed with a state of mediocrity, he might have lived an innocent life, and met a peaceful death. From a critical observation of human life, we shall find reason to subscribe to the wisdom of Agur's prayer, and supplicate Heaven only for a competency. I hope your own mind has suggested the above, or better arguments on the subject. Your mamma and brother join in affectionate salutations with your anxious parent. S. PHILLIPS."

A few days later he reiterates some of the cautions in the preceding letter, respecting the proposed entertainment:—

"September 19, 1793.—My dear son, I think it of consequence that you should endeavor, by all prudent means, to prevent disorder and noise at the approaching interview of your class at your chamber, by securing the influence of the more influential and considerate for this purpose; those who wish to preserve order, are furnished with an argument of weight, from the late conduct of the government, which you observe has been as towards 'young gentlemen.' *Shall they not be encouraged to continue this line of conduct by the experience of its advantages?* I had rather you should give your class two temperate 'treats,' (as they are called,) than one that should be attended with noise or disorder."

This occasion appears to have passed off satisfactorily, and without any unusual excesses. But somewhat later in the season, the spirit of disorder became rife in the College, to which we find allusions in the following letters.

In a long and most interesting communication, dated December 17, 1793, Madam Phillips closes with these earnest words:—

"The troublesome scenes you have been witness to make me blush for human nature; and we cannot but look up to that Divine power who superintends throughout the universe, with peculiar gratitude, that while so many have fallen a sacrifice to the dominion of vile passions, you have been *preserved.* Boast not, my son, nor think your own strength has given you the advantage; remember that is but weakness, without aid from on high; therefore, bend low, let me conjure you, to that Divine power which has been protecting you when in danger of delusion from the path of virtue.

"Now, my dear son, most resolutely determine to give yourself up, soul and body, with all their several important interests, to that God who made you, and has thus far preserved you; to him you owe every thing; own him for your sovereign, and accept that invitation, founded on the highest benevolence to wretched man, to embrace him whom he has announced his well-beloved Son as the Saviour of the world, —give yourself up to this Almighty Saviour,—put your name to the covenant, and may God strengthen you to perform all the requisites to prove your sincerity."

A brief note from Judge Phillips, dated December 31, 1793, suggests, in reference to the vacation:—

"You will be very careful to leave every thing as safe as possible. . . . . The winter vacation is the time when the mischievous are most apt to bestir themselves, and it is possible that the *reforming club* may be more exposed than others. You may mention, as you have opportunity, that Mr. Abiel Abbot, of Wilton, has been written to by a friend, (not one of the electors,) to know whether he would accept the Tutorship if offered, — but he and his friends have great doubt on account of the treatment tutors have met with. It is of consequence that collegians should see how much they injure themselves in discouraging and depriving themselves of some of the best of men, by insulting those in office. I hope to see you with sound limbs and a pure mind in a healthful body."

In the college honors for the junior exhibition, the succeeding year, an oration in Latin was assigned to Phillips, just after he had borne off one of the prizes in his class. At the exhibition, the next spring, 1795, he was honored with a mathematical exercise; and on graduating, as already mentioned, he pronounced the Salutatory Oration. As this era drew near, gratified to the utmost with his deportment and proficiency, and with his honorable rank in his class, his parents were eager to give him such a Commencement, as the judge had sought for himself at the close of his college course.

"I forgot," says his father, June 15, 1795, "in my hurry on Saturday, to ask you respecting your cloths for Commencement, what color you would choose. . . . . I hope you have tried and ascertained what can be done about obtaining one or more upper chambers; also the fourth chamber on the floor you have already secured three upon, if not, do n't delay this matter, and let me know your prospect. Let me know also what you wish for in Boston, that I can procure you. If there must be a curtailing of your oration, I should like to have a copy of the whole in English, so as to form a better opinion what part to omit, unless you are well satisfied yourself on that head. You will devote yourself to the business of your oration this week, as much as you can. If you can't be secure from interruption at your chamber, you had better retire where nobody can find you; the largest edition of Ainsworth may be useful."

In arranging for the entertainment of his class, Mr. Phillips was not only thus liberally aided by his father, but as generously also by his mother, many things being prepared by her own hand, and many by others under her eye at Andover, and sent to Cambridge for the joyful occasion.

It may have been the foreshadowing of this parental zeal for his especial gratification at this juncture, as well as his uniform past experience of their kindnesses, which prompted him, in May of this year, to dwell upon "parental affection" as his theme at a class exercise, a portion of which we here quote:—

"Omnis in Ascanio chari stat cura parentis."

"Parental tenderness is a source of the most refined pleasures to the heart of sensibility. It arises from benevolence directed to its favorite objects. It is an instinctive tenderness impressed on the human mind by the hand of nature, and an emanation from the great fountain of benevolence. It is that tie which holds together society and makes man the friend of man. The full strength of these impressions is only felt by that tender parent whose sublunary happiness or woe depends on the good or ill conduct of his favorite offspring. If, allured by the deceitful charms of vice, they follow in her train, the darts of anguish sink deep within his soul; but if they pass regardless by her tempting doors, and fly to that best retreat where modest virtue stands with open arms for their embrace, language cannot portray the ecstatic feelings of his heart. To such a parent, do not our youthful bosoms burn with desire to express their emotions of filial gratitude? Yes, while he retains the powers of sensibility we will strive to make his joys more exquisite by our obedience; and when impatient angels shall beckon for their long-wished companion, when time shall have poured her richest honors on his head, let ours be the grateful office to soften the pillow of declining age, until relentless death shall cut the knot, and Heaven reward its votary in the bosom of parental affection."

The copy of his Salutatory, in English, which his father desired him to send, is preserved, as is also the original in Latin, together with various other compositions of his in the same tongue, of which he was a great admirer, — and from this we extract a few paragraphs. After suitable addresses to the patriot, Samuel Adams, then Governor, and to President Willard, and others of the Faculty, he suddenly apostrophizes the University, as if the spirit of a past generation were glowing in his breast: —

" Ye sacred, venerable walls, thou school of ancient heroes, thou monument of the magnanimity of our ancestors, we bid you our last, solemn farewell! Thou hast been the guide, the delight of our youth, thou shalt have the support and the filial affection of our riper years. May thy sun continue to ascend till time itself shall die!"

To his class mates he says, in a strain worthy of his Revolutionary father: —

" Let us duly appreciate the inheritance before us, and never forget the toils, the hazards and sufferings of those patriots and heroes by whom it was purchased; despising a life of inglorious ease, let us be ever awake to preserve, and active to improve our glorious patrimony; and, whatever be our station, *the happiness of the great whole be our object — fidelity, our motto!*"

Then with a manly pride and exultation he lingers, in conclusion, upon the present and prospective glory of the nation: —

" While other nations are doomed to distress in various forms, we hail America the favorite of Heaven. While the land and the ocean conspire to our happiness, the city and the country, with the various inhabitants of both, rejoice in their bounties. Behold the forest daily yielding to the hand of culture, and every part of our land bearing marks of improvement. See colleges, and institutions for increasing the knowledge and happiness of mankind, multiplying and progressing. All these are guarded by constitutions and laws, founded on the principles of reason and the rights of man. These constitutions and laws are committed to guardians, whose ability and fidelity their country has proved. Behold at the head of them all that man, who is the ornament, the pride, the glory of his species. Almighty Parent, suffer us to implore but one blessing more: that Thou wouldst teach us the worth of thy mercies, and learn us to improve them, that they may continue as long as time shall endure!"

Graduating from College with such high promise, Mr. Phillips became for a time an assistant teacher in the Academy at Andover, where he united with the church under the pastoral care of Rev. Mr. French, in April, 1796; the assiduous religious culture of his early life, and his own mature convictions, together with the influence of a severe affliction under which the family were then bowed down, conspiring to give a salutary spiritual bias to his feelings. But it had been his own and his parents' settled expectation, that he would devote himself to the legal profession. Accordingly, arrangements were made for his entering upon his professional studies in the autumn of 1796, with the Hon. Samuel Dexter at Charlestown.

A letter from his hand, dated March 22, 1797, when his parents, as we have seen, were consulting for his removal, will give us some idea of his position and promise at this period. We give the letter entire: —

"My Honored Father, — Nothing remarkable has happened since you left Boston. Mr. Dexter returned Saturday night and is well; his future destiny is uncertain. I had yesterday two hours agreeable conversation with him; in the course of which he observed, to my surprise, that I came very near going to Holland as Secretary to Mr. Murray, the new Plenipotentiary. Mr. Dexter was good enough to represent me to Mr. Murray in such a light that had not General Washington obliquely hinted at his former secretary, Mr. Dandridge, who is now out of business, I should have had the appointment.

"I feel grateful to Mr. Dexter for his partiality to me in this instance, especially as his exertions in my favor were used without my request or even previous knowledge. I suspect that Mr. Murray and Mr. Dexter were the two candidates for the office. I have conversed with Mr. Hurd about our business, and he says we may do as much business as we please, with a handsome capital, on a safe foundation. I have been told he says that he wishes I would live in Charlestown; I thank him for his politeness. If the weather be pleasant on Saturday I hope to visit Andover. Please, sir, to give my duty to my honored mamma.

"From, honored sir, your dutiful son,

"John Phillips."

In consequence chiefly of the failure of his health in study, his long-cherished plans for professional life were soon after this interrupted and finally abandoned; and he engaged in mercantile pursuits at Charlestown, where he was married, December 22, 1798, to Miss Lydia Gorham, daughter of Hon. Nathaniel Gorham.

From this time, during his residence there, and afterwards at the paternal homestead in North Andover, the intercourse of the two families was so constant in person, that there was less occasion for correspondence, although we propose yet to introduce in another place some further letters which passed between them.

To both his father and mother, this residence of their son, near them, so happily settled in life, was a source of rich enjoyment; and the filial veneration and love which he so admirably expresses for them in the preceding correspondence, it was his study and joy to manifest, while they lived to be gladdened by it. As a citizen here, he was eminently public-spirited, devoting a large portion of his time and fortune to one and another enterprise for the general good, with little regard for the effect of such a course upon his own interests. It was in this spirit, as well as in the love of Christian learning and in his filial devotion to his mother's wishes, that he joined with prompt magnanimity and zeal in her enterprise of founding a Theological Institution here, and so connected his name with hers in the memory of all who shall ever read its history.[1]

[1] Many of the manuscripts of Col. Phillips in our hands, especially his orations delivered on various occasions, would tempt us to dwell more largely upon his literary history, as affording evidence of rare genius, and felicity of expression; but this would draw us too far aside from our general aims in this memoir. He died at North

But while, through his early years of promise upward to his full manhood of honor, the gratified parents had so well done their duty to this son, and been so well rewarded, they had been called to a far different experience in connection with their younger son Samuel.

Andover, September 10, 1820, aged 44, leaving a family of thirteen children, all of whom are yet living.

To his widow, whose recent decease, June 3, 1856, has been already mentioned, we have been under special obligations in these labors. Her delineation of incidents in Judge Phillips's life, and of traits in his character, with her portraiture of his person, his manner, his whole appearance, has contributed to give distinctness to our conceptions of him; and the affectionate reverence which she has often expressed for him has served to bring down to us, over the wide chasm of years, with vivid freshness the quality as well as the strength of those impressions which he everywhere made. He was embalmed in her memory with all that was gladdening in the palmiest days of her home, before the great shadow of her bereavement fell upon the old mansion, and hid from her sight the husband of her early and ardent love.

The devoted filial reverence of her numerous family, whose training devolved upon her so great a responsibility, at Col. Phillips's decease, is now her best eulogy. Her extraordinary tact and energy, evinced in directing their education and in the oversight of whatever pertained to the family, her quick and affecting sympathy, whenever any of them have been called to taste the bitter cup of affliction, together with her unrivalled social qualities, and her genial beneficence of spirit toward all, guided by her religious habits, have not only enshrined her in the hearts of the family, but made her to others, of every class, an unfailing attraction in the old family centre to the last.

The junior of his brother by nearly six years, he knew nothing of the disquiets of the early family experiences. Though born in one of their transient residences, his earliest recollections of home clustered about their spacious mansion-house, with its ample grounds and commanding site. He grew up amid a style and order of family life, now in the full meridian of its salutary, ennobling refinement. His very nature too, physical and mental, was of the most exquisite mould.

If he resembled either parent more than the other, his was the image of his calm, sedate, considerate father; yet in his deep and tender sensibility, the noble heart of his mother could be seen, reproducing its taste and tone in every winning form. Indeed, there was a peculiarly feminine grace and sweetness in his spirit, and in his manner, which gave a charm to his boyhood, without essentially marring it.

Though often merry and eager in boyish sports, therefore, he would as often suddenly withdraw from these out-of-door scenes, and nestle fondly by his mother's side, to pour into her ear his accents of pity for the poor of whom he had become informed, or of sadness at the misconduct of some playmate that had come to his notice, adding often the exclamation, "O! mamma, how much better it is to be a good boy, than a naughty boy, is n't it!" At any time, if she was at leisure to talk with him, he would hasten to converse upon a variety of subjects with a solidity of views and a forecast far beyond his years, but especially upon plans of doing good, as his favorite theme. Such desires as he would express to make every one happy, such suggestions about denying himself, or taking upon himself the charge of some charity in order to relieve a needy one, such strains of pensive sentiment in regard to usefulness in his subsequent life, often surprised the listening mother's heart, and made it throb with strange emotion. If ever he lapsed into any childish error of conduct, it seemed so slight in comparison with what is to be expected of every child, that none would have marked it; yet he was quick to see it, and to confess it with ingenuous self-reproach. There was a considerable period when he usually slept with his teacher, Mr. Newman; and his gentle heart, on retiring for the night, would habitually first confess the faults of the day unasked, and then with a child's prayer sink to rest.

His education was carefully planned and prosecuted, and his proficiency correspondingly great. At the Academy exhibition, when he was about thirteen years of age, Mr. Newman proposed his reciting upon the stage the lines of Selkirk, "I am monarch of all I survey," etc.; after suitable private drilling, he appeared and rehearsed the verses with so much grace, dignity, and pathos, that his father wept for very joy, which he had too much heart to repress. The child was, at this time, shooting rapidly up to the stature of manhood, and was in every trait so much a man in the type of the father's high ideal, that Judge Phillips weighed every new question respecting his education with especial care.

Of all the long guarded relics in our hands, none appear to have been so often perused in the family, until worn almost to shreds, as a few simple letters from his pen, which we here give entire.

"BOSTON, November 2, 1794.

"HONORED MAMMA, — I have been trying for some time to form an acquaintance with the Muses, but they are afraid to come nigh me, as it were, for fear I should abuse them. On Saturday, I went with my honored aunt to Cambridge, and attended the funeral of our beloved Russell, — hope that instance of mortality will prove a happy lesson to me, and the occasion of my being also ready. I dined at Mr. Gannet's, — just as I had dined I saw my brother, who informed me you was well, which news rejoiced the heart of him who is constantly thinking of you and that last farewell, which I was very sorry was not agreeable to my honored papa; but hope I shall conduct in such manner as ever to merit the approbation of both my parents.

"Please to give my respects to Mr. and Mrs. Newman, and duty to my papa. From your dutiful son,

"S. PHILLIPS."

"BOSTON, November 5, 1795.

"HONORED PAPA, — Yesterday afternoon I received the news that you should send a chaise; I went to my uncle's immediately and delivered the message; my aunt was very glad because she was not ready.

"Please to give my duty to my honored mamma, respects to Mr. and Mrs. Newman, love to brother, and please to receive duty from him who feels the warmest affection towards his parents, who is sincerely sorry for all his missteps, and who hopes, by the assistance of Almighty God, that his conduct will ever recommend him to his parents.

From your dutiful son, S. PHILLIPS."

"ANDOVER, January, 1796.

"HONORED PAPA, — A week has elapsed, and I have not had the pleasure of hearing from you; therefore I conclude it is my duty to remind you of a subject which has been under your consideration for some time, but through the multiplicity of your business may perhaps have at this time escaped your attention, — I mean Greek, sir. On deciding which subject, I suppose depends the part which I am to act on the theatre of life; and therefore must be the result of cool deliberation, and not the hasty effusion of a moment. By means of its not being determined whether I was to go to College or not, you may naturally suppose I have not pursued my studies with that eagerness I otherwise should have done; imagining that the study of the dead languages would be of little or no use to me, unless I put them into execution. 'Riches,' says Dr. Enfield, 'instead of increasing our benevolence in proportion as they enlarge our opportunities of doing it (as might reasonably be expected), how often do they swell the heart with pride, that unsocial and unfriendly passion, and minister to the flame of contention.' . . . 'These, however,' says he, 'are not the necessary consequences of wealth. In the heart which has been carefully cultivated by the hand of wisdom, it produceth far different effects, — it produceth the fruits of piety towards God, and good-will towards man.' . . . And, my honored papa, if fortune prosper me, I hope I shall learn of the good old patriarch, Abraham, not to forget the God who giveth power to get wealth. Till I hear from you, I shall continue to spend my leisure time in writing, not to neglect my other studies. Please to give my duty to my uncle and aunts, and accept the same from your dutiful son. S. PHILLIPS."

Some expressions in this last letter, are supposed to refer to an inquiry, which in some previous communication he had submitted to his father, whether it would not be best to appropriate the money which it would cost to give him a collegiate education to some other useful object, and let him turn to a life of business, as his sphere of usefulness. He is said to have written with great interest and artlessness, to convince his father that so much money would do more good if given to the poor or to some other such use, than if expended on him.

But how soon and suddenly often are the plans of both parents and children dissipated by an all-wise Providence! On the back of this very letter, the date of which he had omitted, is the following memorandum in the handwriting of Judge Phillips: —

"Son Sam'l; say Jan'y 25, '96, ab$^{t}$ studying Greek; the

last communication to his father, before he was seized with the fatal fever which deprived him of reason, and finished his temporal existence Feb'y 8, 1796."

The stroke fell with stunning force upon every heart in the family. It was this great affliction to which we have alluded as having so salutary a religious effect upon the mind of his elder brother.

When first attacked by the prevailing epidemic, which he was supposed to have caught at a funeral, and which, in the short space of three months, swept about twenty others into the grave, the fears of his parents were at once aroused, as he was soon quite disordered in mind, and for a week they were scarcely absent from him an hour; in his aberrations, the loving ascendency of his teacher, Mr. Newman, could recall him, and win him to take his medicines, when he seemed to recognize no other voice.

But there was no "power to retain the spirit" in that fair form. He was to be numbered evermore with the children that are too good for earth; and, drowned in tears together, his parents bowed to the deep affliction, and laid him in their tomb. Those who saw them on that day of sorrow, will never forget how they trembled and sobbed, yet, in all their anguish of spirit, murmured not, but prayed for grace to drink their bitter cup.

Let the voice of the sorrowing father, first break

the silence in which we bow with them in this grief at his death. We extract a paragraph from a brief letter to his wife, dated Boston, February 17, 1796:—

"I feel anxious to hear of your health and state of mind, and of our son's. If it be your present apprehension that you was not thankful enough for the enjoyment of our dear departed son; may we not be hereafter reminded that our grief for his loss produced a forgetfulness of the importance of remaining mercies? These are surely very many and exceeding great, and the general affectionate sympathy of friends ought by no means to be reckoned among the smallest of them."

Two days later, he adds the following:—

"BOSTON, February 19, 17°

"I am much obliged by your favor of yesterday, and the useful reflections which it contained;—I have no desire that you should forget the dear object of our affections, which we have been lately called to surrender back to the God who lent him to us. It would be in vain, if I were to desire it, because it would be impossible; and I believe it would be wrong to do it if we could.

"Much advantage may be derived to ourselves, and at the same time honor may be done to religion, and the divine object of it, by a suitable remembrance of this precious LOAN OF HEAVEN,—a LOAN, I call it, because I think all our richest temporal comforts may be more properly considered in this light than as gifts. The Author of this mercy never relinquished his right in it; we from his birth, recognized this right, and took the first opportunity, in the presence of the congregation, as well as in the view of Heaven, to surrender back the lovely visitant to its Creator, acknowledging his perfect right to dispose of him as should seem best to him. We must be fully convinced that the best possible disposition *is now* made of our dear child; and should not this conviction produce entire resignation? Should we be willing to oppose and disappoint the purpose of *Infinite Wisdom*, if it was in our power? The very idea excites horror!

"Let us, then, in humble, filial submission, acknowledge that the *Supreme Ruler* has done perfectly right, and entreat that we and others may learn those lessons of wisdom which this dispensation is designed to teach us.

"Perhaps one of the first of these lessons is our entire, absolute, universal dependence on the Infinite Lord and proprietor of all; we are extremely apt to consider the enjoyments we possess as *our own*, as having a complete right in them; whereas, we are only tenants at pleasure; and every day which the rightful owner protracts our possession of any of his favors, he increases our obligation. . . .

"I am yours, with sincere affection, S. P."

In a letter to his only surviving son, he says: —

"Boston, February 24, 1796.

"My dear Son, — . . . The dispensations of Providence seem plainly to admonish me, that it is time to abstract my attention more from the concerns of time, and to direct it to higher objects; within a few years, I have followed to the grave both my parents, a beloved uncle, who was as a father, and a very desirable child; the last bereavement speaks an emphatic language to the afflicted parents and brother in particular; and it ought to be our daily study and prayer to learn the intention of Heaven in respect to us personally; if every instance of mortality is a loud call to the living, as it undoubtedly is, what careful heed is to be given to the solemn messenger when he comes into our chamber to our bed and takes a part of ourselves! It is proper on such an occasion to recollect what was amiable in the deceased, and to endeavor to transcribe into our lives whatever was conformable to our divine Exemplar. I was pleased to find you employed in writing a character of your dear brother; and though the kindness of friends rendered your care unnecessary for the particular purpose for which it was intended, yet I think a part of your time would be well employed in making a delineation of his character somewhat particular; it would afford much satisfaction to us and his particular friends in the review, and might be useful to youth who might be made acquainted with it; for it would be difficult for us to name the youth whose character might with more propriety be held up as a model for imitation.[1]

[1] The following paper, in the handwriting of Mr. John Phillips, but without signature, is preserved in the family, and is doubtless the "character" which his father found him engaged in writing: —

"Died, at Andover, February 8th, 1796, Samuel Phillips, Jr., Æt. 14; the youngest son of the Hon. Samuel Phillips, Esq."

"He 'remembered his Creator in the days of his youth;' while tenderness and filial gratitude marked every feature of his countenance; his every action was dictated by benevolence. Seldom does the age of *childhood* exhibit the actions of a *man;* but here the age of *manhood* would have been adorned by the virtues of a *child.*

"The *young* were ever happy in the embraces of his friendship;

"It is natural for us, also, to inquire how far we discharged our duty to the object of our affections, who is separated from us; and would to Heaven I had less cause for regret on my part than I have upon this review! I desire, on this account, to humble myself in the presence of my Maker; to implore his forgiveness, and to supplicate his grace to quicken me in the discharge of remaining duty. The time, my dear son, is short — how short, is known only to Omniscience! How greatly does it concern us to have our hearts formed to the love — the Supreme love — of infinite perfection! — and what depravity must possess those hearts that are so averse to the love of such an object! What cause for humility! What cause for earnest importunity for purifying and renovating grace! What will kingdoms avail without it! In that situation where I lately beheld my dear child, how trifling is every object compared with the favor of the Eternal MAJESTY OF HEAVEN! and this favor is to be obtained in the days of health and ease, rather than at any period; it is hazardous in the extreme to depend on securing it at any other."

As an illustration of "the general affectionate sym-

the *aged* viewed with fond anticipation his conduct, which fairly warranted future usefulness. His parents flattered themselves with hopes, founded upon the strength of his mind, and on the goodness of his heart. But alas! the tender heart of youth must weep; old age must shed a tear over his sleeping ashes; and the well-founded hopes of an anxious father and a tender mother must be in a moment blasted. Early his Heavenly Father called him to his bosom. He with joy obeyed, smiled duty to his earthly parents, then gave his heart to Heaven."

pathy of friends," to which Judge Phillips refers, we will here insert a letter written now to the only son, by Professor Pearson, of Harvard College:—

"CAMBRIDGE, 15th February, 1796.

"My young friend, son of my friend, permit me to express on paper, what words failed me to utter when I last met you. Believe me, my dear sir, my heart was wrung with anguish for you, as well as for your most excellent, most afflicted parents. Though urged on by an irresistible impulse, it was the first time I ever approached your papa's hospitable dome, but with lively emotions of pleasure. But on that sad, that mournful day, my fortitude forsook me, and a strange reluctance and dread of meeting my distressed friends had seized my mind. This I offer as an apology for my not being able to address you as I wished, on that melancholy occasion. Nor am I now able to express how much I feel for your situation. Suddenly bereaved of a beloved, an only brother, possessed of every quality that could render him dear and amiable, the wound without doubt appears incurable. Your high expectations are instantly disappointed, and every purpose of your heart concerning him broken off. But you will remember that this is the good pleasure of your Father in heaven, who knows what is necessary and best for us, whose object is invariably the same, both when he gives and when he takes away. To unerring wisdom it has seemed good, that you should bear the yoke in your youth. God grant you every needed support, and by this dispensation teach you thus early to realize the danger of depending on any of the objects of time and sense!

"You are just entering, my dear young friend, upon the

giddy theatre of the present life; such a visitation is admirably adapted to curb our ambition, to moderate our desires, and to tarnish in our view the dazzling objects of this vain world. Should this be the happy consequence of this event; should you be enabled hereby to adopt with sincerity the language of David, 'whom have I in heaven but thee, and there is none upon earth that I desire besides thee,' you would have reason to bless God for this early chastisement all the days of your life. Your dear brother, I trust, is happy. Prepare to meet, and enjoy him forever. Be on your guard against the snares of this delusive, enchanting world; and daily seek the protection and blessing of heaven. Forget not to pray for your afflicted parents; and be all that to them, that the best of parents can wish, or that affectionate gratitude can dictate. Not that I suspect the goodness of your heart; for with unspeakable satisfaction have I frequently noticed your filial respect and anxiety; but because I feel every thing for your bereaved parents, that the sincerest friendship can suffer; and because I have loved you from the moment of your birth to this instant. As a pledge of this, accept these hasty lines, with my best wishes for your real happiness in the present and the future life. I shall always be happy to see you, but especially at my own house; let me request this pleasure soon, and believe me as ever, your affectionate and now your tenderly sympathetic friend and humble servant, E. PEARSON.

"Mr. JOHN PHILLIPS."

In the filial tenderness of their first-born son and especially in his deep religious sympathy with them, the parents, in this crisis, had a rich solace; but no balm, human or divine, could at once heal their deep wound; nor did it ever, especially in her heart, fail to bleed afresh, at the mention of Samuel's name. She could never hear him alluded to, years afterwards, even to the last day of her own life, it is said, without bursting into tears, though she loved still to talk of him, and disciplined herself in all her sensibility to speak not only submissively but cheerfully.

The room where he had studied and slept, was not allowed to be disturbed in the slightest particular for nearly fifteen years, until the removal of the family compelled it. His little slate, and writing-book, his pen, and sealingwax, his half-burned candle, his violin, of which he was very fond, his daily text-books in study, his child's bed, his clothing, every thing lay or hung precisely as he left it, a sacred memento; and so he, though dead, spoke daily to their hearts, lingering in their memory and tinging all their habitual life.

While thus sharing in the various experiences of his strictly domestic life, with his rare treasures in his wife and children, Judge Phillips and his family held a social position, in his town and in the country, of no less interest. It will be remembered how early he was the people's candidate for public offices and trusts, and with how much steadiness through all changes they showed their partiality for him, by their full votes year after year. This was the result of his personal popularity, not less than of the unlimited confidence which was reposed in his ability and integrity. Even the exasperated partisan strifes of the Federalists and anti-Federalists did not alienate from him the cordial good-will of his fellow-citizens, although he was incapable of trimming between the two parties, or of concealing, in the least degree, his own political preferences. The popular feeling toward him, as a man and a friend, was always stronger than any merely political prejudice, throughout the length and breadth of the town.

In the village around his mansion, especially, the willing deference paid to him was acknowledged with so much simplicity and grace of manner as to make him a universal favorite. On the Sabbath and other days of public concourse, as he passed to or from the church, no bow was made to him which he did not cordially return, and men have repeatedly told us that in these exchanges of village courtesy they have seen him with his hat off half of the time from the church door to his own.

His more general connections, socially, with various classes of eminent individuals or families in the Commonwealth, were in part a necessary consequence of his own civil labors in such a variety of stations, but still more of the attractiveness and weight of his character. Judges and senators, clergymen, and all men of letters, eminent merchants, and honored patriots, officers in the army, and distinguished strangers from other lands, received his highbred civilities without stint, and returned them without measure. When he was in the meridian of his long civil career, if any had a higher social position, no man in the State had a wider or more elect circle of honored and honorable personal friends.

He was among the few whom Washington, in his Presidential tour, honored with a visit at his mansion in 1789. The personal acquaintance of Judge Phillips with this illustrious Father of his country, began, as we have already stated, in July, 1775, at Cambridge. During the sessions of the Provincial Congress, at Watertown, he had been repeatedly appointed on a committee to confer with the Commander-in-Chief, and from this period all his early impressions respecting this great man were intensified. With him, as with all others, the nearest intercourse with Washington only served to deepen his admiring reverence for him. At every turn in the fortunes of the war, Judge Phillips watched his consummate generalship with eager interest; and when upon the reconstruction of the form of government, Washington was elected to the Chief Magistracy by acclamation, Judge Phillips was filled with exulting confidence in the success of the great republican experiment.

With a succession of greetings, which made his

journey from Mount Vernon a triumphal march, Washington had repaired to New York, where he was inaugurated on the 30th of April. After thoroughly organizing the new government, and setting all its wheels in motion, he deemed it due to himself and the country to make a tour through the Eastern States in the autumn. His arrival at Boston was on Saturday, October 24th, mounted on a milk-white charger, and escorted by a long and brilliant military and civic procession, which had met him on the Neck in Roxbury.

"The number of people collected to see their beloved President," says the Centinel of October 31st, "it is almost impossible to compute. The streets were crowded, —

'You would have thought the very windows moved,
To see him as he passed; so many young and old
Through casements darting their desiring eyes.'"

When he reached the Old State House, and stepped out upon the temporary balcony in view of the people, a select choir instantly sang an original Ode in several stanzas, of which the first was, —

"Great Washington the hero comes,
Each heart exulting hears the sound,
Thousands to their Deliverer throng,
And shout him welcome all around,
Now in full chorus join the song,
And shout aloud Great Washington."[1]

[1] The streets through which Washington rode from the Neck were then called Orange, Newbury, Marlborough, and Cornhill, but were henceforth named collectively *Washington* street.

On the Sabbath he left his quarters, on the corner of Tremont and Court streets, where the store of Pierce now stands, only to attend divine worship both parts of the day in company with the Hon. James Bowdoin.

On Tuesday he received formal complimentary addresses from Governor Hancock, in the name of the Commonwealth, from President Willard on behalf of the University at Cambridge, and from the Society of the Cincinnati, to all of which he made replies; and on Wednesday, he sat down to a public dinner with the elite of the city in Faneuil Hall.

On Thursday morning Washington pursued his journey to Salem, where he was met, escorted, addressed, and entertained with the same enthusiasm. An incident here occurred which greatly pleased him. On being introduced to the selectmen, their chairman, a sturdy Quaker, "being covered, took him by the hand and said, Friend Washington, we are glad to see thee, and in behalf of the inhabitants, bid thee a hearty welcome." On his way from Boston to Salem, a corps of horse from Andover, under Captain Osgood, joined his escort at Lynn, consisting of upwards of fifty men, in red uniforms faced with green; and this company, which had rallied at the instance of Judge Phillips, continued to escort the President on his tour as far as Portsmouth.

When he left Salem on Friday, to please the citizens,

he rode out on horseback, crossing the Essex bridge, then recently erected between Salem and Beverly; and it is chronicled as an illustration of his practical inquisitiveness, that after passing the draw at the channel, he dismounted and went back to examine carefully its mechanism, which had struck him as very ingenious. Proceeding through Beverly, he halted at Ipswich, and was duly welcomed by an address, to which he replied; and in the afternoon he reached Newburyport, where he was received with the same ceremonies.

On Saturday he was welcomed to Portsmouth by Governor Sullivan, who had served under him as a General in the Revolution; the civic and military array here, at his reception, surpassing any thing that had yet been collected, except at Boston; and the enthusiasm of all classes being at the very highest pitch, as they had been hearing day after day of his progress in state from Boston eastward.

Here, as at Boston, he sacredly observed the Sabbath, the Rev. Mr. Ogden at Queen's Chapel in the morning, and Rev. Mr. Buckminster at the Congregational church in the afternoon, having the illustrious guest for a hearer, and both, in the style of the times, "felicitating" their audience upon the great occasion of his visit. At Boston he had sat for his portrait to the artist Johnson, at the request of the selectmen, who designed the painting for Faneuil Hall. A rival Boston artist, Gullaher, followed in his train to Portsmouth, and there the President did him the honor to sit to him also.

But here despatches reached him which led him to cut short his tour, and hasten to the seat of government. On Wednesday, November 4th, he reached Haverhill, where he lodged for the night. Thursday morning he drove early to Andover and breakfasted at Deacon Isaac Abbott's tavern, in the house now owned by Hon. Amos Abbott and lately occupied by Capt. Edward West. Here, as he stood in front of the house, some of our most aged citizens remember to have seen him.

While tarrying here, he asked the little daughter of Deacon Abbott to mend his riding glove for him; and when she had done it, took her upon his knee and gave her a kiss, which so elated Miss Priscilla, that she would not allow her face to be washed again for a week!

Leaving the inn now, the President, escorted by Judge Phillips, and many others, passed along by the Old South Church up what is now School street, to the mansion of his friend, in the south-east parlor of which he was entertained for half an hour or more by the Judge and Madam Phillips with their children and guests. The moment he left the house, Madam Phillips tied a piece of ribbon upon the chair which he had occupied during the interview, and there it remained ever afterwards until the day of his death, when she substituted for it a band of crape.

Before leaving the village, General Washington sat a while upon his horse, on the common opposite the mansion-house, receiving the greetings of the crowd, and gratifying them by a full view of his majestic person; and then, accompanied still by Judge Phillips and the cavalcade which he had collected, the party passed down what is now Phillips street westward, and taking the old Wilmington road across the plain, drove to Lexington, where they dined. Here with Judge Phillips and a few others, General Washington went leisurely over the Revolutionary battle ground; and the General, among other things related, it is said, "with a degree of good-humor," an anecdote of Dr. Franklin. "The British," he said, "complained to Dr. Franklin of the ill usage their troops met at Lexington, by the Yankees getting behind stonewalls and firing at them; — the Doctor replied, by asking them, *whether there were not two sides to the wall!*"

Parting from the Judge here, the General hastened onward in his return, lodging at Watertown that night; the place of so many interesting reminiscences to them both; the next night he was at Uxbridge, and on Saturday of the next week he reached New York. These reminiscences of the first President's tour, in connection with his visit to Judge Phillips, prepare us to appreciate the feelings which both he and Madam Phillips so fully expressed, in letters which they exchanged at the death of Washington. We find a letter from his pen, in these words: —

"Boston, January 9, 1800.

"This day has been devoted by the town of Boston to commemorate the virtues of that eminent benefactor of his country, and distinguished ornament of his species, whose death we all deplore. The orders of procession and of performances, which will be herewith forwarded, will give you a better idea of the plan projected than I can communicate in other words; and it was executed to admiration. Were I to undertake to describe which of the performances was most excellent, the task would be difficult. The prayer by Dr. Eckley was not exceeded by any of the other exercises. The eulogium, by Judge Minot, was composed and spoken in a manner that did honor to himself and to the town, as well as justice to the occasion.[1] The hymn, the ode, and the concluding lines will speak for themselves, and the music was equal to the compositions.

"The whole commanded the undiverted, solemn attention of a crowded audience; and the countenances of thousands expressed, more forcibly than language can describe, that unfeigned grief of heart, which is an higher encomium upon the virtues and services of our deceased *Father* than ten thousand eulogies. Happy will it be for us, if the people of the United States act consistently with themselves. But how absurd will they appear, if, after these high professions of sorrow, they should trample underfoot those important instructions of wisdom, which he gave to us with the solemnity of a dying man. You will probably soon have an op-

[1] This eulogy may be found in a volume of "Eulogies and Orations on the Life and Death of General George Washington," published in Boston in 1800, p. 19–29.

portunity of reading the eulogium; and I wish I could obtain a copy of the prayer; they would afford you a pleasing and profitable repast."

From a letter of hers, dated February 23, 1800, we select the following: —

"Yesterday being fine, I attended the performance of those resolutions made by the town to meet at the North Parish, for the purpose of testifying sorrow for the removal of so great and good a man as General Washington from the world.

"We had two excellent prayers by Messrs. Symmes and French, and an oration by Son, who behaved with dignified composure and respect for his subject and the numerous audience. I do n't pretend to judgment in composition, — have seen but few; those seemed pleased, and 't is said, all were gratified. Mr. B. will be in town soon, and if opportunity favors, will be better able to give you the truth than I am. The music was very pleasing. I believe Son is very glad it is over, and I hope it may be of advantage to him, by giving him a hint not to lay aside valuable books, and may lead him to attend still more to the improvement of his mind, as he must find it *necessary*, that he may step forth on any public occasion, with *confidence* in his abilities to do justice to his subject, and thereby produce good and pleasing effects to the world.

"I am sorry you could not have been here, but suppose you was agreeably employed at the time at the church in Brattle street. . . . . Here allow me to request you would be particularly careful on your return; doubtless, as you have been so long absent, this air and our accommodations may affect you disagreeably, therefore think it will be wise in you to fortify yourself as to clothing, and be *seasonable* in your return if possible; you will excuse me, I am very loth you should suffer by giving us pleasure.

"Mr. French has given us two good sermons to-day, on the subject of the loss of near friends, with some good directions for our improvement under afflictions; and we have had an affecting scene in the baptism of the good doctor's babe, whom he has given the name of *Samuel Moody*.[1] This will gratify you very much; for this I mention it. I am rejoiced you are so well; pray be careful; certainly, you must have very strong inducements when you reflect how much pleasure you afford your friends, and what benefit your services are to the public.

"Present my duty, if you please; I am very glad friends enjoy so much as they do; and pray when the times of suffering come, support from an Almighty God and All-sufficient Saviour may be their portion."

These eager listenings, on the part of Madam Phillips, to every new suggestion for the comfort or profit of the afflicted, coupled with such significant cautions respecting his health, were not wholly retrospective. They had, it is true, gone down together often into the valley of the shadow of death, with departing friends of public fame, and with beloved ones from the circle of their family kindred; and the thought of death

[1] The name of Judge Phillips's early instructor at Dummer Academy.

could never now come up without reproducing the fair image of that dear son for whom they were still grieving. But already the dim presentiment of another and yet greater sorrow in reserve for them, was at times flitting across their minds.

Before we proceed to speak of this, however, we must return again, and trace the life of Judge Phillips in other aspects, as connected with enterprises and characteristics which distinguished him, even more than all we have yet mentioned, from his earliest manhood to his latest age.

# CHAPTER X.

## HIS INTEREST AND AGENCY IN THE CAUSE OF EDUCATION.

It has been shown in a former chapter, with what zeal and ability Judge Phillips contributed, in every practicable way, to the great work of the Revolution, and how persistently, year after year, he discharged the various civic trusts committed to him. Yet, however useful, or honored, or interested he was in such spheres, it was his sense of duty in obedience to the calls of Providence and in his desire to promote the public good, more than his natural taste, or any existing inclination, which riveted him to these various engagements. The times had made him a man of business; had associated him with powder and politics; had agitated him with public cares, and consumed him with public toils; but in all this he had shown how completely a far-seeing patriot scholar can sacrifice his predilections in great public exigencies. Neither "General Court life," as we have seen, nor life on the bench, was entirely congenial to him; although at a time, and amid a generation of statesmen, which made any such station a high honor, especially for a young man.

While faithful to all such trusts, therefore, and unrivalled for his industry and efficiency, he was continually indulging other impulses, more akin to his native temperament and his purely intellectual and moral affinities.

There was, as we have seen, a hereditary love of learning in the Phillips family. The father and one of the uncles of Judge Phillips had not only received a collegiate training, but on graduating had successively taught the grammar-school, for a time, in his native village, while his revered grandfather was exerting his commanding influence over the schools in the south precinct of the town. Yet, when he came to fit for College, he had sought the advantages of the infant and unincorporated Academy at Byfield, as the best within his reach. Nothing had yet been devised in the town to meet the wants of its youth, in a course of liberal study. The town grammar-school was, however, sustained with various success, year after year; and on completing his college curriculum, Judge Phillips became at once conspicuous for the interest which he manifested in this school and the others throughout the town. His influence was constantly exerted to procure the best instructors, and to enlist the zeal of both the children and their parents in improving the standard of scholarship. He was himself a frequent visitor at the schools; and, to the end of his life, with all his deep interest in other forms of education, he continued to watch over the common schools here, and to devise methods of improving them, with a solicitude which could scarcely have been greater, if each one of them had been sustained at his own cost, as his personal enterprise.

Some years after his removal to the South Parish, Mr. William Foster proposed to open a select school for a limited number of young lads, most of whom were to be also members of his family. To this effort Judge Phillips gave the aid of his personal inspection, as well as his hearty recommendation, and for a period of many years, "Master Foster's school" was widely known.[1]

Nor was it in his own town merely, that his habitual zeal in the cause of education manifested itself. In his address to the grand-jury, from which we have quoted, it will be remembered how sagaciously he watched for the welfare of the public schools in the county; calling attention to the demands of the law, and enforcing legal obligation by the lessons of reason and experience. His office as senator, also, placed him for twenty years upon the Board of Overseers of Harvard College, where his pertinent addresses at the close of the class examinations, from time to time, are still remembered by his surviving friends. "It was a rare thing," says Dr. Eliot, "to find him absent from the Board of Overseers of the University. He was often

[1] Records of Phillips Academy, p. 117.

on committees, and improved the opportunities to render essential services to the place of his education."[1] An outline of one of his addresses to the Senior Class at their final examination, is preserved.

"We have received," he says, "much satisfaction in the examination which has now closed; not only in the evidence given of your improvement in the various branches of study you have pursued, — evidence which at once bears honorable testimony of the ability and fidelity of your instructors, as well as of the docility and application of the pupil; but especially from observing that order, regularity, and decorum, which have done credit to the first class of the first University in the United States.

"Your last examination in the ancient and respectable seat of science being closed, it may not be deemed improper for those who sustain the office, and ought to possess the affection of guardians, to make some expression of that affection at this last opportunity of the kind they will have for it. After closing your collegiate life, it will be natural to make a solemn pause, and take a serious review of the scenes you have passed, and at the bar of your own breasts to decide impartially upon the several parts of your characters and conduct, so far as you can recollect them; those of them which receive the honest approbation of cool, unprejudiced reason, will prove a fruitful source of enjoyment through life, and afford a powerful incentive to the practice of wisdom in future.

"If, in the course of your scrutiny, you find occasions for

[1] Eliot's Biog. Dic. p. 379, 380.

regret, (and you will be fortunate beyond the lot of other mortals if you do not,) it will be natural to place a double guard against those dispositions or habits which furnished these occasions, and to caution others against the errors which may have marred your comfort.

"You will soon enter upon the broad theatre of active life; and fortunate, indeed, will you be, if you each select that part to act, which you are qualified to perform, with most advantage to the public, and reputation to yourselves.

"The field for usefulness is immense; the number of skilful, faithful laborers is small. Perhaps at no period has your country had larger claims on the abilities and virtue of its present citizens, and of those who will soon coöperate with or succeed them. Those who are the best husbands of time and opportunities for improvement, will never have occasion to complain of redundant qualifications for any important department; multitudes have lamented their deficiency in them.

"As the season for acquiring these qualifications is short, it is important that your attention should be mainly directed to those studies which are best adapted to qualify you for your intended profession; and let your intended profession or pursuit be what it may, we feel ourselves authorized to say, that no book will so well recompense your study of it, as the Holy Scriptures; nay, that a whole life spent in the closest researches to all other books, will leave you essentially wanting, if you neglect this treasury of Divine knowledge."

In these labors connected with the University, Judge Phillips not only had opportunities for imparting such well-considered counsel to the students, but was kept in constant intercourse with the Faculty, and with a large circle of literary friends, of which Cambridge was the centre. It was here that "the American Academy of Arts and Sciences" originated in 1780, of which he was one of the members named in the Act of Incorporation, which was passed on the 4th of May, before the new Constitution of the State had been completed. Besides the President and Professors of Harvard College, and distinguished clergymen in Boston and the vicinity, many of his associates in this society were the same eminent men with whom he had labored in the Constitutional Convention of that year, and in the Legislature during the previous five years.[1]

During the collegiate course of his son, in the year 1793, the University conferred upon him the honorary degree of Doctor of Laws, as a just tribute to his various public services, and to his zeal in promoting the cause of learning through so many years, and in such a variety of forms; an honor which, at that day, was enjoyed by but few among all the eminent Alumni of the College.

It was not, however, by any such general services in connection with Harvard or elsewhere, that he earned a title, above others, to special consideration as a patron of learning, although in every such agency

[1] Acts and Laws of Massachusetts, 1780, Chap. XVI.

he was second to none. Another and more lasting work in the cause was also occupying him, as we have already intimated, from his early manhood, through his entire career. HE WAS THE PROJECTOR AND CHIEF PATRON OF PHILLIPS ACADEMY.

His plans and efforts to establish this Institution were the favorite work of his life. We have seen with what ardor he enlisted in the great Revolutionary struggle; how laboriously he discharged his various civic trusts; how carefully he inspected his numerous private affairs; with what watchfulness he sought the welfare of his family, and with how much interest he identified himself for the time with every other work, however transient, in which he engaged; yet in all this he did not once forget his foster-child, the Academy; but bore it on his heart and in his hand, with an intensity of devotion to its interests greater than he ever manifested for any other object. His zeal here was like the life-long enthusiasm of an inventor, watching the machinery which he has constructed, and meditating every possible improvement upon it; or the glow of an artist in his studio, admiring and retouching the best productions of his creative mind. We should, therefore, do special injustice to him, and to our own aims in this Memoir, if we did not enter with some degree of minuteness into the history of his connection with so great a work.

It will be remembered that when he graduated from College, it was with such distinction as gave the highest promise of future eminence in professional life. His talents, scholarship, character, and social rank, all justified the highest aspirations. He was, moreover, an only son, the heir to ample estates, which parental industry and frugality were still augmenting; and his childless uncle, Dr. John Phillips, at Exeter, had conceived a special fondness for him, and had intimated his intention of making him the chief heir to his large fortune also. If the prospect of wealth, enriched by the kindliest attachments, could have dazzled him, it was here. There was an affair of the heart, too, exerting its full influence over him; and because of this, the dark cloud of parental displeasure was hanging over his head, and reflecting its shadow into his heart; while, to crown all, the liberties of his country were in extreme peril, and he was drawn irresistibly into the vortex of war.

Yet it was in the very midst of influences within and without so alien from any new literary project, that he gradually developed the plan of establishing a Classical Academy in his native town! and the mode in which he proposed to execute the enterprise, was especially in conflict with these obstacles. His plan was first to persuade his exact and frugal father,—now in a measure inclined to distrust his judgment, since the matrimonial misstep, as he considered it,—

and then his partial uncle, to endow the school as its joint FOUNDERS; thus diverting from himself, as their prospective heir, the property which they should consent to devote to this object. These proposed founders were men to appreciate his plan, but not to have originated it; although in his modesty, he was inclined sometimes to ascribe this honor to his uncle, whose zeal in prosecuting the enterprise was especially conspicuous.

It was a great era in their lives, when they took his project into serious consideration. Trained to habits of rigid economy, their energy in business had hitherto expended itself chiefly in the work of accumulating and investing property successfully; now the greater work of using, or rather of appropriating their property wisely, was to be decided. With what misgivings or modifications they at first encouraged the enterprise, and finally committed themselves fully to it, we are unable to state; but it is well ascertained, that, in their minds and his own, there were very material changes from the inception of the project to its completion; especially in respect to the character and location of the contemplated School, if not as to its existence. Doubtless the solid judgment and enlarged experience of two such liberally educated men, both of whom had been teachers, helped to give some valuable features to the proposed effort; but there is abundant evidence, that the originating process was distinctively his; and that in the ultimate embodying of their combined counsels, he had a leading agency to which they deferred.

At first, as we learn from one of the documents in our hands, the proposed Institution was designed by the Founders to be rather a private establishment, under his personal supervision, than a public High School. The entire endowment, in lands, buildings, and funds, was to be made over to him personally in trust, and to vest in him; and the Founders with seven others, were to be Trustees of the School, under a Constitution in many important particulars like the one finally adopted; while he, in the language of the Indenture which was drawn between the parties, covenanted to "stand seized forever of the lands and monies aforesaid to and for the uses and purposes, and upon the *trusts* aforesaid, and for no other purpose whatsoever."

The manuscript of this Indenture before us, in his hand, is a literary curiosity. It embodies, almost as fully as the subsequent Constitution of the Academy does, and to a large extent in the same phraseology, his long-pondered and thoroughly matured ideas of the character of his School, while the hundreds of changes in its diction, page after page, from the first form of expression used, show that every sentence was most carefully elaborated, every word repeatedly weighed. The instrument is without date, but was written some time in 1777.

While thus digesting his views and approximating his ideal of the projected Institution, the question of its location was agitated. Earnest and repeated efforts were made to obtain a suitable site for it in the North Parish, near his own and his father's residence. It was a wise point entirely settled in the plan of the founders to have ample grounds, even if they should not have at first an expensive building. But no negotiation could procure the locality which they were most anxious to have, — the present site of Dr. Kittridge's house, and adjacent grounds, — and with deep regret they were compelled to look elsewhere.

In January, 1777, — a single year only subsequent to the first movement in the powder-mill enterprise, — the first purchase of lands for founding the Academy was made of Solomon Wardwell,[1] in the South Parish; in March another tract was bought, and in January, 1778, still another, making together about one hundred and forty acres.[2] Upon the tract included in the second purchase, was the old dwelling, to which Judge Phillips first moved from the North Parish; taking possession, so far as can be ascertained, very soon after the purchase, as it was his wish to be constantly able

[1] Father of the late Dr. Daniel Wardwell of Andover.

[2] A tract of 200 acres in New Hampshire was also added.

to direct in person the arrangements for the opening of the school.[1] Soon after completing these purchases, all of which were made in his father's name and at his father's expense, he obtained from his uncle at Exeter a bond for the payment of his proposed share of the endowment in money. This bond is dated May 29, 1777, and is in Judge Phillips's handwriting, together with the various indorsements of payments on it; as, indeed, is nearly every other paper also connected with the whole transaction.

An old joiner's shop, included in the first purchase, was immediately removed and fitted up as the first school-room for the Institution, standing on the corner of our present Main and Phillips streets, upon the south side of Mr. Farrar's door-yard. It was a rude building, of one story, about thirty-five by twenty feet, done off temporarily in the plainest manner for the purpose, and not intended to accommodate more than thirty or forty scholars. Meanwhile the proposed constitution of the Academy was again and again retouched, until, as the time for opening the Institution drew near, the plan of vesting the whole directly in the Board of Trustees, rather than in Judge Phillips personally, was adopted; and the deed of gift and constitution were modified in conformity with this view.

There is one most important paragraph of consid-

[1] See Appendix G.

erable length in the constitution as finally adopted, which appears in the draught of the Indenture already referred to, not as it was first written, but inserted on a separate leaf as an after-thought. It is the passage commencing with the words, "and whereas many of the students in this Seminary may be devoted to the sacred work of the Gospel ministry" — toward the end of the instrument, in which so much prominence is given to the anticipated *religious* character of the institution, and which embodies a summary of the doctrines which were to be inculcated. This paragraph, a *fac simile* of which, as originally written, we here insert, not only gave emphasis to the entire religious tone of the constitution, but was the germ of a course of Theological study which was, at a later day, introduced into the Academy, and led, at last, to the founding of a separate Theological Department.

Yet with all this slow growth, and these many revisions, the copy of the constitution, as engrossed and adopted at the founding of the school, shows an occasional erasure or interlineation, by the careful hand that had drawn it, in order to make its diction still more perfect. This document, written by Judge Phillips, with even more than his usual neatness, was preserved as a keepsake, after his decease, by Madam Phillips, until, at her death, it was, by her request, deposited in the Archives of the Institution. With these statements respecting it, we here insert it in full.



× This plate was destroyed in the Boston Fire.

## CONSTITUTION OF PHILLIPS ACADEMY.

" A short reflection upon the grand design of the great Parent of the Universe in the creation of mankind, and the improvements of which the mind is capable, both in knowledge and virtue, as well as upon the prevalence of ignorance and vice, disorder and wickedness, and upon the direct tendency and certain issue of such a course of things, must occasion, in a thoughtful mind, an earnest solicitude to find the source of these evils and their remedy; and a small acquaintance with the qualities of young minds,—how susceptible and tenacious they are of impressions, evidences that youth is the important period, on the improvement or neglect of which depend the most important consequences to individuals themselves and the community.

" A serious consideration of the premises, and an observation of the growing neglect of youth, have excited in us a painful anxiety for the event, and determined us to make, in the following conveyance, a humble dedication to our Heavenly Benefactor of the ability wherewith he hath blessed us, to lay the foundation of a public free School or Academy for the purpose of instructing youth, not only in English and Latin Grammar, Writing, Arithmetic, and those sciences, wherein they are commonly taught; but more especially to learn them the great end and real business of living.

" Earnestly wishing that this Institution may grow and flourish; that the advantages of it may be extensive and lasting; that its usefulness may be so manifest, as to lead the way to other establishments on the same principles; and that it may finally prove an eminent means of advancing the interest of the great Redeemer, to His patronage and blessing we humbly commit it.

"KNOW ALL MEN BY THESE PRESENTS, that we, Samuel Phillips of Andover in the County of Essex and State of Massachusetts Bay, Esquire, and John Phillips of Exeter in the County of Rockingham and State of New Hampshire, Esquire, for the causes and considerations, and for the uses and purposes, hereinafter expressed, have granted, and do by these presents grant unto the Hon. William Phillips, Esq., Oliver Wendell and John Lowell, Esquires, of Boston in the County of Suffolk and State of Massachusetts Bay, the Rev. Josiah Stearns of Epping in the County of Rockingham aforesaid, Elias Smith of Middleton, William Symmes and Jonathan French, Clerks, Messrs. Samuel Phillips, Jun., and Eliphalet Pearson, Gentlemen, and Mr. Nehemiah Abbot, Yeoman, all of Andover aforesaid, and to their heirs, all the Right, Title, and Interest, either of us have in certain parcels of land, hereafter mentioned, namely.

"In three several pieces of land, situate in Andover aforesaid; the first of which contains about twelve acres, the second piece contains about twenty-eight acres, the third piece contains about thirty acres, being lately part of the estate of George Abbot, Esq., deceased, and conveyed by Capt. Joshua Holt, Administrator on said estate, to Samuel Phillips, Esq., aforesaid, March first, one thousand seven hundred and seventy-seven; — likewise two other parcels of land in said Andover, situate near the two first-mentioned pieces, containing about thirty-nine acres, conveyed by Solomon Wardwell to said Phillips, January twenty-fourth, one thousand seven hundred and seventy-seven, together with all the buildings on said lands; — likewise two other pieces of woodland, situate in said Andover, containing about thirty-two acres, conveyed by Nehemiah Abbot to said Phillips, January twelfth, one thousand seven hundred and seventy-eight; — likewise about two hundred acres of land in the town of Jaffrey in the county of Cheshire and State of New Hampshire, conveyed by John Little to said Phillips, September fourth, one thousand seven hundred and seventy-seven.

"And the said Samuel Phillips and John Phillips do also further give, assign, and set over unto the said William Phillips, Oliver Wendell, John Lowell, Josiah Stearns, William Symmes, Elias Smith, Jonathan French, Samuel Phillips, Jr., Eliphalet Pearson, and Nehemiah Abbot, and to their heirs, the sum of one thousand six hundred and fourteen pounds, to have and to hold the same land and the same sum of money to them and to their heirs, to the use and upon the trust, hereafter mentioned.

"The lands shall be let out on proper terms, and the said sum of money put to interest on good security, or both improved in such way as shall be found on the whole most beneficial; and the whole of the Rents, Profits, Issues, and Interest of said land, and of said sum of money, shall be for ever appropriated, laid out, and expended, for the support of a public free School, or Academy, in the south parish in the town of Andover aforesaid, in manner and form following.

"The said Samuel Phillips and John Phillips shall, together with the before-named William Phillips, Oliver Wendell, John Lowell, Josiah Stearns, William Symmes, Elias Smith, Jonathan French, Samuel Phillips, Jr., Eliphalet Pearson, and Nehemiah Abbot, be Trustees of said School; and hereafter the Master, for the time being, shall ever be one of the Trustees; a major part shall be laymen and respectable freeholders; also a major part shall not consist of the inhabitants of the town where the Seminary is situate.

"The Trustees shall meet on the last Tuesday of April instant; and ever after, once in every year, on such day as they shall appoint; also, upon emergencies, when called thereto, as hereafter directed; and a major part of the Trustees shall, when regularly convened, be a quorum; of which quorum a major part shall have power to transact the business of their trust, except in cases hereafter excepted; and their first meeting shall be at the dwelling-house on the lands purchased of Captain Joshua Holt, where Samuel Phillips, Jr. now resides, at which shall be chosen the officers of the Trust; a name shall be given to this Seminary and its principal Instructor; and such other business relating to this Institution transacted, as the Trustees shall think proper.

"There shall be chosen annually a President, Clerk, and Treasurer, as officers of the Trust, out of their own number, who shall continue in their respective offices till their places are supplied by a new election; and, upon the decease of either of them, another shall be chosen in his room at the next meeting. The Master shall not be chosen President, and no member shall sustain the office of Clerk and Treasurer at the same time.

"The President shall, in all cases, give his voice and vote in common with any other member; and, whenever there shall be an equal division of the members on any question, it shall determine on that side, whereon the President shall have given his vote; and in his absence, at any meeting of the Trustees, another shall be appointed, who shall be vested with the same power, during such absence;—he shall call special meetings upon the application of any three of the Trustees, or upon the concurrence of any two of the Trustees in sentiment with him on the occasion of such meeting. And upon the decease of the President, a special meeting may be called by any three of the Trustees. All notifications for special meetings shall express the business to be transacted, if convenient; and be given at least one month previous to such meeting, if not incompatible with the welfare of the Seminary; and, when a special meeting shall be called for the appointment of an Instructor, or to transact other business of material consequence, information shall be given by leaving a written notification at the house of each Trustee, or in such other way, as that the President, or members notifying, shall have good reason to believe that each member has received the notice.

"The Clerk shall record all votes of the Trustees, inserting the names of those present at every meeting. He shall keep a fair record of every donation, with the name of each benefactor; the purpose, to which it is appropriated, if expressed; and of all expenditures; and a true copy of the whole shall be taken, and kept in the Seminary, to be open for the perusal of all men; and, if he shall be absent at any meeting of the Trustees, another shall be appointed, to serve in his room, during such absence.

"The Treasurer shall, previous to his receiving the interest of the Seminary into his hands, give bond for the faithful discharge of his office, in such sum as the Trustees shall direct, with sufficient sureties, to the Trustees of the Seminary for the time being by name; said bond to express the use both in the obligatory part and in the condition. He shall give duplicate receipts for all monies received, countersigned by one of the Trustees; one to the donor, the other to be lodged with such member as the Trustees shall from time to time direct; and the Trustees shall take such other measures as they shall judge requisite, to make the Treasurer accountable, and effectually to secure the interest of the Seminary.

"The Trustees shall let or rent out the lands in such a manner, as they shall find on the whole most profitable. They may make sale of any kind of estate, make purchases, or improve the property of the Seminary in any way, which they judge will best serve its interest.

"Upon the death, resignation, or removal of the Master, appointed by the said Samuel Phillips and John Phillips, the Trustees shall appoint another in his stead; and ever after from time to time, as there shall happen any vacancy in this office, they shall supply it.

"Whereas the success of this Institution much depends, under Providence, on a discreet appointment of the principal Instructor, and the human mind is liable to imperceptible bias; it is therefore required, that when any candidate for election, as a principal Instructor, is so near akin to any member of the Trust, as a nephew or cousin, in determining that election, any member, to whom the candidate is so related, shall not sit.

"The Trustees are empowered to appoint such assistant or assistants in and for the service of the Seminary, as they shall judge will best promote its usefulness, and as may be duly encouraged.

"No person shall be chosen, as a principal Instructor, unless a professor of the Christian Religion, of exemplary manners, of good natural abilities and literary acquirements, of a good acquaintance with human nature, of a natural aptitude for instruction and government; and, in the appointment of any Instructor, regard shall be had to qualifications only, without preference of kindred or friend, place of birth, education, or residence.

"The Trustees shall make a contract with each Master and Assistant, before their entrance upon office, as to salary; of which there shall be no alteration but in their favor; which the said Trustees are empowered to make, as to them shall appear reasonable, and as the income of the Seminary will admit.

"It shall be their duty, to inquire into the conduct of the Master and Assistant, or Assistants; and, if they or either of them be found justly chargeable with such misconduct, neglect of duty, or incapacity, as the said Trustees shall judge renders them, or either of them, unfit to continue in office, they shall remove the Master or any Assistant, so chargeable.

"The Trustees shall determine the qualifications, requisite to entitle youth to an admission into this Seminary.

"As the welfare of the Seminary will be greatly promoted by its members being conversant with persons of good character only; no scholar may enjoy the privileges of this Institution, who shall board in any family, which is not licensed by the Trustees.

"And, in order to preserve this Seminary from the baneful influence of the incorrigibly vicious, the Trustees shall determine, for what reasons a scholar shall be expelled, and the manner in which the sentence shall be administered.

"The Trustees, at their annual meeting, shall visit the Seminary, and examine into the proficiency of the scholars; examine and adjust all accounts relative to the Seminary; and make any farther rules and orders which they find necessary, and not inconsistent with any rule that is or may be established by the Founders.

"They shall, as the funds will permit, without affecting the support of the Master or any assistant, have power to erect such buildings as they may think necessary; and, at a convenient season, when of sufficient ability, shall erect a large, decent building, sufficient to accommodate at least fifty scholars with boarding, beside the master and his family; unless it shall be the determination of a major part of the Trustees, that the true design of this Institution may be better promoted by the scholars boarding in private families, and by some other improvement of the interest of the Seminary. They shall, from time to time, order such repairs as they shall judge necessary.

"Upon the death, resignation, or incapacity for the service, by reason of age or otherwise, of any of the Trustees, the remaining Trustees shall supply the vacancy by a new election.

"In settling the salary and perquisites of the Master, and in the consideration of every other question, in which the Master is particularly interested, he shall not sit. And, if any question shall come before the Trustees, wherein the town or parish, where the Seminary is situate, may be a party or particularly interested, and any minister belonging to such town is a Trustee; in the consideration of such question he shall not sit.

"At the meetings of the Trustees, there shall be made decent, not extravagant, entertainment. Economy is to be ever viewed by the Trustees and Instructors in their respective capacities, as an object worthy their particular recommendation.

"The Master, when appointed, shall receive applications for the admission of scholars, and determine them agreeably to the rules respecting the same.

"He shall conform himself to the Regulations established by the Founders and Trustees, and have power, from time to time, to make such other consistent Rules and Orders, as he shall find necessary for the internal management and regulation of the Seminary; which Rules and Orders shall be subject to the examination, amendment, or discontinuance of the Trustees, at their discretion.

"It shall be ever considered as the first and principal duty of the Master, to regulate the tempers, to enlarge the minds, and form the morals of the youth committed to his care.

"There shall be taught in this Seminary the English, Latin, and Greek Languages, Writing, Arithmetic, Music, and the Art of Speaking; also practical Geometry, Logic, and any other of the liberal arts and sciences, or languages, as opportunity and ability may hereafter admit, and as the Trustees shall direct.

"The Master is to give special attention to the health of the scholars, and ever to urge the importance of a habit of industry. For these purposes it is to be a part of his duty, to encourage the scholars to perform some manual labor, such as gardening, or the like; so far as it is consistent with cleanliness and the inclination of their parents; and the fruit of their labor shall be applied, at the discretion of the Trustees, for procuring a Library, or in some other way increasing the usefulness of this Seminary.

"But, above all, it is expected, that the Master's attention to the disposition of the *minds* and *morals* of the youth, under his charge, will exceed every other care; well considering that, though goodness without knowledge (as it respects others) is weak and feeble; yet knowledge without goodness is dangerous; and that both united, form the noblest character, and lay the surest foundation of usefulness to mankind.

" It is therefore required, that he most attentively and vigorously guard against the earliest irregularities; that he frequently delineate, in their natural colors, the deformity and odiousness of vice, and the beauty and amiableness of virtue; that he spare no pains, to convince them of their numberless and indispensable obligations to abhor and avoid the former, and to love and practise the latter; of the several great duties they owe to God, their country, their parents, their neighbor, and themselves; that he critically and constantly observe the variety of their natural tempers, and solicitously endeavor to bring them under such discipline, as may tend most effectually to promote their own satisfaction and the happiness of others; that he early inure them to contemplate the several connections and various scenes, incident to human life; furnishing such general maxims of conduct, as may best enable them to pass through all with ease, reputation, and comfort.

" And whereas many of the Students in this Seminary may be devoted to the sacred work of the gospel ministry; that the true and fundamental principles of the Christian Religion may be cultivated, established, and perpetuated in the Christian Church, so far as this Institution may have influence; it shall be the duty of the Master, as the age and capacities of the Scholars will admit, not only to instruct and establish them in the truth of Christianity; but also early and diligently to inculcate upon them the great and important Scripture doctrines of the existence of One true God, the Father, Son, and Holy Ghost; of the fall of man, the depravity of human nature; the necessity of an atonement, and of our being renewed in the spirit of our minds; the doctrines of repentance toward God and of faith toward our Lord Jesus Christ; of sanctification by the Holy Spirit, and of justification by the free grace of God, through the redemption, that is in Jesus Christ, (in opposition to the erroneous and dangerous doctrine of justification by our own merit, or a dependence on self-righteousness,) together with the other important doctrines and duties of our Holy Christian Religion.

" And, whereas the most wholesome precepts, without frequent repetition, may prove ineffectual; it is further required of the Master, that he not only urge and re-urge; but continue from day to day, to impress these instructions.

" And let him ever remember that the design of this Institution can never be answered, without his persevering, incessant attention to this duty.

" Protestants only shall ever be concerned in the Trust or Instruction of this Seminary.

" The election of all Officers shall be by *ballot* only.

" This Seminary shall be ever equally open to Youth, of requisite qualifications, from every quarter; provided, that none be admitted, till in common parlance they can read English well, excepting such particular numbers, as the Trustees may hereafter license.

" And in order to prevent the smallest perversion of the true intent of this Foundation, it is again declared, that the *first* and *principal* object of this Institution is the promotion of true Piety and Virtue; the *second*, instruction in the English, Latin, and Greek Languages, together with Writing, Arithmetic, Music, and the Art of Speaking; the *third*, practical Geometry, Logic, and Geography; and the *fourth*, such other of the liberal Arts and Sciences or Languages, as opportunity and ability may hereafter admit, and as the Trustees shall direct. And these Regulations shall be read by the President, at the annual meetings of the Trustees.

" Whereas, in the course of human events, the period may arrive, when the prosperity of this Institution may be promoted by removing it from the place where it is founded; if it shall hereafter be judged, upon mature and impartial consideration of all circumstances, by two thirds of the Trustees, that for good and substantial reasons, which at this time do not exist, the true design, herein expressed, will be better served, by removing the Seminary to some other place; it shall be in their power to remove it accordingly; provided, that if this event shall ever take place, there shall be fairly and truly entered on the Clerk's records all the reasons, whereon the determination was grounded; and the same shall be subscribed by the members, who effected the determination; but unless the good of mankind shall manifestly require it, this Seminary shall never be removed from the South Parish in the town of Andover.

" And we hereby reserve to ourselves, during any part of our natural lives, the full right, jointly to make any special Rules for the perpetual Government of this Institution; which shall be equally binding on those, whom they may concern, with any clause in these Regulations; provided, no such Rule shall be subversive of the true design herein expressed. We also reserve to ourselves a right, jointly to appoint one person, to succeed in the Trust after our decease or resignation; to whom shall be transferred the same right of appointment, and to his Successors in the said Trust for ever.

" In witness whereof we, the Subscribers, have hereunto set

18 *

our hands and seals this twenty-first day of April, in the year of our Lord one thousand seven hundred and seventy-eight.

"Signed, sealed, and delivered in presence of — SAMUEL PHILLIPS (S.)

"JOHN ABBOT,

"HANNAH HOLT. — JOHN PHILLIPS (S.)"

It is now nearly eighty years since this constitution was written, yet scarce a word in it is obsolete; and there is not a paragraph nor a phrase which it would be desirable to alter. The purity, the ease, the perspicuity and precision of the style, and the sagacious drift and scope of the plan here embodied, have been the admiration of all who have ever been concerned in the oversight or administration of the Academy.[1] The Institution has continued to be, in all its distinctive features, precisely what its revered projector intended it to be, with no change but expansion, and this such as he anticipated might ensue. To appreciate the honor due to him here, it should be noticed that, in this case, as in the form of civil government which he was helping to construct, there was nothing to copy, but every thing to originate. No such school was then known; no such constitution had ever been seen. He was planning a model classical school, for boys only,

[1] One who was for forty years a trustee of the Institution has often been heard to remark, that as the constitution was read year after year at the meetings of the Board, its language seemed to him more like *inspiration* than any thing else, except the Bible!

which should be in the highest sense FREE, — not as the word is now used, and as some still understand it, free from all charge for tuition or other costs; for his own action immediately after the opening of the school disproves this, — but open to all, and furnishing ample facilities for a wide range of study, especially in the first years of a liberal education; not a sectarian school, and not a mere scientific school; but a classical and Christian gymnasium, in close alliance with the University and the learned professions. It was his distinct aim and hope, so to shape this Academy, that it would soon lead to others of a similar character, as it in fact did. He was thus to be the parent not of Phillips Academy alone, but of its many imitators and co-workers in the cause of learning elsewhere.

With such antecedents, the formal act of founding the Academy took place, as will be seen from the date of the deed of gift, on the 21st of April, 1778. The first meeting of the trustees, as prescribed by the constitution, was held on Tuesday, April 28, at which the organization of the Board took place, and the name of Phillips *School* was given to the institution. The number of scholars to be admitted was limited to *thirty*, preference being given to those who were "to be instructed in the learned languages," and no *others* to be received unless the full number should be incomplete for a month. Mr. Eliphalet Pearson, one of the trustees, who was then teacher of the town grammar-school, and had been freely consulted in the whole process of drafting the constitution, was elected Preceptor; and it was decided that there should be two vacations a year, one in April, the other in October, of three weeks each.

At this very meeting, the war was also before their minds; for a vote was passed to apply to the General Court for an appropriation of books to the school, from the libraries "of the absentees;" referring to persons who had withdrawn from the country and joined the British in the contest. There was another formality, also, connected with the organization. The Rev. Mr. French preached a sermon upon the occasion, the manuscript of which is still preserved by his son. On the morning of Thursday, April 30, the school was opened in due form, with an attendance of *thirteen* pupils, and in less than a month the full complement of *thirty* was made up.

In all this *organic* period, Judge Phillips was the master-spirit of the enterprise, as he had been in the various preliminary steps. The meetings of the Board were at his house; he suggested their course of action, and was made chairman of most of their committees. He began at once to keep their records, although another was nominally clerk; and with these, a complete catalogue of all the pupils admitted, with their place of residence, age, etc. etc.: he acted in like manner as treasurer, taking upon himself the labor, while another person held the seal of the office.

We have before alluded to the historic interest with which the old house, in which he now resided, became in this way invested. It has the honor not only of having been his residence for a period, but of being the birthplace of the Academy. While he lived in it, the meetings of the trustees continued to be held here, as the first had been, in the west room; now used as a dining-room by the Academic Club. When he removed from it, it became the residence of the successive preceptors of the school, Mr. Pearson, Mr. Pemberton, and Mr. Newman. When the Theological Seminary was founded, this house was occupied by Dr. Woods; and here, in the same room, his first course of Lectures in Divinity was delivered.

The only other buildings at this time, on all the territory now known as "Andover Hill," were the new academy on the corner of the same street, and two old dwelling-houses, belonging to the estates of Stephen Abbott and Samuel Abbott, deceased; one near the site of the Abbott Professor's house,[1] and the other a few rods south of the printing house. We give, in this connection, the best representation which we have been able to sketch of "the Hill," as it then appeared.

The very first term of the school not only confirmed, but enlarged the views of its indefatigable pro-

[1] Lately occupied by Dr. Woods.

x See page 17 (error in binding)

jector respecting it. Such numbers pressed for admission to its privileges, that the opening arrangements were soon materially modified; and at the close of the term a charge was, by vote of the trustees, at his suggestion, made upon each scholar, to pay the salary of an assistant, and other necessary expenses incident to an enlargement of the plan:[1] a practice which was continued, with various modifications, through his lifetime; and is still, as then, found necessary, for the want of more ample endowments.

With the rapid expansion of the school, another question began now to occupy his thoughts, — the question of obtaining for it an act of incorporation; and in October of this year a committee was appointed to apply, at such time as they should judge best, to the General Court for such an act. In connection with this application, it was also voted to change the name of the Institution from Phillips *School* to Phillips *Academy;* under which title it was incorporated on the 4th of October, 1780.

There are some circumstances connected with this Act which deserve to be mentioned. By it, Phillips Academy had the distinction of being the *first* incorporated academy in the Commonwealth. The Act had to be drafted without any aids from precedent. On examining the original paper as engrossed, now in the

[1] Academy Records, p. 30, etc.

archives of the State, we find that the preamble is in the handwriting of Judge Phillips, and a portion of the first enacting clause; the remainder of the document appears to have been copied by a different hand; but that the composition of the whole was his work there can be no question.[1] In a letter to his uncle at Exeter, dated Andover, September 6, 1780, speaking of various hindrances to his being at Dartmouth College, of which he had been chosen a trustee, at the ensuing commencement, as Dr. Phillips desired, he says: —

"I am under a still further difficulty on account of an act of incorporation for Phillips School, which I am solicitous to get through this session, by reason of Mr. Lowell's being a member of the General Assembly, as well as for other reasons; — this school is in a flourishing state, in the estimation of those who have children here; and I trust you will give yourself opportunity, this fall, to acquaint yourself in person with the situation of it."

The Act, thus originated, was the *last* legislative act of the General Court, under the old regime, the new State Government, under the Constitution which Judge Phillips had assisted to frame, being organized early in the November following, thus reminding us again of the Revolutionary scenes in the midst of which the Institution was evolved: and, as if to make the recollection still more vivid, the act next preceding this

[1] See Appendix, H.

related to a powder-house in Boston, and the newspapers of the very next day contained the startling intelligence of Arnold's treason! Nor can we omit to notice here, in passing, the fact that the ever memorable *hard winter* had ushered in this year; when for forty days from the first of January the cold was most intense; and the no less memorable *dark day* had occurred in the spring, on the 19th of May.[1] At the

[1] Rev. Mr. French, one of the trustees, gives the following account of this phenomenon: "The morning was ushered in with a very dark cloud hanging over the west and north-west, attended with thunder. It settled into the north. The wind at south-west, brought over a number of clouds from that quarter. The darkness began about nine, and at twelve o'clock it was as dark as evening. Candles were lighted; domestic fowls repaired to their roosts; frogs peeped; night birds appeared; cattle repaired to their barns. Objects could be discerned at a small distance only. The clouds put on a strange kind of brassy, copper color, and every thing conspired to make the appearance exceedingly gloomy.

"It abated after twelve, and after three in the afternoon the appearance was no other than a dark, cloudy day. Though the moon fulled the day before, and was at a considerable height, in the evening the darkness returned, and soon became total, as if there had been no such thing as vision, and continued till about midnight.

"The darkness of the day and evening lasted about fourteen hours. Concern and terror seemed to sit on the countenances of the people.

"The darkness extended over all the New England States; westward, it reached to Albany; at the southward, it was observed all along the sea-coast; and to the north, as far as the settlements extend, though not in all places equally dark." — *Abbott's History of Andover*, p. 189, 190.

date of its incorporation, the academy had received in all ninety seven scholars, and the number then in attendance was about sixty.

An exceedingly interesting and important aspect of this academy enterprise now began to present itself. In the constitution the projector of the school represents it as one of the earnest wishes of the founders, "*that its usefulness may be so manifest, as to lead the way to other establishments on the same principles.*" In this respect, as well as in others, its history outran his prophecy. It had been only two or three years in operation, and was but just formally incorporated, when his uncle at Exeter began to confer with him upon the subject of founding another academy like it, at that place.

It has been said that Judge Phillips was the prime mover in this project also; but we are inclined rather, on the ground of various evidences in the case, to ascribe the honor to his uncle. That Judge Phillips took the most eager interest in it, and rejoiced over it, and coöperated with Dr. Phillips in it at every step, we have abundant proof; but in the communications which passed between them, Dr. Phillips seems naturally to speak of the enterprise as moving forward under his hand, very much as Phillips Academy had done under the eye of Judge Phillips; while the latter, as naturally, writes of the satisfaction which he derives from his uncle's plans and efforts, as they are from time to time made known to him. The truth was, Judge Phillips had, in the process of originating Phillips Academy, so infused his spirit into his uncle, that he needed no other stimulus to such a work. He saw that his nephew would have no need of his fortune, except to consecrate it to some such public use. He had no children on whom to bestow it. He could alone most amply endow a school, which would be a lasting monument of his zeal for Christian learning, and in the few years since his attention had been first called to this great subject by his nephew he appears to have already matured his noble project. The first allusion to this topic, which we find in their letters, appears in the following: —

"ANDOVER, February 26, 1781.

"HONORED SIR, — As I have so good a conveyance, I can't consent to its passing unimproved, though the bearer can tarry but little longer than while I acknowledge the receipt of your very valuable favor of the 24th ultimo; for which I beg your acceptance of my warmest acknowledgments: — the contents are important, and if I was capable of returning an answer which would be worth your perusal, it is out of my power to do so now. . . . Mrs. Phillips and the little boy join in a tender of duty to our uncle and aunt, with

"Your for ever obliged and most dutiful nephew,

"S. PHILLIPS, JR."

Two months later, in a letter from Boston, April 23, 1781, he writes, in connection with other business: —

"HONORED SIR, — . . . Since receiving your last favor, I have been chiefly from home, and when at home have been so unfortunate as not to obtain Messrs. French's and Pearson's opinion of the dimensions of a building that would be most convenient for an Academy: — this I hope for speedily, and shall with great pleasure transmit it. The joy I felt, on finding that you had it in contemplation to lay the foundation of another Academy, was great indeed: so great, that I hardly know of any thing within human reach that could have given me more satisfaction, save the intelligence that your purpose was executed. May my honored uncle *long* enjoy the fruits of his pious cares and projections, in seeing those who are furnished with the best principles filling the most important places in Church and State, and doing worthily for the kingdom of our glorious Saviour. The impatience of the bearer forbids my adding more than my dutiful addresses to my honored aunt, and that I am,

"With the warmest sentiments of gratitude and respect,

"Your very dutiful nephew, S. PHILLIPS, JR."

To this his uncle replied: —

"EXETER, April 27, 1781.

"DEAR SIR: — . . . Your concurring sentiments and warm expressions respecting another Academy, are very refreshing and highly animating; and will greatly endear you to my friends here, who were encouraged to expect the help of your advice, and such assistance as might, in a course of time, when you shall have more leisure especially, greatly increase the benefit of such an institution. The motion was exceedingly agreeable to the General Court, who have incorporated the Academy, by the name of the Phillips Exeter Academy, for the purposes mentioned in yours; and the trustees nominated and appointed (besides myself) are, Daniel Tilton and Thomas Odiorne, Esquires, of this town, John Pickering, Esq., of Portsmouth, David Maclure, of Northampton, Clerk, the Hon. S. Phillips, Jr. Esq., Andover, and the Preceptor, Mr. Benjamin Thurston — the estate allowed the same with yours — and might have been twice so much (I doubt not) had it been asked; and the Act concludes thus: 'And whereas the said Institution may be of very great and general advantage to this State, and deserves every encouragement; be it therefore enacted, by the authority aforesaid, that all the lands, tenements, and personal estate, that shall be given to the said Trustees for the use of said Academy, shall be and hereby are forever exempted from all taxes whatsoever;' which very encouraging clause concludes me, Most affectionately yours,

"J. Phillips.

"Hon. S. Phillips, Jr., Esq."

The "purpose" of Dr. Phillips, it appears, "was executed." The Act of Incorporation bears date the third of April, 1781; the school, which was so carefully in all respects taking its predecessor at Andover for a model, being endowed by his munificence as its sole Founder. Fifty thousand dollars were given by him at the outset for this purpose.

The opening of the school, however, was deferred until a suitable building could be erected and a preceptor found: and was still further delayed by some opposition to his wishes in regard to its location; concerning which he writes freely as follows to Judge Phillips: —

"EXETER, September 13, 1781.

"DEAR KINSMAN, — The Trustees in town met soon after you left us, and could agree no better than before. I recollected a word you dropped, — that if people in town insisted on building upon the spot first proposed, and would convert the building to some *other* purpose if it was found by experience not to answer *this*, it might put an end to the *present* difficulty; I ventured to propose the question as a thought of my own; the *two* gentlemen were so confident that it would answer the purpose, that they manifested a willingness to take that risk upon themselves: it must lie there, for all the other Trustees are differently minded. Mr. Pickering, indeed, says he did not give his opinion, when in town before, *officially;* and upon reading the Act, said it was not the Trustees' business to determine the matter — suppose he meant without a trial — I sent for Mr. Maclure. He was fully of your opinion, — spake his mind with great freedom and solemnity. Mr. Thurston and I have often repeated our own sentiments, and have continued our endeavors to obtain another spot more suitable. The gentleman who owns the land, where you were pleased to say it might give the pleasure of inspecting to some advantage, has been waited on, and consented to sell half an acre, with the addition of a convenient way to the finest spring in town, within about eight or ten rods of it; but the two gentlemen with a number of others to the west of the town, say 't is an inconvenient place, and pay little or no attention to it. They have treated with General Folsom for half an acre bordering upon the Common, but say his price is very unreasonable. They have again treated with the man whose land joins upon mine at the little precipice; he will not spare the quantity which I insist upon as necessary in that very confined situation. They can have half an acre at *three* fold the value, and are so attached to the spot, I hear, they mean to purchase it; hoping it may reconcile the Trustees to continue it there. They know it (the school) must be opened in town; and if they will run the hazard of its removal, what shall — what can we say more! . . . .

"I wish to know in time, *this fall*, when you suppose you can attend a Trustee meeting here; if you judge it necessary there should be one. The frame was ready to be erected last Friday. I suspect they will purchase the additional half acre to-day; if they proceed, one room, at least, will, they say, be in readiness by the first day of November. . . . . In tenders of love to you and your other self and Johnny, your aunt joins with your uncle JOHN."

Another letter soon followed.

"EXETER, October 5, 1781.

"DEAR KINSMAN, — Having a favorable opportunity by Mr. Thurston, I write, hoping he will more fully communicate matters respecting himself and the school here. . . . . The building is erected where the builders pleased; and suppose one room may be finished this month. But whether it would be best to desire a gentleman so out of health as Mr. Thurston really is, to enter for so short a time, or to wait till spring in order to procure an Instructor who might be employed and settled to his own and others' advantage, is the question.

"Your sentiments herein would lay a fresh obligation upon your loving uncle, JOHN PHILLIPS."

The opening of the school, which had been retarded by these obstacles, finally took place on the 1st of May, 1783, and from this time its Founder had the satisfaction of watching its prosperity and usefulness for many years, parallel with the history of its earlier compeer at Andover.[1] During these conferences of Judge Phillips with his uncle in reference to this Academy in 1781, he repeatedly alludes, in his letters, to the subject of building a house, at last, for his own family residence; such a step as he now felt had become a necessity. And here we shall see how his deliberation and forecast, in planning for his own home, resulted, ultimately, in important advantages to his cherished school. Early in the spring of 1782, he purchased of one of the heirs of Samuel Abbott, deceased, a tract adjoining the lands of the Trustees on the south, on which the residence of the late Professor Stuart was afterwards built. A few days later he concluded a contract made nearly a year before, with William Foster, for a tract of several acres, now included in the Seminary grounds, upon the southerly side on Salem street, and extending around a short distance upon Main street; and on

[1] See Appendix I.

the same day he obtained, of Asa Holt, a small tract more remote from the Academy, near the southerly section of its lands obtained from the estate of George Abbott. By these purchases nearly the whole of "Andover Hill" came into his own and the Trustees' hands. Soon after this he negotiated with the Trustees for the site of his mansion-house, adjoining his recent purchases, on the south-east corner of the tract originally obtained of Solomon Wardwell, exchanging for an acre and a half here about three acres on the corner where the new Academy was soon erected. A little later he purchased for his father and uncle, in the name of the Trustees, the "old training field," on the corner opposite.[1] After he had erected his mansion-house here, as described in a preceding chapter, and had taken possession of it, his uncle, in a long communication respecting the affairs of his Academy, greeted him in these cordial words: —

"Exeter, January 14, 1783.

"Dear Kinsman, — Your very kind favor of the 31st of December I received, and heartily congratulate you on your removal into your new habitation, after the uncomfortable situation you have lately been in. Heaven grant the devout wishes of your heart respecting this residence, — a heart which is, I trust, the habitation of God, through the Spirit, and rejoiceth in Him more than in all worldly accommoda-

[1] See again Appendix G.

tions and successes, which justly merit and happily excite your dutiful and grateful acknowledgments. . . . .

"I am, with love to your whole self,

"Most affectionately yours,

"JOHN PHILLIPS."

In this connection we give also an extract from another letter of later date, as both give important intimations of the freedom with which Judge Phillips suggested his characteristic views to his uncle, and of the great weight which was attached to them.

"EXETER, August 18, 1783.

"DEAR SIR, — Your favor of the 16th I received; am sorry to hear of our dear sister's illness. . . . . May Heaven continue so great a blessing with us; her dearest connections in particular. . . . .

"Your very rational, generous, and religious plan of improving moneys for the advantage of the public, in promoting education, must meet my fullest approbation; and in consequence, command my future, as well as present, attention, — how to come at the means is the only obstacle. The agreeableness of your neighbor gives me pleasure. Under your very many cares and labors, kind Heaven affords you many comfortable enjoyments, — his name be praised, and Himself will doubtless be the supreme object of your confidence and joy. Oh, pray that it may be so with your poor unworthy uncle, whose love to yourself and the whole family is most cordially returned. JOHN PHILLIPS."

In speaking of the erection of his mansion, we have

stated that one reason for his building so large a house was Judge Phillips's desire to show suitable hospitality to his numerous friends. Another reason was his wish to have a few members of the Academy in his family from term to term. For the sake of the school generally, and in the hope of special usefulness to such as became members of his family, though so much absent himself, he cherished this as a favorite feature of his work, and Madam Phillips warmly seconded his views. From this date, therefore, a few of the scholars found a home here year after year. A sketch of "Mayor" Phillips of Boston, in 1825, from the pen of S. L. Knapp, in the Boston Monthly Magazine, incidentally shows us how admirably this arrangement subserved the great ends of the school. After speaking of the Academy itself, he says:—

"Young Phillips had other high advantages for improving his mind and manners, for he lived in the house of his kinsman, Samuel Phillips, which was also an admirable school for youth. The master of the mansion was truly a great man, distinguished not only for the numerous offices he held in civil and political life, but for his ardent desire to promote the cause of religion and learning in the land, *believing that the permanency of our freedom depended upon the diffusion of knowledge amongst the rising generations.* . . . Many young men were permitted to live in his house, and he took so deep an interest in the pupils of the Academy, as constantly to keep in view their course of study, and frequently to question them on the subject.

"In these dialogues he used the choicest language himself, and was careful to correct the youths who suffered a low, inappropriate, or equivocal word or expression to escape them. In all this his manner, though solemn, was kind, and encouraged the most timid to answer his inquiries, and put interrogatories with freedom.

"Mrs. Phillips, his lady, was of still more importance to those under their care than her husband. She possessed a mind cultivated by extensive reading, and manners refined by early advantages, and a long acquaintance with the best society. She was blest with a fine flow of spirits, a rich imagination, an affectionate heart; and acted the fond mother to all under her roof, or within the reach of her care. It was impossible for any one to live with her a month, without understanding the value of a pure, elevated, and polished woman in the education of men." [1]

Still another reason for a large edifice was, the wish of Judge Phillips always to have the Trustees meet at his house and share in his hospitalities. This practice of entertaining them, gratuitously, at their various official meetings, he introduced at the founding of the School, and continued while he lived, as Madam Phillips did afterwards during her lifetime.

And once fairly in the occupancy of his new residence, with such views and aims in reference to the Academy, he was soon engaged in another effort to improve the Institution.

[1] Pages. 282, 283.

The first Academy building, even if it had been intended for permanent use, was too small for the enlarged work now done in it. Indeed, it had been apparent, after only two years' trial, that such would be the case, and as early as 1780, the subject of erecting a new edifice began to be agitated; in 1784, the plan and location of it were determined, and a committee was instructed to build it as soon as the necessary means could be procured; during the year 1785, the building was completed; and, on the 30th of January, 1786, the school was removed to it, in the last week of Mr. Pearson's service as Principal, his election as Professor at Cambridge having been already accepted.[1] This "New Academy," as it was then called, stood near the south-west corner of the present Seminary lawn, opposite the Abbott Professor's house. It was a two-story edifice of wood, with recitation rooms and a study room on the lower floor, arranged for one hundred pupils, and a spacious hall for exhibitions and other public purposes on the second floor. The old Academy remained for many years on its original site, where it was for a time used as a singing-room, then as a store-room for paper rags, etc., until, in 1803, it was sold and removed about half a mile eastward, to be fitted up for a dwelling-house,[2] in which form it

[1] Academy Records, p. 40, 45, 53, 55, 60.

[2] The residence for many years of widow Hannah Berry.

remained until it was torn down, about ten years since, to make room for a new house on the same spot.

The "New Academy" was worthy of the growing reputation of the School. But how were the means obtained to erect and furnish it? It was located on a portion of one of Judge Phillips's recent purchases, which he had transferred to the Trustees in exchange for the site of his mansion-house; the building was erected under his direction, at the joint expense of the two original Founders, and their brother, Hon. William Phillips of Boston; "they," as the entry in the Journal states, "having given the same to the Trustees in equal parts," together with the training field on the south side of the road. The whole cost was three thousand one hundred and sixty-six dollars and sixty-six cents; for which the Institution was not only indebted to their liberality, but to the influence of Judge Phillips in eliciting it. Prior to the erection of this commodious building, the exhibitions of the School had been held in the village church. In 1788, two years after it was completed, the use of the Hall on the Sabbath was tendered by the Trustees to the Parish as a place of worship, while the old meeting-house could be demolished and a new one built, Judge Phillips being appointed to communicate the vote.[1]

While these changes were in progress, both in connection with the school and with his private affairs, he

[1] Appendix, J.

had erected a store, East of the old Academy, on the opposite side of the highway, near the present front entrance to the Seminary grounds. In this state "the Hill" remained now for a considerable period, the mansion-house, the new Academy,[1] and the store being the only additions as yet to the buildings which were in existence at the opening of the School. Such was the aspect of things here, at the time of Washington's visit. An old stone wall inclosed the tract now in front of the Seminary buildings, in which the rocks, birches, alders, bushes, and briars of every sort were still undisturbed; the lands south and north of the old Academy were occupied as a farm for tillage and pasturage; there was a plain face wall along the front line of Judge Phillips's house lot, and the area in front of his mansion was an open common, as seen in the accompanying outline.

Before the new Academy was completed, Dr. Phillips had often expressed the desire that Judge Phillips would do him the favor to sit for his portrait, respecting which we insert the following extract as an illustration of their mutual regard: —

"BOSTON, February 7, 1785.

"HONORED SIR, — . . . Your repeated mention of a subject, which is a farther evidence of your partiality for your

[1] The "New Academy," which is remembered by large numbers of the Alumni of the School as their literary home, was destroyed by fire on the night of January 30, 1818.

× See page 193 (error in binding.)

unworthy nephew, demands my warmest acknowledgments. To comply with your desire while the Court is sitting is not in my power, being constantly taken up from ten in the morning till nine at night, with only a short intermission at noon; and I hope to obtain my uncle's consent for a delay, for the present at least. The hurry of the gentleman who will carry this to Haverhill, gives me only time to add that we have the prospect of a permanent bridge of Charles River,[1] that friends at Boston are well, and that I am,

"With the most dutiful respect,

"Your obliged nephew, S. P., JR."

[1] "This was the first effort," says Dr. Dwight, "to erect a bridge over a broad river in the American States. A brief account of its origin will not be destitute of interest.

"Judge Russell, the gentleman whom I have already respectfully mentioned, was long and ardently desirous that a bridge should be erected between these towns. As he advanced in years he became more and more solicitous to see the work accomplished. His son, the late Hon. Thomas Russell, and his son-in-law, the late Hon. John Lowell, District Judge of Massachusetts, together with several other gentlemen connected with them, were earnestly desirous to see the wishes of this venerable man realized. At that time it was universally believed, that for a river so wide and a current so strong, a floating bridge was the only practicable structure of this nature. They, therefore, engaged a gentleman to obtain for them a correct account of the construction, expense, convenience, and security, of the floating bridge, then lying on the Schuylkill at Philadelphia. Several other persons, at that time bound for Europe, they requested also to furnish them with similar information concerning bridges in that quarter of the globe. While this business was in agitation, both the gentlemen being on a visit at Cambridge during the session of

Not unwilling to gratify his uncle, he is yet so intent on other cares that he cannot find the time for an act so personal! And it was this absorbing devotion to his life's work, which drew the heart of his uncle toward him with so much affectionate confidence.

After a brief interval, therefore, we find them again

the Supreme Judicial Court, they made the projected bridge a subject of conversation with the Hon. David Sewall, one of the judges. In the course of this conversation, the designs mentioned above were particularly stated. On his return to York, the place of his residence, Judge Sewall communicated this information to his brother, Major Sewall, a gentleman distinguished for peculiar mechanical talents. After being informed that the difficulties presented by the stream furnished the only reason for erecting a floating bridge, Major Sewall observed that a fixed bridge might be constructed, as easily and certainly, to be secure from the dangers of the current. His brother requested him to state his views to the gentlemen concerned. Accordingly he formed, and communicated, a scheme for the intended structure. After this scheme had been thoroughly examined, the original design was relinquished, and the present bridge begun. At the request of the undertakers, Major Sewall came to Boston, and continued to superintend the work, until he had completely possessed the builders of the principles on which it was to be accomplished." . . . "Charlestown bridge was finished in 1787. It is built on seventy-five wooden piers, and is forty-two feet in breadth, and one thousand five hundred and three in length; the river being here two hundred and eighty feet wider than the Thames at Westminster, and six hundred and three feet wider than the same river at London bridge. It is also deeper." . . . "The bridge was built by two able and ingenious American artists, Messrs. Cox and Stone, and cost fifty thousand dollars." — *Dwight's Travels*, Vol. I. p. 495–497.

interchanging letters in reference to the Academy at Andover, which resulted in giving it an entirely new and most important feature. The Institution was now, for the time, amply furnished with lands and buildings; but Judge Phillips, who had from the first wished to make it as far as possible an inexpensive school, was specially interested to connect with it every practicable aid to the indigent, and particularly to candidates for the gospel ministry; nor had Dr. Phillips, in all his efforts at Exeter, lost sight of this great want at Andover. We introduce here a portion of their correspondence on this subject.

"EXETER, March 15, 1789.

"DEAR KINSMAN, — I thank you for your kind concern for my health, expressed in polite and endearing terms; may your pious wishes with respect to any future usefulness be answered: and particularly with regard to our Academies. Gracious Heaven bless *them both*, in this and future generations! And may your cares, labors, and experience, be eternally and most bountifully rewarded; your numbers exceed those here — and of Latin pupils especially. I think Mr. Abbott has forty-five this spring, and proves a faithful instructor. . . .

"President Wheelock was with me about five weeks. The Court allowed payment of my donation in *State notes*. . . . As for obtaining help from Government, towards support of a Professor of Divinity, there is no prospect of it. I purchased of the President five hundred acres of College land, at an easy rate, and promised to quit it, provided the

Trustees would appropriate *this*, and *all other lands* I had given them, to the support of a Professor of Divinity."

"EXETER, April 20, 1789.

"MY DEAR SIR, — I received your kind favor of the 16th instant, and am much obliged by your just and useful observations with respect to Academy instructors. I have had your Bradford scholar much in my mind; but upon your recommendation shall turn my attention more upon Dana.

"With regard to your acceptance of an office, you may very soon be elected to, what shall or can I be expected to say? especially as I am ignorant of the salary. Your great and constant attention to the public interest, since you entered upon the stage of business, has, it seems, exposed you to losses and embarrassments in your private concerns, — and you are now become more sensible of the importance and even the necessity of providing for your family, making payments, etc. etc. In this you are undoubtedly right: — what very clear and indisputable tendency your closing with a certain offer would have hereto, all circumstances considered, yourself, and your nearest and most dear connections are much better judges than I can be; especially in my present weak state of body and mind, which forbids any very intense thought.

"With respect to our Andover Academy, *your* personal oversight was what I had in view, at the first; and have hitherto rejoiced in the peculiar benefit of it. The expense arising from the late elegant building, you will be so good as to acquaint me with. I have long been thinking whether the donation for pious and charitable uses might not be best secured by the *whole* number of Trustees, because they are a *body politic;* and may very judiciously order and improve that part of the Academy estate, as may best answer the design. Ten years are past since I first wrote about such a donation; and 'tis likely as many more may pass, before payments on the notes of hand will be generally obtained. What will you and your judicious father and uncle William object to the admitting into the Academy a number of poor children of good morals, and a very promising genius, and support in part or wholly till they are sufficiently proved?

"As to a college education, 'tis what I never had in view,—some, however, will not be contented without it; and those of ability will act their pleasure. The very best *Academical* education may surely answer some of the best and most valuable purposes. And if the Trustees of our Academies, in some future time, employ a very sound Theological Professor, why may not some of the most orthodox and pious preachers proceed from them? or why may not charity scholars be expected to obtain a degree, if well qualified therefor, at some of our Colleges? . . . May you, my dear and loving kinsman, be under the Divine direction. As duty appears, you will act. If God calls you, his presence will go with you, and *this* shall be my comfort!

"I am, with our love to your whole self and the children,

"Most affectionately yours, J. PHILLIPS.

"Hon. SAMUEL PHILLIPS, JR., Esq."

"BOSTON, May 30, 1789.

"HONORED SIR,—I have attempted repeatedly to write to you, but have been as often prevented by one means and another. . . . Will it not be best that charity scholars should, in all cases, be required to do what they can for themselves?

I mean without interfering with their studies, in order that the Academy Fund may be made as extensively useful as possible? Some precaution of this nature I had in my mind to suggest the expediency of, now you are putting your donation for pious and charitable uses into the hands of the Trustees: — and one more I will venture to hint; where a charity scholar, after having obtained a competent share of knowledge, shall from inclination pursue any other study and Profession than that of Divinity, — or where a person, after having received the benefit of this donation, shall engage in trade or any other lucrative business, and thereby advance his interest, or be guilty of any foul immorality, — in either of those cases, should not the favored person be held to repay the money expended for his benefit, in whole or in part, and with or without interest, according as his circumstances may enable him? Will it not be proper to require, that none shall enjoy the benefit of this donation but persons of truth and fidelity, and such as give good evidence of their *piety* and *virtue?*

"Will it not be desirable to empower the Trustees to expend *part* of the income for some other special purpose, when two thirds of them shall judge that the *great objects in view* will be better promoted by any other particular appropriation of such part than by the support of charity scholars? Your own consent, where the opinion of the majority shall be in favor of such other appropriation, should authorize it; important advantages might arise from such a liberty, if *due care* be taken to *prevent misapplication.*

"Would it not have this tendency, if you should reserve the right of naming some person, before your decease, whose consent afterwards should be necessary, in order to justify such different appropriation, — he to have no power in the case, unless one half or two thirds of the board should be in favor of the measure? Such person, being the object of special confidence, would, if deserving it, feel a special obligation to *vigilance*, and *to see that the intention of the donor was executed.* I hope the right will be reserved of making any such other special appropriation of such part of the interest as you shall judge proper, during your lifetime, perpetual.

"Will not the state of your health admit of your affording us the pleasure of your company at the Trustee meeting of your Andover Academy? I presume my uncle William will be there; — your meeting the brethren would be very pleasing, and the other Trustees will be highly gratified, but none more than he who has received so many expressions of affection, though so unworthy of them; — you doubtless remember that the meeting is to be on Tuesday, in the week before Commencement at Cambridge, which will be the 7th of July. If the proposed transfer of your donation should take place at this meeting, that will afford a further reason for your being present; . . . but any or all the reasons together will not be sufficient to justify your exposing yourself. . . .

"Please to present my duty to my aunt.

"I am with unfeigned gratitude,

"Your much obliged and dutiful nephew,

"S. PHILLIPS, JR."

The donation to the Andover Academy referred to in these letters, amounting to more than twenty thousand dollars, was finally made in October, 1789, and communicated in due form to the Trustees at their next annual meeting in July, 1790. As the deed of gift, conveying this munificent sum, is not now to be found among the files of the Institution, his aim in the donation, and the connection of Judge Phillips with it, must be inferred from their letters, and from the following record.

On receiving the donation, the Trustees immediately "Voted, That the Honorable Samuel Phillips, Jr., Rev. Mr. Tappan, and Mr. Pearson be a committee, to draft a vote of thanks to the Honorable John Phillips, Esq., for his very generous donation to the Academy." Their draft, which was reported and adopted, was in these words:—

"The Board, having been made acquainted by a legal instrument, bearing date the 16th day of October, 1789, this day communicated, that the Honorable John Phillips, Esq., of Exeter, one of the founders of this Academy, 'for and in consideration of further promoting the virtuous and pious education of youth, (poor children of genius, and of serious disposition especially,) in Phillips Academy, founded in Andover, in the State of Massachusetts,' has given and granted to the Trustees of said Academy and their successors, or their order, certain notes of hand, therein described, to a very large amount, under certain reservations, therein mentioned,

"*Voted*, That the thanks of the Board be presented to the Honorable John Phillips, Esq., for his before-cited pious and liberal donation, whereby he has still further manifested his generous and ardent zeal for the promotion of knowledge, virtue, and piety, and conferred an additional and lasting obligation upon the Academy.

"Upon this occasion, the Trustees cannot but add their fervent wish and prayer, that the DONOR, the distinguished *Friend* and *Patron* of science and religion, may live to behold, with increasing joy and satisfaction, the happy fruits of this, and of all his other pious liberalities; and at a very remote period, his numerous acts of benevolence may receive that reward, which original and infinite goodness can bestow."[1]

We have thus far been the more particular in our statements of the varied agency which Judge Phillips had in enlisting the coöperation of this uncle, and also of his father and other relatives in his plans, because, while ascribing so high an honor to him, we have wished also to do ample justice to them.

It is a remarkable circumstance, that this noble donation of his uncle at Exeter was communicated to the Board at the last meeting which his father, the elder brother, ever attended; and we cannot so well pay the tribute, which we have contemplated, to these three brothers, at any other stage of our narrative, as by presenting them in a group in this connection.

The eldest of this distinguished trio, *Samuel Phillips*, Esq., of North Andover, has been already somewhat distinctly brought before the reader, by our incidental references to him in the progress of this memoir. After graduating at Harvard College in 1734, he for a

[1] Academy Records, p. 77, 78.

short period instructed the grammar-school in his native town; but soon devoted himself mainly to mercantile pursuits, in the North Parish, where he continued to reside for more than fifty years.

Of his college life or his earlier years, we have learned no important particulars, except that from his childhood upward his intellectual and moral traits bore a remarkable resemblance to his revered father's; and as these became stereotyped in his full manhood, the other sons, who were several years his juniors, honored him with a deference similar to that which they all felt for their father.

He had more of the reverend clergyman's exact, rigid, inflexible, commanding spirit, than they; and less opportunity or disposition to temper it, by an enlarged intercourse with the world; yet, with the advantages of his home education and his collegiate course, he was in mind and manners, a man of letters, not less than a man of business. There is not, in the entire gallery of the family portraits, one which catches the eye sooner than his, for its courtly and dignified mien. He has been sometimes represented as unduly precise and exacting, both as a merchant and a magistrate; as insisting too tenaciously upon mere rights, to the neglect of expediencies and amenities. If this was ever the case, it may have been as justly chargeable to the times as to the man; or it may have resulted from the very virtues for which he is to be honored; his exalted love of justice, his high-toned patriotism, his primitive simplicity and frugality, his fervent religious faith and zeal.

In the great struggle of the country for its liberties, no man was more steadfast, or more ardent than he. Other civil services he appears to have carefully performed, from a sense of duty chiefly, and not from any special interest in them, — but in the Revolution his whole heart became enlisted. The entire action of the town in the contest, so much of which we have in a former chapter detailed, was spontaneous, — it was such action as a community of patriots would most naturally have taken, — yet it was specially stimulated by him, as an acknowledged leader. When they gave him "instructions" how to act as their representative, it was at his suggestion; and with his own pen the instructions were carefully drafted, which he was as careful to obey. Even the ever active zeal of his son here did not surpass the heartiness and energy of the father's patriotic impulses; and it has seemed to us that all of his strongest characteristics shine out with more lustre here than anywhere else.

One can read, without special note, of his having been long a Justice of the Peace and of the Quorum, of his being chosen Representative to the General Court and the Convention of Deputies, of his election as one of the Governor's Council, of the various civil and religious offices which were conferred upon him in his native town, and which he discharged with acceptance, as well as of his unsullied probity and great success in business; but when we see how eagerly his best efforts were put forth, year after year, among the very foremost of the Revolutionary patriots, we most heartily admire and revere him.

His connection with Phillips Academy, however, as one of its *founders,* is the fact in his history, which, more than any thing else, will give him a lasting name. Though so deeply involved in the Revolutionary struggle, like his son, he found time and inclination minutely to scan this literary project in all its bearings; and, as it came to maturity, devoted to it his time and counsel and money, with an intelligent interest commensurate with its importance. Residing so near the Institution, however, and in almost daily conference as he was with his son, there are few memorials of his agency left in letters or other manuscripts, except the Records of the Board of Trustees.

At the organization of this Board he was unanimously chosen President, and was annually reëlected to this office until his decease. Scarcely a meeting of the Trustees was held, for this whole period of more than twelve years, which he did not attend; although the details of service in various particulars were usually assigned to the younger members, under the lead of his son. No feature of the school appears to have interested him so much as its religious aims and tendencies; devoted as he had ever been in his attachment to the sound and vital faith of his fathers.

Coöperating thus actively with his son in plans and efforts to benefit the Academy, and often renewing his gifts to relieve its exigencies or to augment its usefulness, he had the great joy, at last, of seeing its endowments munificently reinforced by the ample donation of his brother and co-founder; and then he could well say, "Lord, now lettest thou thy servant depart in peace." He died shortly after this donation was tendered to the Board, August 21, 1790, aged seventy-five years and six months; and as his death thus began to dissolve the band of the Academy's originators and patrons, all who were connected with the Institution united in paying their tribute to his memory.

An obituary notice in the "Centinel" states that,—

"His funeral was attended with great solemnity. The order of procession was as follows:—

The Students of the Academy.
The Assistant and Writing Instructor.
The Principal.
The Trustees, all with the usual badge of mourning.
The Corpse,
Followed by the mourners, and a numerous train of respectable friends and acquaintances.

In this order they proceeded from the late mansion of the deceased to the meeting-house; where, after a very pertinent prayer by the Rev. Mr. Symmes, a judicious and pathetic oration was delivered by *Mr. Pemberton*, Principal of the Academy. . . . . The solemnities were introduced by a hymn and closed by an anthem, excellently adapted to the occasion. In the same order the procession moved from the meeting-house to the place of interment. . . . . It is but a just tribute to uncommon merit to observe, that if integrity of heart, and purity of morals, an exemplary conduct in private life, a conscientious, faithful discharge of the various offices he sustained, and singular liberality in the cause of religion and learning, constitute a good and great character, it was eminently his."[1]

The second of the three brothers, Hon. John Phillips, LL. D., of Exeter, now claims our notice. Of his connection with the chief subject of this memoir, in the founding and endowment of Phillips Academy, and also of Phillips Exeter Academy, we have spoken at large heretofore. His regard for Judge Phillips, which so often throws its fascination around us, was doubtless the incentive with him to not a little of all this varied generosity. Yet the more we have studied and admired them together, the more have they seemed to us to be linked with each other in such deeds by a strong native congeniality of spirit.

[1] His wife, Mrs. Elizabeth Phillips had died, the previous autumn, aged seventy-one; an obituary notice of whom, at the time, closes with these lines: —

"Think what the mother, Christian, friend, should be,
You 've then her character, for such was she."

We do not conceive it possible to say any thing more just or honorable to Dr. Phillips, than to characterize him as eminently like his nephew, the Judge.

Dr. Phillips, like his elder brother, had obtained a liberal education; and after graduating from Harvard College, in 1735, but one year later than his brother, had engaged in teaching for a short period, when, with such preparation as the times afforded, he began to preach the Gospel. Numbers of the sermons which he wrote are still preserved; and it could not have been from any want of regard for the profession, or any want of encouragement in it, that he finally relinquished it; for in subsequent years, after settling in business at Exeter, and teaching a classical school there for a time, when the church in that village, in which he was a ruling elder, was seeking a new pastor, he was unanimously invited to accept that office. He is said to have often stated, and especially after he had repeatedly listened to the preaching of Whitefield, that he did not feel qualified for the ministry.

Turning, therefore, to pursuits for which he deemed himself better fitted, he became distinguished not only for his hearty sympathy with the clergy, but for his zeal in fostering institutions to educate them. It was with the most liberal and far-reaching views that he dispensed his gifts in this great work. Instead of withdrawing his aid from Andover, after he had undertaken so much at Exeter, he added donation to donation, until his gifts to Phillips Academy, including a legacy by his will, amounted to more than thirty thousand dollars. To his Academy at Exeter his donations were much larger. With other friends of learning in New England, he contributed also liberally to the funds of Princeton College. In Dartmouth College, of which he was for twenty years a trustee, he endowed a Professorship of Theology; and wherever his money was thus bestowed, his heart went with it.

Had he not left these various monuments to his memory, his rare capacity and success as a merchant, his aptness as a teacher, his honors as colonel of the militia, or as one of the special justices of the Superior Court, might have been thought worthy of note; but it is as the liberal patron of institutions of learning that he has been, and deserves to be, especially honored.

After the decease of his elder brother, he was chosen President of the Board of Trustees at Andover, which office he held until his death, April 21, 1795, at the age of seventy-five years and eight months; and the inscription which Professor Pearson is said to have proposed for his monument, has seemed to us an admirable expression of the spirit in which so beneficent a life was closed at last. By his will, two thirds of his estate was bequeathed to the Exeter Academy, and one third to the Academy at Andover; and this was the proposed epitaph: —

"*Without natural issue, he made posterity his heir.*"[1]

The younger brother, Hon. William Phillips of Boston, had already begun to catch the spirit of the others, with reference to the endowment of institutions of learning, but was for the most part engaged in prosecuting other enterprises. Without the advantages of a liberal education, he had so much native force of mind, and so much practical culture from his intercourse with men of eminence in every profession, that there were few in our metropolis who exerted a more marked or salutary influence. Repairing at the early age of fifteen to the city as a clerk to Edward Bromfield, Esq., and subsequently marrying the daughter of his employer,[2] he became a partner with him in the firm, and rapidly amassed a large fortune.

As a representative from Boston in the General Court, as a member of the Senate and of the Governor's Council, as a delegate to the Convention for rat-

[1] This epitaph reminds one of the memorable saying in regard to Washington, "*Heaven wrote him childless, that millions might find him a Father!*" — *Knapp's Sketches*, under the signature of Ignatius Loyola Robinson, LL. D., p. 253.

[2] By this marriage a great-great-grandson of the first minister of Watertown, was united to a great-great-granddaughter of the first minister of Boston, Rev. John Wilson, who had come from England, it will be remembered, in the same company.

ifying the Constitution of the United States, and in other offices, he had a long and honorable career of civil service; in every stage of which he was prominent among the men of the period, especially in those emergencies which called for the highest judgment and resolution. Throughout the entire period of the Revolution, his name will be found constantly associated with the Adamses, and Bowdoin, and Hancock, and other leading patriots.[1] His eldest daughter was married to Josiah Quincy, Jr., and had taken refuge with the family in Norwich during the siege of Boston, when that heroic young orator died on his return voyage from England. With the firmest and stoutest of heart, he bore the very brunt of the conflict with Governor Gage; boldly protesting, in person, against his arbitrary measures, and resisting him at every step.

But as these scenes, which so well elicited his zeal and decision, passed away, the current of his life moved on again calm and clear in its old channels; and from spending his fortune freely in the cause of liberty, he began to make it more directly tributary to the cause of education and religion. Retaining still his carefulness and exactness in all the daily details of business, his house was the hospitable home of the clergy from

[1] The "Committee of Safety," for example, chosen in Boston, July 26, 1774, were James Bowdoin, Samuel Adams, John Adams, John Hancock, William Phillips, Joseph Warren, and Josiah Quincy. — *Frothingham's History of the Siege of Boston*, p. 29.

every quarter; and whenever they or others sought the aid of his hand in any work of charity, it was freely bestowed.

It was at his house that Judge Phillips usually stayed, year after year, during his long service in the General Court; so unwilling were the family ever to have him go elsewhere. There are numerous passages in the letters of Judge Phillips, in which, with a touching fulness of heart, he expresses his sense of the kindness which he here received. One of these acknowledgments we cannot forbear to extract. "January 26, 1795," he writes, when suffering from illness: "My uncle and aunt are very cautious of my doing any thing that may hazard an exposure. They show me all the attention, care, and affection that they could, if I was their child, and an only child." . . . In the same letter he says, in reference to the devoted attentions of his aunt: "I can hardly realize that the disciple who washed the feet of our *Divine Saviour* and wiped them with her hair, had a better heart than this Christian." . . . "This instance of condescending goodness in the lady of a gentleman of the first fortune in New England, and one of the first in the United States," as he characterizes it, he gives "as a *specimen* of that unwearied kindness which is shown" him.

To the Academy at Andover, which his beloved nephew was ever fostering, this uncle had already made liberal donations; having, besides other gifts, borne his third with the other brothers of the expense of erecting the new building. On the 12th of March, 1797, Judge Phillips writes in haste to Madam Phillips:—

"My dear Friend,—If this reaches you before you have sent a horse and chaise for me, please to omit it till Tuesday. My uncle has desired me to assist him about a piece of business this week that *I know you will be pleased with.* Indeed, it is doubtful whether I shall be able to get home before Thursday.

"I am affectionately yours, S. P."

The explanation of this hint is found in the codicil to his uncle's will, dated April 18, 1797, devising, with other charitable bequests, the sum of four thousand dollars to Phillips Academy, as a fund for aiding indigent scholars.

With many such works of beneficence in the use of his large fortune, he was now preparing to leave both his estate and his Christian munificence of spirit to be inherited by his honored son. On the 15th of January, 1804, "he died, in a good old age, full of days, riches, and honor."

Thus lived and died the "three sons" of our venerable clergyman, in the very spirit of that religious injunction in his will, "to serve their generation according to y[e] will of God, by doing good, as they shall have y[e] opportunity, unto all men, and especially to y$^{e}$ household of faith; as knowing y$^{t}$ it is more blessed to give than to receive!"

Excellent portraits of these three distinguished patrons of learning, and of Judge Phillips, presented to the Institution which they had originated by *His Honor William Phillips*, of whom we shall hereafter speak, now adorn its halls; and at every annual exhibition of the school, these four are seen together, as if in mid life yet upon the stage, watching the ever growing success of the great enterprise in which they so long labored.

After the decease of Dr. John Phillips, Hon. William Phillips was chosen President of the Board of Trustees, until his age and infirmities led him to decline the office, when Judge Phillips was elected.

The Academy was now in the full tide of a most gratifying prosperity: well endowed, though less amply so than the school at Exeter; well instructed, and already widely known as a model institution. Having with so much perseverance and success concentrated upon it the good-will of its family of patrons, Judge Phillips sought also now to enlist in its behalf the patronage of the State. His brother-in-law, Hon. John Foxcroft, had, through his agency, made a donation to the Academy of some lands in the District of Maine, valued at several hundred dollars. Judge Phillips was himself largely concerned in various operations connected with the lands of the Commonwealth in this

District. The State had for a succession of years honored him with important commissions, pertaining to its lands, so far as they had become a subject of dispute, or were to be offered for sale. The Records of the General Court show, that, from 1783 to the year of his decease, he was seldom free from trusts of this kind.[1]

Connecting with his own Academy others of a similar character which had already sprung up, he succeeded now in obtaining, amid these labors, from the General Court, a grant of a half township of these lands to each institution, estimated at the time to be worth nearly $2,000;[2] and the tract which was finally conveyed to Phillips Academy, was selected under his own eye; but though it was a new proof of his deep interest in the school, this grant has never realized his expectations, and has been of comparatively little advantage to the Institution. During his lifetime, no income was received from this source; but the school was sustained, and year after year enlarged, from the income of its various endowments by his relatives, and by means of its regular charges for tuition, while its advantages were made free to indigent young men from all sections of the country, by means of its beneficiary funds.

Before it had been a score of years in operation, it had attained so wide a celebrity that not only the sons

[1] See Appendix K. [2] Ibid. L.

of gentlemen from the various New England States, but from the South, and from the West Indies, and from France and other foreign countries, resorted to it; and Judge Phillips, who was now President of the Board of Trustees, was so identified in the public mind with the Institution, that his personal correspondence and intercourse with the young men and with their parents became very extensive. A few years after Washington's visit to Andover, and while he was President of the United States, at his suggestion his nephew, William Augustus Washington, sent two sons to the Academy, and Charles Lee sent the two sons of his deceased brother, Richard Henry Lee; after a brief interval, three more of the Washington family joined the school. When Colonel Washington and lady came on with their sons, Judge Phillips wrote to Madam Phillips: —

> "I hope you will be able to make their time agreeable; I feel powerfully inclined to show every token of respect that is proper to the representative of that eminent instrument of political salvation to his country. It is not improbable that the General means to adopt one or both of the youths bearing his name, if worthy of it."

Occasionally remittances were made through the President, who had interested himself so much in the arrangement. Among the letters now in our hands, is one from his pen, which we here insert, with the reply of Judge Phillips, a memorandum of which is entered upon the same sheet: —

"Mount Vernon, 28th Sept., 1796.

"Sir.

The enclosed letter, from my Nephew to me, accompanying one from him to you (which have been to Philadelphia and back), must be my apology for giving you the trouble of reading this address.

I shall only add, that if there are arrearages yet due to you, and you will let me know the amount, it shall be remitted from Philadelphia; at which place I expect to be by the first of November.

I am, Sir,

Your Most Obed$^{t}$ H$^{ble}$ Serv$^{t}$,

" G$^{o}$ Washington.

The Hon$^{ble}$ Sam'l Phillips, Esq$^{r}$."

"Oct'r 28 '96.

"Sir.

I have been honored with your favor of the 28$^{th}$ Ultimo, enclosing a letter from Col$^{o}$ Washington, in which were received one hundred and fifty dollars, and take the liberty to enclose an answer.

You are pleased to authorize me to give you notice of any arrears on account of the sons of your Nephew; it gives me pleasure to say, there are none of any consequence now due to me.

With the highest respect,

I am Sir

Your Most Obed$^{t}$

And very h$^{ble}$ Serv$^{t}$,

Samuel Phillips.

To the President of the United States."

The young Washingtons were in the family of Rev. Mr. French; the Lees were with Judge Phillips, for whom, with Madam Phillips and their son, they had the warmest regard. The elder of these brothers died soon after entering College at Princeton, and in the last lines he ever wrote, after speaking of his wishes respecting several other friends, he said: — "My friendship for the Phillips family cannot be buried with me in the grave, but it will live with me in the immortal life. Perhaps some little article presented to each of them, Mr. and Mrs. Phillips and their son, as at my request, would please them." A copy of the paper left by him containing these parting messages, which was sent by his uncle with an account of his last hours to Judge Phillips, was carefully preserved, and bears this touching indorsement by his hand — "pretious!" — so deeply was his heart affected by such expressions of attachment. In a letter of Judge Phillips to Mr. Lee, written after he had received this paper, there is a passage which shows with what spirit in this case, as in many others, he interested himself in the pupils of the Academy: —

"The observation," he says, "expressed in your introductory letter, that 'one of your principal inducements in sending him and his brother so far from Virginia and their friends, was that they might be brought up in the purest principles of religion, morality, and virtue,' accorded so perfectly with my ideas of the essential part of education, that

I took more pleasure in urging remarks tending to that object; the unremitted and serious attention with which these remarks were received by our departed friend, heightened the pleasure of the duty; the satisfaction you are pleased to express in the conduct of his education is highly grateful; and the cordial expressions of attachment to our family in his last letter to you, will be among the sources of our most pleasing reflections through the remainder of life."

Had Judge Phillips been the acting Principal of the Academy, and the daily teacher of the pupils, instead of a Trustee merely, he could not have used language more expressive of his personal activity in guiding those who were thus sent to enjoy its advantages.

And this accords perfectly with his whole habit toward the students. He had not taken more interest in originating the Academy than he now continued to take in its daily work. The instructors were selected by him with the greatest care, and were stimulated in all their duties by his aid. The pupils revered and loved him, remembering well, for long years afterwards, his kindly looks and paternal counsels, and repeating incidents, without number, illustrative of his intercourse with them. It was emphatically *his* Academy, the favorite work of his hand, fashioned and animated in the highest possible degree by his spirit; and as such it stands his noblest monument.

More than seven hundred pupils were admitted to its

*Wm. Phillips.*

course of study, during his own lifetime, among whom he could number many who were called to the highest stations. And it is but continuing the sketch of *his* enterprise, to add here, that the Academy, thus originated and prosperous under his eye, has moved onward from strength to strength in its career, for a half century since he passed away. Largely indebted to the later as well as the earlier patronage of the Phillips family, and especially to the liberal hand of His Honor the late Lieutenant-Governor, William Phillips, and attracting to itself a full attendance of pupils, the Institution has been singularly prosperous.

We cannot, as we surely would not, here pass over the name of His Honor, William Phillips, without a brief notice of the impulse which his liberality imparted to the school. The only surviving son of his honored father, he succeeded not only to his large fortune, but to his virtues. Of frail constitution and delicate health in early life, he rose above the consequent defects of his education, by the force of a sagacious, well-balanced mind, animated by steady religious impulses. He was the senior of his distinguished cousin at Andover by about two years; and between the two there were some strong points of resemblance, as well as an affectionate intimacy; both were intensely patriotic, and made strenuous efforts to promote the Revolution; both were specially distinguished for soundness of judgment. Governor Brooks, with whom, as well as with Governor Strong, His Honor William Phillips was long associated, is said to have remarked, "that in all their consultations and deliberations, he had never known him to give an erroneous opinion:" both were mild and winning in manners, while yet of inflexible firmness in their principles; both were eminently sincere and unpretending, showing everywhere their real character with no glosses; both were eager patrons of sound learning, and of a most devout, religious spirit. In 1773, as the Revolutionary contest was thickening, while one was entering upon his long career of civil service at Andover, the other set sail, from Boston, for England. After an extended tour through Great Britain, and various countries on the continent, he returned, in 1774, in one of the tea ships, and immediately began to take part in the councils of the patriots.

At a later period, he was called to a large experience in legislative life: for many years a representative from Boston, he was finally chosen Lieutenant-Governor of the State in twelve successive elections, during which period he was also repeatedly one of the Presidential electors.

But, conspicuous as he was as a civilian, both for his offices and for the qualities by which he honored every office more than it could honor him, he was yet more eminent for his leading participation in all the great philanthropic and religious enterprises of his day. It was not his money only, nor chiefly, which he freely bestowed upon such enterprises. They were aided as constantly by his far-seeing counsels, and by the whole weight of his personal influence.

At Andover, his very name was a tower of strength. Early elected a Trustee, and entering with all his heart into the views of his cousin, which he had known minutely from the first, he began also early to be a most liberal donor to the Institution; and the long catalogue of his gifts is a most animating record. For a period of nearly fifteen years he gave five hundred dollars annually to aid needy students in the Academy. Prior to this, he had made repeated donations in lands and books, valued at more than a thousand dollars; and while making such large charitable contributions to aid the young men, he gave also five thousand dollars toward rebuilding the Academy, after it had been burnt, and then, in his will, left the Institution a bequest of fifteen thousand dollars.

Nor were his liberalities at Andover confined to the Academy. The Theological Seminary, which the widow and son of his revered cousin, with others, had founded under the same Board of Trustees with the Academy, he also largely aided in his lifetime, and at his death left it a legacy of ten thousand dollars. The whole amount of his gifts to these institutions, not including the invaluable portraits already mentioned, was more than forty thousand dollars. With the same liberal hand he dispensed his wealth, through a long life, in aid of every good cause.

"I confess," said Dr. Wisner at his funeral, after glancing at his career, "that when I consider all these circumstances, I look with wonder — and I hope with gratitude to God, whose grace made him what he was — at the variety and the amount of his charities. They have been for a *series* of years from eight to eleven thousand dollars a year. And by his will he has contributed to various benevolent objects, most of them religious charities, sixty-two thousand dollars."[1]

At his death, which did not take place until a quarter of a century after Judge Phillips's decease, in May, 1827, when he was in his seventy-eighth year, there were, in every section of the Commonwealth, expressions of the most hearty sorrow and of the highest eulogy.[2] An engraving of his portrait, which hangs in × the Library of the Seminary, is here presented.

[1] Dr. Wisner's Funeral Discourse, p. 31, 32.

[2] It is due to the memory of the four, whose donations have created and sustained so important an institution as Phillips Academy, to state here summarily, the amount of their several gifts. These are as follows, in round numbers: —

| | |
|---|---|
| Hon. Samuel Phillips, of North Andover . . . . . . . . . | $6,000 |
| Hon. John Phillips, LL. D., of Exeter . . . . . . . . . | 31,000 |
| Hon. William Phillips, of Boston . . . . . . . . . . . | 6,000 |
| His Honor, William Phillips, of Boston, to the Academy . . | 28,000 |
| " " " " " to the Seminary . . | 14,000 |
| | $85,000 |

Others of the family name have also made donations of consid-

× See page 254 (error in binding.)

The plan of Judge Phillips originally contemplated the possible, and indeed probable, outgrowth of a College, or of some equivalent institution, from the Academy; and the Constitution was drafted with this point distinctly in view; but especially with reference to an institution, or to a development of the classical Academy itself, which would provide special facilities for the study of Divinity.

One memorable conversation especially which he once held with his clerk, Mr. Moses Abbott, as they sat under the old oak, now standing just in the rear of the Seminary Chapel, is still narrated by his surviving friend; in which Judge Phillips pointed out the very site of the present Seminary buildings, as the probable location of the future College. Treatises upon Christianity had long been regular text-books in the Academy. Arrangements had also been made for the separate instruction of a class of students in Divinity, so that, what was not realized until after his death, the distinct endowment and opening of a Theological Department, was at last most naturally inaugurated by his widow and son, as if moved yet by an impulse from his own living spirit.

erable amount, to one or the other of these Institutions, besides the large endowment of Madam Phillips and her son, in founding the Theological Seminary, which, of itself, was nearly $20,000; so that a sum total of more than $100,000 has been concentrated here by this family; and its wide spread results are carrying their name to the remotest lands, as benefactors of the race.

But while in its growth, after itself receiving about twenty students in Theology, the Academy threw out its vital and vigorous offshoot in that direction, its genius was so elastic, and its foundation so broad, that the germ of yet another department in a different direction was beginning to appear; and, in process of time, after the legacy of his Honor William Phillips, who regarded the project with especial favor, an English Department, designed as a Teachers Seminary or Normal High School, was organized. The intention at first was to keep this Department distinct from the Classical School, as had been done with the Theological Department, and a commodious building was erected for its use. But with no endowments, and with an inadequate support from its term-bills, although largely attended, experience wrought a change in the plan, and the Academy has for many years embraced an extended course of both Classical and English study under one *regime*, while it continues to give especial prominence, as it did when first opened, to instruction "in the learned languages."

Such have been the natural, and almost necessary, unfoldings of the comprehensive plan of the Founders of the Institution. Calling it at first a *School* merely, and not aspiring ever to term it more than an *Academy*, they virtually originated little less than a University of the highest type. Not attempting too much at once, their sagacious scheme has led especially to a course of Classical and Theological instruction, nowhere surpassed now, if equalled, in thoroughness or in scholarly symmetry, or in the earnest religious life which electrifies it all.

In the Classical Department a careful register of all who have ever been admitted has been kept, and is now a volume of very great interest. Nearly *four thousand* pupils have, for a longer or shorter period, been thus connected with the Institution, among whom are many of the most eminent names of the past half century; while not less than *twenty-seven hundred* have been members of the English Department, and from the Theological Department, besides the many who have pursued their studies here for a part of their professional course, nearly *thirteen hundred* have regularly graduated.[1] The spirit and drift of the Academy, which after a quarter of a century from its origin gave birth to the first Theological Seminary in the world, must be ascribed to Judge Phillips, more than to any other person, however far from even his best thoughts so broad a scheme as was ultimately adopted may have been, and whatever other issues or interests may have arisen to modify it.

As we thus contemplate his life-long efforts for the Academy, so persistently prosecuted, so nobly seconded

[1] See Appendix, M.

by his family, so successful in all their immediate aims, revealing at last in this new form the strong undercurrent of religious power, which had visibly animated them from the very beginning, we come naturally to notice his character and life in yet one more essential aspect.

# CHAPTER XI.

## HIS RELIGIOUS SPIRIT AND EFFORTS.

To his careful religious training, with its consequent early religious tendencies, repeated reference has been incidentally made already. He was constitutionally susceptible, in a remarkable degree, to such culture, whether it sought to mould his conscience or his feelings. None would accept with more reverence and sympathy the heritage of ancestral piety which distinguished the family with the race of Puritans to which they belonged. What these old New England Fathers thought and did was always a stirring consideration with him, to which he often alluded when stimulating himself or others. He admired their type of character. It was one of his most cherished aims, not only to be himself of the same spirit with them, but to do whatever was in his power toward perpetuating such a spirit in society.

We have never studied the character of one, among the living or the dead, in whom the various forces of religion seemed more symmetrically blended. He was religious in study, in trade, in neighborly kindness, in domestic life, in politics, in every civil office, and in his zeal to promote learning, as well as in public worship or public charities. It was emphatically a religious institution, which he was intent upon establishing; a religious vitality which he sought to breathe into all education within its atmosphere. Such we are sure must have been the inference of the reader from his various papers as they have been here cited: and we have nowhere found a line in all his manuscripts, or heard a word from any who remember him, that does not tend to confirm this impression.

In the place of his residence — from his birth to his death — he has left a name for genial, consistent, winning, zealous piety, more fresh than the memory of his highest honors. As the result in part, doubtless, of that discipline of sorrow through which the family passed in his childhood, and partly of the reiterated bereavements afterwards which he so keenly felt, together with his own frequent illness, there was a subdued tenderness of sensibility in his religion, which added to its impressiveness.

It was with such a charm about him, that he drew near to the students, as in the case of young Lee, and opened to them the treasures of Heavenly wisdom, seeking, in the spirit of a pastor, or a father, to guide their feet into the way of peace. With the same ever wakeful tact, he often made his correspondence almost entirely religious in its tenor; seizing with avidity upon occasions of every kind, which would help him to pour out his full heart with the best effect.

We have stated that during his confinement at Medford with his fractured leg, his cousin, Miss Sally Phillips, was much with him. It appears from the following letters, that on their return to Andover together the subject of her uniting with the church was suggested to her, and the time of her taking this step was soon decided. We give now his letters to her on this occasion, as worthy of special note, not only for their delicate aptness, as addressed to her, but for the justness with which they at the same time commend this duty to the young generally.

Soon after reaching his home he writes, —

"ANDOVER, May 4, 1794.

"MY DEAR MISS PHILLIPS, — You have this day made a public declaration of your belief in, and regard for, the religion of the blessed Jesus. Will you permit me in the sincerity of my heart to congratulate you on this joyful event, — an event which has, beyond all doubt, caused much joy in heaven as well as on earth. Openly and explicitly to declare on the Lord's side, and in the face of the world to subscribe with your own hand to his covenant, cannot fail of pleasing that Almighty Being, who hath declared, 'before all the people I will be glorified:' — for the same reason, it must give joy to all good beings who come to the knowledge of it; — and among the inhabitants of this globe, those who feel most interested in your happiness, will feel most gratified and delighted; — for, by the same act which does honor to religion, and the glorious Founder of it, you take the most effectual measure to promote and secure your own peace and comfort, usefulness and happiness in this world, and bliss everlasting.

"Such a transaction, duly performed (as I doubt not yours has been) by persons of any age or class, tends directly to subserve both the important purposes above expressed; — but when it is performed, in the early part of life, by a person in the midst of gay and pleasing scenes, whom friends caress and the world flatters, surrounded with objects and under circumstances calculated to rivet the affections to the present state, and obscure the realities of futurity; — when this person is of the tender sex, (who are sometimes restrained by mistaken delicacy or unjustifiable diffidence,) possessing an uncommon share of sensibility; — then is signal honor and benefit derived to the best of all causes, and peculiar joy afforded to all its friends and advocates; at the same time, a foundation is laid for a rich and increasing harvest of blessings to the happy possessor.

"These blessings are great and numerous; — the satisfaction derived from a reflection on the consequences above hinted at is not inconsiderable; an early public dedication is expressive of a consideration and thoughtfulness which does credit to any character, and of that filial love and reverence which are the best affections of the heart; it affords a longer opportunity of usefulness to mankind, and by example, that most powerful of all persuasives, may allure many to similar reflections and resolutions.

"May such be the happy consequence of this day's transaction, and, when your days of usefulness on earth shall be finished, may your spirit be frequently delighted, in the regions of immortality, with the glorious tidings of the increasing happy fruits of this example among the children of men! With these wishes (in which Mrs. Phillips very cordially joins me) for the present I will bid you adieu, after begging you to believe that I am

"Truly your affectionate friend,

"SAMUEL PHILLIPS."

"ANDOVER, May 14, 1794.

"MY DEAR MISS PHILLIPS, — Your very obliging favor of the 10th instant, afforded me a degree of pleasure that will not suffer me to rest easy in delaying to return you my hearty thanks for it. . . . After perusing your favor repeatedly, and with increasing satisfaction, it was difficult to determine which part was the most pleasing, unless it was that in which you say, 'upon a late compliance with duty I have the most reason I ever had to congratulate myself;' — and surely the declaration was founded in the highest reason; for to comply with the charge — the dying charge — of a Father and a friend, who claims (and most justly too) an infinite superiority to every other friend, must afford to the heart of pious sensibility, a joy which beggars the power of language to describe; — and how is this joy enhanced, when, by the same act which expresses our obedience and fidelity to our Divine Master, we receive a most affecting token of his love and friendship for us? for, (according to the author you entertained me with at Medford,) 'when my Lord at the table says, *Take and eat, this is my body*, this is infinitely more and better than if a rich man should say to me, *take my estate;* or than if an emperor should say to me, *take my crown and diadem;* or than if all the kingdoms of the world and the glory of them were offered me.'

" The gratitude you express to me on this occasion is too generous; my reward was abundant, and of the highest possible value, in the welcome reception you gave to my proposition and the consequences which have followed.

" Will you allow me to suggest a caution, which I have constant need to have more forcibly impressed on my own mind, — *that we do not ascribe to the instrument that honor and praise which are due to the power which actuates it.* Let us not in the present case, overlook that overruling Providence, which gave so favorable an opportunity for entering on such a subject, in our journey to Andover — which overcame an embarrassment on my mind that prevented my introducing it till near the close of the journey, although a desire of doing it had existed for months before, and particularly at the commencement of that journey — and which inclined you to give such a cordial entertainment to the proposal. Neither should we overlook the same universal Ruler, who guided the operations of your mind in contemplating the subject, who influenced it to the happy result, and smiled on the first attempt for executing your purpose. Indeed, every encouraging and animating consideration which preceded and attended the weighty transaction, and every happifying reflection which followed it, are so many claims on our fervent gratitude to that all-pervading Spirit, which inspired, sustains, and regulates the vital principle. . . .

" I am yours, with great esteem and affection,

" S. Phillips."

In all the family correspondence, it is most instructive to notice with what spontaneous ease his pen turned often from the business or news of which he was writing, to some high religious view or use of his topic, or was diverted to some kindred strain of ethical discussion. Very many of his letters to Madam Phillips contain passages with regard to the religious instruction of their children, the spirit of which she was transfusing into their hearts, while to the children themselves, early and late, he was often writing upon the same great themes. A most touching letter to his younger son, on the occasion of his fifth birth-day, which we feel restrained from citing, shows at what a tender age that young and pure spirit was preparing for its early exit from earth.

To the elder son he frequently gave invaluable religious hints, as he wrote upon other topics; and on many a special occasion, religion, in some of its most important aspects and claims, was the only theme of his communications. Through the entire period of his minority, and even after his connection with the church and his marriage, the son was thus with the tenderest affection kept near to the father's heart. The following letters, in addition to those which we have cited heretofore, of the same general tenor, may serve as an illustration of the spirit of this correspondence; the facts which some of them incidentally disclose in his personal and family history, will not be regarded as detracting from their excellence, but rather as enhancing it.

"ANDOVER, November 24, Sabbath evening, 1793.

"MY DEAR SON, — Your letter of the 12th and 15th instant has been received, and the contents gave me pleasure. . . . We have this morning been much affected by the information of the sudden and unexpected death of Deacon Abbott; . . . thus we are deprived, in a very affecting manner, of one of the best men the town afforded: — what a shock to his poor distressed wife and beloved children, to the neighborhood, to the church, to the town and the public; — when a man of exemplary piety, integrity, prudence, virtue, and general goodness is taken from among us, how universally is the loss felt and lamented. In many instances the rich, the mighty, and the honorable leave the stage, while few regret the loss of them, and some are glad to succeed them; but when a good man departs, we read sadness in every countenance, and the serious who survive are prompted to exclaim, 'Help, Lord, for the godly man ceaseth, and the faithful fail from among the children of men.' What a call to survivors, to double their diligence in their Master's service, when we see the uncertainty of the event of an hour!

"Such a family as his was rarely to be met with; — not only the heads of it exemplary for the Christian character, but all the children treading in their steps; at every communion, how pleasing to behold parents and children all approaching the altar of the Lord, and with one heart and one voice commemorating that wonderful love of the glorious Saviour which astonishes angels! Is it not strange that these instances are so rare? Does the blame lie with the parents or the children? probably in most cases with both!

"I take it to myself, that I have omitted to urge this great duty upon the child to whom I am now writing. Let me, then, without losing another hour, seriously ask, my dear son, do you not believe your lost and undone condition by nature, your misery without a Saviour, that the Son of God has undertaken the mighty task, that he condescended to take our nature, that he obeyed the whole law, that he suffered and died to purchase your ransom from endless misery? Do you believe the necessity of repentance, love, and new obedience, in order to be qualified for enjoying the benefits of Christ's purchase? and is it not your daily prayer and labor to obtain these gifts and graces? If not, what will all your other cares, studies, and labors amount to? How infinitely light and trifling will every attainment, without an interest in the blessed Redeemer, appear at the hour of death, that honest hour, which speaks a language that must be heard by all the children of Adam, a language which is frequently sounding in our ears!

"That you and I and all of us may be prepared for our own turn, which will soon arrive, is the fervent prayer of your affectionate parent, SAMUEL PHILLIPS."

"ANDOVER, December 17, 1793.

"MY DEAR SON, — I received your letter of a late date and was much pleased with it. . . . In this hour of danger, remember that "soft words turn away anger;" and *whatever provocation you may receive, do n't lose the perfect command of yourself.* . . . You will not be safer in any situation, than in your chamber or study, with your door fastened, and your mind intent on your book, unless when you are on your knees imploring your infinitely wise and good Father in heaven, *to direct, preserve, strengthen, and defend you: — what a blessed privilege to be admitted to solicit such high favor of the King of Kings, with hopes of success, if the supplicant have the true spirit of prayer;* and when nearest the throne of grace, forget not to return humble, fervent thanks, that you have been preserved from the vices which have plunged others into so much misery, and also to pray for their repentance and reformation. . . . We think much of you and pray for you, and hope these trials will issue in your final advantage.

"I am your affectionate, anxious Parent,

"S. PHILLIPS."

The occasion and the effect of such letters as the preceding, are indicated by the following brief note from an intimate friend of the family, alluding to scenes of which we have spoken heretofore, as will be remembered, in connection with another portion of the family correspondence: —

"CAMBRIDGE, January 1, 1794.

"DEAR SIR, — After fervently wishing a happy new year to you and yours, I take the liberty to thank you for your friendly advice. . . .

"You have doubtless heard of the uncommon scenes, both of irregularity and of public censure, which have distinguished the last term at College. The immediate government has exercised the greatest industry, patience, and impartiality in their inquiries, deliberations, and decisions upon these painful subjects; and we flatter ourselves that our conduct will be sanctioned by the approving voice of the sober public, and particularly of the Board of Overseers.

"I congratulate you on the manly, honorable, and virtuous

part which your son, as well as many of his fellow-students, has acted, amidst the late scenes of temptation and trial.

"With sentiments of great esteem, I am, Sir,

"Your affectionate friend and servant,

"D. TAPPAN.

"Honorable Mr. PHILLIPS."

Amid all his anxieties respecting the religious state of his son, Judge Phillips was cheered by many hopes; and, as in the case of Miss Sally Phillips, endeavored to lead him to a full and public consecration of himself to God, as we see in the ensuing earnest appeal:—

"BOSTON, January 26, 1794.

"MY DEAR CHILD,—I have been this day celebrating the stupendous love of the Divine Saviour, at the feast of the supper; and my thoughts were exercised, in no inconsiderable degree, for the dear youth to whom I stand in one of the nearest relations, and whose spiritual as well as temporal happiness I am under the most solemn obligations to promote by all proper means in my power;—I then felt, and still feel, a solicitude to know whether any, and if any, what effect has been produced by some remarks lately made in writing, on the subject of taking upon yourself the bonds of the covenant; to these remarks you replied, that the subject of them was under consideration;—do they still remain so, or are they dismissed for others of trifling moment, as all temporal concerns must be when compared with those which respect our future existence? If not dismissed, how does the subject appear to you? Does it not appear reasonable to obey the command of our Sovereign—of a Sovereign who has given himself up to the sufferings of death to save us from everlasting misery? — especially to give the readiest obedience to his dying charge? You feel yourself under obligations to obey the commands of your earthly parents, and a concern when any instance of disobedience comes to our knowledge; and it is right you should; but any human authority is of little force, compared with that which exists with that Supreme Being, who gave us existence, is continually upholding us, and withheld not his own most precious life to save us.

"Do you believe, my dear child, that Christ died to save sinners? that endless misery must have been your and my portion, inevitably, had it not been for this infinitely costly sacrifice? Do you believe that this sacrifice, costly as it was, will be of no avail, unless we become qualified to receive the blessings which the Saviour died to purchase, by repentance for all our sins, and that faith in the Redeemer and his Gospel which shall have a commanding influence over the heart and the life, the temper and conversation, the powers of the body and affections of the soul, and, in short, over the whole man? This repentance and this faith are God's gift; but he must be sought to, and inquired of, to grant it; if it is not worth praying for, and striving after, it is not worth giving. If these graces of repentance and faith are not worth praying for, then heaven and the happiness of it are not worth praying for. You have every encouragement to beg the bestowment of these blessings, for your Heavenly Father is perfectly ready and willing to bestow them, if you ask aright; more ready than any earthly parent can be to bestow the good things of this life on his dear offspring. If you do not possess them, and do n't even desire them, how awfully hazardous your state! What must be your position, if called out of time, in such a situation! A serious consideration of this question is of infinite moment; no subject of consideration is of any moment, compared with this. Therefore let me entreat and conjure you, by all the affection and authority of a father, to dwell upon the thought, till you find the stream of genuine contrition and pious affections to flow plentifully.

"If you do possess these graces, you have the highest reason to give praise, *humble, fervent, unceasing praise to that infinitely merciful God*, who has redeemed you with the blood of his own Son, and hath given his blessed Spirit to apply his redemption.

"How can you do enough to show forth your gratitude to such a Saviour? Among other tokens of this gratitude, is it not highly becoming to commemorate the last tragical scene of his sufferings, with his disciples, in the sacrament of the supper? — especially, considering this duty was given in command by himself, among the last orders which he delivered while on earth.

"I was charmed to-day with the sight of a young family of Mr. Salsbury's, all joining with their dear parents in celebrating this feast. How happy, thought I, if our dear children would enable their anxious parents to say to the Almighty, HERE ARE WE AND THE CHILDREN THOU HAST GIVEN US! If you have difficulties on your mind open them to me freely, and I shall delight to assist; and rejoice that you have a mighty Counsellor, who invites you to his throne for advice, at all times: improve this exalted privilege diligently, and do not forget to return some of the prayers which are frequently poured out for you by your anxious parent, S. PHILLIPS."

The occasion of the two following letters is indicated in the letters themselves. The first, we regret to say, is incomplete; the manuscript in our hands being evidently the original outline of the communication, without the final revision and concluding paragraphs. It is in these words:—

"ANDOVER, October 17, 1797.

"'*Finis origine pendet.*'

"MY DEAR SON,—To-morrow will complete twenty-one years of your life. As, at that period, youth are generally considered as released from that parental authority which they are the subjects of before, it may not be improper to offer at this moment some hints, and give you some advice dictated by the feelings of a parent, whose affection gives rise to much anxiety for your welfare.

"You will consider them with that attention which is due to the last counsel you will ever receive while (in a legal sense) in a state of minority, from one standing in the class of relations which is nearer to you than any other on earth.

"As this may be considered one of the most memorable eras of your life, I would recommend to you to set apart Wednesday, the 18th of October, 1797, for the purpose of serious recollection, meditation, humiliation, thanksgiving, and prayer; and for adopting those resolutions which that occasion will dictate as proper.

"Although the state of your business may render it inconvenient to comply with this advice, yet I can hardly realize it to be such as would prevent you from absenting yourself from the store on occasions far less important than this.

"It has been the practice of the best men that ever lived, to set apart every anniversary of their birth, as well as other days in the year, for purposes similar to those I have mentioned; and they have given full testimony to the advantage they have experienced from the practice.

"After humbly presenting yourself before the heart-searching God, and earnestly imploring his direction and benediction in the duties before you; it will be highly proper on that day to take a careful and minute review of the past years of your life; and, in doing this, it will be useful to inquire, how you have discharged the various duties which have resulted from the various relations you have sustained to God as your Creator, Preserver, Redeemer, constant and unwearied Benefactor; to your parents and other dear relatives; to your Instructors and governors; to your superiors, equals, and inferiors; what duties in these several relations have been wholly omitted or carelessly performed; and what obligations have been violated; what improvement you have made of *time*, especially of *holy time;* of the various *advantages* you have enjoyed for improving your mind and storing up useful knowledge; for correcting the disorders of your temper, and any vicious and irregular propensities; how far you have been influenced by the counsel and instruction that have been given to you from the Sacred Volume by your parents, by godly ministers, and by friends; what improvement you have made of your various opportunities for getting and doing good; how you have regarded the providences of God, not only those of a public nature, but those which respect the family of which you are a member, and yourself personally. If, on such a review, you don't find the humiliation I recommend, will there not be reason to fear you have not been sufficiently thorough in the examination?

" On that day, it will be proper to review the distinguished mercies you have received, in your preservation in life to this time, in the health you have enjoyed; and may you not reckon it in the number of your mercies, that your parents have been spared to watch over, to advise and counsel you, through the precipitate years of youth, even unto manhood.

" You will consider, my dear son, the circumstances of your lot have been uncommonly favorable; your life thus far has been devoted to improvement; you have had a succession in general of uncommonly able and faithful Instructors from your early childhood; you have had no material avocations to divert your attention from useful studies. Your advantages have been great, and (except in a father who this day laments, in tears, his numerous defects in duty toward you, both in precept and example) may I not say they have been equalled by few, and surpassed scarcely by any; and forget not the goodness of Heaven in preserving you from gross immoralities, amid the snares and temptations that have attended your youth, and the situations of danger in which you have been placed, and which have proved fatal to others. Restraining and rescuing influences are too little thought of by most.

" That you have been disposed, at an early period, to make a public surrender of yourself to your Maker, and subscribe with your hand to his Covenant, is a further cause of thankfulness. As your cup has overflown with mercies, let your heart overflow with gratitude to the infinite Source of them all. Much fruit, then, may justly be expected from you by

God and man, and your own conscience will justify the demand.

" After spending a suitable portion of time in reviewing the past, and in those exercises of mind which that review will suggest, you will judge whether it is not a very seasonable duty to make a renewed, solemn, and unreserved dedication of yourself, and of all your powers and faculties, of all that you have and are to your Heavenly Father; and to implore his direction and guidance in forming suitable resolutions for the time to come. The 17th chapter in Doddridge's Rise and Progress, will be of great use to you in such a work.

" You will remember, my son, that all your pursuits must be regulated by a supreme regard to the Divine honor. Let the fear and love of Jehovah possess your heart, dictate every purpose, and influence every action. This fear, we are taught by inspiration, is the *beginning* of wisdom; without this foundation all your superstructure will be as wood, hay, and stubble. Possessing this filial fear, you will seriously resolve to begin and close every day of your life with the most solemn acts of devotion. If the blessings of Providence and grace are not worth asking, they are not worth bestowing; and what day of your life is there in which you do not need them.

" You will, doubtless, judge it reasonable to make it part of your plan, to read some portion of Scripture at those stated periods; and, that you may read them to more advantage, I now present you with Henry's Exposition of the Old and New Testament, and Doddridge's Exposition of the latter. The first of these books was estimated by a late pious deceased friend and relative, (from whose prayers you and I have doubtless reaped unknown benefits,) to be of more value than gold, yea, than much fine gold. In these volumes, if read in a proper temper of mind, will be found inestimable treasures of wisdom and knowledge. Let them be the man of your counsel at all times. The proverbs of Solomon can't be too often consulted; they will form the richest furniture with which your mind can be stored, for every situation, condition, and relation of life. They contain, as Mr. Henry observes, in a little compass, a complete body of Divine ethics, politics, and oeconomics: and whensoever reading the sacred Scriptures, we ought to consider ourselves as in the more immediate presence of the great God; and if we do n't pay a serious regard to him, when speaking to us in his word, how can we expect him to regard our petitions to him? These books, my son, are the best estate I can give you.

"If the want of time be offered as an objection to the execution of such a plan, may it not be asked whether we can justify the denial of a small portion of our time to the service of him who gives us all the time we enjoy, and who can with the utmost ease cut short or protract our days, according to his own sovereign pleasure? and what benefits can result from any business, that will counterbalance the advantages to be hoped for from the appropriation of a small portion of our time to such a purpose?

"If company at any time interfere, what company will make amends for the loss of a humble, solemn interview with the Sovereign of the universe, who exercises infinite condescension in inviting us into his presence? By husbanding our time properly, we shall not find it difficult to gain a small portion of it, at the beginning and close of each day, for the discharge of this important duty: and here let me recommend a careful perusal of the 19th chapter in Dr. Doddridge's 'Rise and Progress,' containing directions how we should be in the fear of God all the day long, with a serious resolution to come as near to the plan there proposed as possible.

"But of all your time, be persuaded, my son, to entertain the firmest resolution, that you will pay the strictest regard to the holy Sabbath. The injunctions of Scripture are often repeated, and very solemn, on this head; and your improvement in the most valuable of all knowledge, your progress in virtue and piety, and your usefulness to others, will depend much, very much indeed, on your discharge of this duty. On account of your vicinity to the metropolis, you will be a witness to a melancholy disregard of holy time. On this account, your guard ought to be much increased, to prevent your respect for that day being insensibly diminished, and in order that your example may contribute to stem the torrent of impiety, which is breaking in upon us like a flood, and threatens the judgments of Heaven upon our country.

"To regulate your dealings with others, you can't propose to yourself a better rule than that of our Saviour, in Matthew vii. 12,—'all things whatsoever ye would that men should do to you, do ye even so to them;' you will often call to mind that comprehensive injunction in Micah vi. 8,—'to do justly, love mercy, and walk humbly with thy God,'—and what more 'doth the Lord require of thee?'

"Let me earnestly recommend the cultivation of a meek and humble frame of mind. The more attention will be necessary to acquire and preserve these virtues, if a state of worldly prosperity should attend you; because the natural tendency of such a state is to inflate the mind with pride. We ought to remember that a state of prosperity very often proves unfriendly to virtue; and the Divine caution, 'let him that thinketh he standeth, take heed lest he fall,' should be ever in mind. What higher inducement can be given us to cultivate meekness, than to be assured that 'the meek he (the Lord) will guide in judgment; the meek he will teach his way,'—and that 'the ornament of a meek and quiet spirit is, in the sight of God, of great price.' The highest reason have we then to labor, that we may be clothed with humility. . . ."

"MY EVER HONORED AND BELOVED FATHER,—The eighteenth of October, 1797, has introduced a set of ideas which I never before felt. Your letter, which I esteem the most valuable fortune you can give me, while it impresses on my mind an idea of the importance of the era which I have now reached, and with a firm belief that my future happiness and usefulness will depend on my setting out, inspires me with increased affection and respect for the hand that penned and the heart that dictated it. May the precepts it contains be indelibly engraven on my mind! for they only can insure my present and future happiness.

"My intention has been to endeavor on this day to express my filial gratitude for the former unremitted care, tenderness, and anxiety of my parents, who are nearer and dearer to me than any other beings on earth; but my feelings will not permit me. The only alteration that the day produces in my situation is, that it devolves on me an increased responsibility. Hitherto I have leaned on my parent's reputation, and have in every instance wherein I could know his will, been guided thereby. *Now* I only am answerable for my every action,— but shall ever feel the same veneration for their opinion I ever have done, and still feel in a state of minority as far as relates to them. This day I have been engaged in the manner which you recommended: I have received Dr. Doddridge's Exposition of the New Testament, and one volume of Mr. Henry, for which I am thankful, and promise that want of time shall not be an excuse for my neglecting a daily application to them.

"I have now, sir, to make one earnest request; which is, that you would not consider me as freed from your authority until I shall cease to be the object of your parental affection, —that I may still have those rules of conduct repeated, which had so much influence in helping me to avoid the almost fatal temptations of a college life.

"I will conclude, at present, by earnestly praying, that the lives, happiness, and usefulness of my earthly parents, may be the peculiar care of my Father in Heaven, and that his assisting grace may enable me to follow through my life the precepts of their lips exemplified by their conduct.

"I am, with increasing respect, your dutiful son,

"JOHN PHILLIPS.

"The Honorable SAMUEL PHILLIPS."

"ANDOVER, January 1, 1800, 3 o'clock in the morning.

"MY DEAR SON,—On this first morning of a New Year, I awoke early; and the activity of my mind having banished sleep from my eyes, I rose and betook myself to such exercises as are proper for the season.

"Influenced by the example of those whose characters I revere, as well as by a conviction of the utility of the practice, I have heretofore aimed to appropriate a more than usual share of the first day of the year, as well as the anniversary of my birthday, to such exercises as were adapted to qualify me better to answer the end of my creation. I hope I have derived some advantage from the practice; it would doubtless have been greater, had not I been too remiss in performing the duty, and too unmindful afterwards of the purposes formed at these seasons.

"The present period appears to call for more close attention to every religious duty than any we have seen; and one object of this letter, is to invite you to join me this day in the exercises I have mentioned; and though we are not in the same house, or in the same society, let us kneel before the same Throne to lament and beg forgiveness for our past defects, neglects, and transgressions; and to implore Divine mercy for ourselves and each other, for our families, for our friends and connections, for our mourning and threatened country, and for a convulsed world.

"We shall find ample field for a long day's close, uninterrupted employment; and though cares and business may strive to intrude and divert our attention from the duty proposed, let us summon up a holy resolution to appropriate this day to the more immediate service of the *all glorious Being* who is *Lord of all our time.*

"Let us begin with imploring the Divine presence, direction, and benediction on the exercises of the day; then read some portion or portions of the Sacred Scriptures that are proper for the occasion; afterwards apply ourselves solemnly to the duty of serious meditation and reflection, *self-examination, humiliation*, and *prayer*. This will be a proper season, also, to renew our dedication of ourselves to the special service of our Divine Master; and let us not fail, in his strength, to form such resolutions as a review of our past lives suggests to be needful, such as shall tend to make us better men, better husbands, better parents, better heads of families, better members of society, and better Christians.

"It will increase the solemnity and utility of the work, if we commit as many of our thoughts as we can to writing. This will be quite necessary for our resolutions, that we may frequently review them, and see how far we have fulfilled them.

"An agreeable and profitable variety may be made by reading some pertinent sermons or other tracts; the sermons of the pious Mr. Foxcroft, on the last and first day of the year, which I put into your hands yesterday, I have repeatedly read with much satisfaction, and, hope with some profit. Doctor Doddridge's Rise and Progress furnishes more chapters than one that may be useful on this occasion. The Book of Psalms abounds with matter, admirably adapted to excite, direct, and animate our devotion. An observation of the day by fasting is recommended by the experience and example of many worthies; at least, an abstinence from our usual quantity of food and drink appears to me will be highly proper and beneficial.

"If you approve of my proposition, you will probably order a fire in the most retired chamber, and give notice to suitable persons in your family, that your engagements to-day don't admit of interruption, unless upon some very special occasion. And let us engage in these exercises with a seriousness and devotion becoming those who are utterly uncertain whether we shall have leave to unite in similar duties on another New Year's day ever again on earth.

"Wishing you and your dear consort may enjoy many years more useful and happy than any that have passed, with best wishes for your mamma and beloved offspring,

"I am your affectionate father, SAMUEL PHILLIPS."

"ANDOVER, January 1, 1800.

"MY HONORED FATHER, — I have received your excellent letter of this morning. It witnesseth that the virtues and piety of the fathers have descended to the offspring; and O that the example of both might be imitated by the children's children! To this end I will endeavor to pass this day in the manner recommended in your letter.

"May He who giveth the increase so bless our endeavors, so strengthen us, and all who this day form virtuous purposes, to perform them in such a manner that harvests of honor may arise to himself, and our own happiness and usefulness be increased.

"Be pleased, Sir, to offer our duty to my honored mamma, and accept the same through your ever dutiful son,

"JOHN PHILLIPS, JR."

"ANDOVER, January 4, 1801. Sabbath Eve.

"MY DEAR SON, — Having arrived to the first Sabbath of a New Year and of a new century, I have been reviewing some of the past scenes and occurrences of my life; and the review affords me ground for deep humiliation, as well as for admiration, gratitude, and praise.

"Among the numberless causes for unfeigned self-abasement, I may enumerate neglects of duty to my Maker, my fellow-creatures, especially my *family*, and to myself; and have great reason to lament, that I have *improved time* to no better purpose, and that I have no better answered the design of my creation.

"Without being particular under each class, I might state a long catalogue of family duties which have not been discharged, as they ought to have been; and I here record my hearty regrets, therefore, to you, my dear son, that you may take warning from my errors, and lay a foundation for more agreeable reflections in the future periods of your life. To this end, let me urge you to remember that the duties of heads of families are numerous and very solemn.

"Their duties to each other, — to love, comfort, support, and encourage each other in every thing virtuous and praiseworthy, as well as to watch over, admonish, advise, and guard against every thing unbecoming the Christian profession, are solemn indeed. Those whom Providence has brought into the tender relation of husband and wife, have far greater advantages for promoting each others' spiritual as well as temporal felicity, than any other created beings. They ought frequently to bear in mind that sooner or later they must part; not unfrequently they are called to this distressing trial much sooner than they expected, and sometimes suddenly. What anguish must fill the mind of the survivor, if the reflection should arise that any thing has been neglected to preserve or reclaim from error, or to stimulate and encourage in duty!

"When Heaven bestows the blessing of children, new obligations, and those of the most serious nature, are brought with them. To provide for their comfortable support is not the greatest, although this calls for our industry, care, and economy, and the necessity for these increases with the increase of our families; but to use our utmost vigilance and diligence to regulate their tempers, to instruct them in the principles and duties of the Christian religion, and duly to impress them with a sense of their infinite moment, is as much more important than any thing which relates merely to the present life, as eternity is longer than time.

"For the discharge of these duties, the Author of our nature has given to parents special advantages, — particularly by impressing on the minds of children that awe, reverence, and respect for their parents, which they feel toward no other mortal. Indeed, the Creator seems, in some sort, to have made parents his substitutes, to form, mould, and train up their offspring for glory.

"This remarkable and universal impression upon the minds of children, and which rarely ceases, especially through the years of minority, where the precepts, deportment, and *example* of parents are such as to justify it, proves more forcibly than a thousand arguments their obligation to improve this influence for the honor of its Author, and their high accountability for the manner of their using it. Next to our children, those of our household claim our inspection, instruction, and example, to restrain or recover them from the paths of sin, and to guide and establish them in the ways of piety and virtue.

"To discharge these duties to the tolerable satisfaction of our own minds, we have need to labor, and watch, and strive, and pray, not only in private, but with our families, without ceasing.

"Indeed those who neglect a regular, daily, and devotional acknowledgment of the Supreme Being, with their families, not only forfeit the Divine direction, support, and blessing, where they most need it, but deprive themselves of the best argument to enforce any religious or moral instruction. May I not add, that those who live in the neglect of this duty expose themselves to the charge of hypocrisy in the view of their children and domestics, whenever they inculcate any virtuous instructions? For may they not with reason ask, in their own hearts, if they do not openly state the question, with what propriety do you urge upon us duties under the authority of a Being whose authority you do not acknowledge?

"Indeed, those who neglect family prayer, seldom subject themselves to this charge, for with this they generally fall into the neglect of most other religious duties of the family. And for these neglects, among other sins, it is my serious belief the Almighty has been, and is now, holding the rod of his anger over us, and that we shall feel the weight of it, unless we reform.

"It affords me unspeakable satisfaction to be a witness, that yours was not in the dark catalogue of prayerless families. Having begun well in this respect, it is my humble, fervent prayer, that *no* considerations of business, pleasure, ease, or *company*, may ever tempt you to omit this daily acknowledgment of our dependence on the Supreme Being. Business has sometimes so incumbered me, that I have found it difficult to command time for the performance of the duty; but let us carefully weigh the importance of that business which will justify our neglecting the best interests of our own souls, and the souls of our children and domestics, and risking their everlasting perdition.

"Order in our arrangements, so essential for every other purpose, is particularly so to prevent disappointment or embarrassment here. Until the close of life, or very near it, my honored parents devoted their first attention, after the family had risen, to this duty; and always rose at an early hour when they were well. But if no opportunity offered before, the family were generally collected together immediately after breakfast, and it is easier to retain than to collect them after they are dispersed. It is, however, far better to perform the duty with a small portion of the family, when more cannot be obtained, than to omit it. If people are waiting on business, they will think it as reasonable to allow a little time to pay your acknowledgments to your Maker, as for refreshing your nature. If they do not, it is no matter how little concern you have with such characters. If the duty or the refreshment must be omitted, is it not far safest to deny ourselves, at least curtail, the latter? Sometimes persons in waiting have been invited to join in this devotion, and have been glad of the opportunity; and whether they join or not, who can tell what blessed effects may result from the example!

"The presence of visitors, particularly those of respectability in the view of the world, and especially if they were disposed to think lightly of the duty, has sometimes, in the earlier part of my life, put my fortitude to the trial; — but that awful denunciation of our Saviour in the 38th verse of the 8th chapter of Mark, 'whosoever shall be ashamed of me and of my words in this adulterous and sinful generation, of him also shall the Son of Man be ashamed when he cometh in the glory of his Father with the holy angels,' has caused me to shudder at the thought of being restrained by the fear of man.

"The venerable ancestor from whom our family proceeded, the Reverend George Phillips, (who arrived in Charlestown in the year 1630, and afterwards settled and died in the ministry in the town of Watertown,) was eminent for piety, and has been handsomely spoken of for his literature. It is written of him, that he commonly read the Bible through six times in a year, and through four generations from him to my father, and including him, I trust that a good portion of the spirit of their progenitor descended. I can fully testify that the two last, namely, my father and grandfather, with their consorts, were remarkably constant in their devotions, both of the family and closet; and my mother informed me that she never knew my father to omit family prayer, when he was well and at home, but once from the time he began to keep house, although he was for many years much engaged in business both public and private.

"Who can tell how many blessings the prayers of our pious ancestors have procured for their descendants! Let us, my dear son, be equally faithful even unto death, to our God, to ourselves, and to those who shall be born after us. Greatly aggravated will be our condemnation, if we should degenerate with such examples before us. Should we ever be left to such a woful defection, (which God forbid!) what reason will our posterity have to upbraid us therefor!

"December 5, 1801.

"The foregoing was written at the time of its date, but want of health and unforeseen events prevented my finishing the letter, or even copying what was written. Fearing longer to delay communicating the thoughts which were penned upon a subject which has excited many painful reflections on my pillow, and at other times, I have asked your honored mother to finish copying what I had begun.

"When I began the copy, I left a margin, with a view, if I should communicate my thoughts on other subjects, that you might easily connect the letters, if you judged them worth preserving; but as it is very doubtful whether I shall ever be able to write you again on any subject of moment, you will pay such regard to this as the importance of the subject demands.

"With most anxious solicitude for the happiness of yourself, your beloved spouse, and dear offspring, both here and hereafter, I am Your affectionate parent,

"Samuel Phillips."

The spirit of Christian solicitude and fidelity which thus, to the last, poured out its full tide around his son, as it did in other forms about the daily path of the students in the Academy, made Judge Phillips also a pillar in the church of which he was a member. After his removal to the South Parish, and the transfer of his connection from the North to the South Church, his hand and heart were with his pastor in every good work. It was through his influence that Mr. French had settled here. They were not only class mates, but congenial spirits; and it was with a warm personal regard, as well as Christian interest, that Judge Phillips coöperated with him in his ministry.

For many years he was active in sustaining the practice of reading to the people at noon on the Sabbath; even after his health became greatly enfeebled, he would still tarry and read for the hour from some favorite doctrinal or devotional treatise, and by his zealous example and his dying requests he left such an impression of the importance of this exercise, that it was continued for a long period afterwards. So when perplexing cases of discipline occurred, or when exciting discussions in the church or parish arose, though never a partisan, but always a peacemaker, his course was uniformly a rebuke to the lax and the factious. The building of the new church soon after Mr. French's settlement, was so hotly contested, that it came near dividing the parish; yet with friends in both parties, Judge Phillips, little leisure as he had for such work, was made chairman of the building committee, and managed the whole affair so dispassionately as to satisfy all with himself, if not with the project.

In his day ministers were usually "settled for life." But with all his conservatism he was an innovator. His fertile mind was intent upon improvements; upon discussing principles and devising schemes, which would break in salutarily upon the old order of things. Sometimes his best friends, and especially his father and uncles, who were yet sure to second his projects, would hint that he had a little too much of the spirit of what we, in our day, term "Young America." Proverb as he was for caution, his foresight seemed to them a species of adventurousness. Thus, as early as the year 1788, we find him elaborately discussing with his uncle at Exeter, the question whether "the interests of religion and the general good might not be advanced, by removing gentlemen of the clergy from places of less to those of greater consequence in particular cases." The views which he expresses are intermingled with so many personal matters, that we cannot properly quote them; but they show with what care he was accustomed, like a judge, to sum up such cases of interest to the public, and state all their important bearings, far in advance of any existing public sentiment. When a council was convened in 1792 at Newbury, in the case of his friend Dr. Tappan's call from that church to the Professorship of Divinity at Cambridge, he attended as delegate with his pastor, and assisted in adjusting the very delicate questions which were mooted.

Among the schemes which are most characteristic of him, and which show in the strongest light how his mind would link the future with the present, or his growing country with his native village, the *Charitable Donations* which were made by him, in the following instruments, stand conspicuous: —

"Wishing to contribute to the promotion of Christian knowledge and piety a part of the substance wherewith God has blessed me, and out of respect and affection to my native town, I, Samuel Phillips, of Andover, in the county of Essex, and Commonwealth of Massachusetts, Esquire, do make the following donation, for the purposes hereinafter mentioned, and I do hereby direct my heirs, executors, and administrators, within one year after my decease, to pay to the Trustees of Phillips Academy in Andover, or their successors in office, the sum of one thousand dollars, in trust for the purposes hereinafter mentioned; to the payment of which, well and truly to be made, I bind my heirs, executors, and administrators firmly by these presents:

"The said sum to be by the Trustees aforesaid and their successors always kept out at interest upon good security, and the interest thence arising to be disposed of in the manner following, namely: one sixth part to be annually added to the principal sum for ever; and the other five sixth parts to be laid out in the purchase of the following books, namely:— Dr. Doddridge's Address to the Master of a Family on Family Religion, the Westminster Assembly's Shorter Catechism, Dr. Watts's Divine Songs, Dr. Hemmenway's Discourse to Children; and, when the income shall permit, Dr. Doddridge's Rise and Progress of Religion in the Soul, and other like pious writings, to be by the said Trustees and their successors as aforesaid, or by a committee of their appointment, distributed among the inhabitants, who do now or may hereafter reside within the present boundaries of the said town of Andover.

"That is to say, the aforesaid Address to the Master of a Family on Family Religion to be given to every young man who may be about to enter into the family state, and to such others being already heads of families, as to them shall seem best; and the other books aforesaid to be annually distributed in such manner as to the said Trustees shall appear best calculated to promote the pious design of said Treatises, and the real object of this appropriation; and in the said distribution, it is desired, that the friendly advice and assistance of the Congregational Ministers within the limits aforesaid may be requested.

" And whenever, in process of time, the income of said fund shall, in the judgment of the said Trustees or their successors as aforesaid, be more than sufficient to supply the several families within the limits aforesaid, and the said families shall in fact have been so supplied, the surplus of said income to be applied, at the discretion of the said Trustees and their successors as aforesaid, to the use of Phillips Academy aforesaid, and the further promotion of the pious designs of the honorable Founders thereof.

" And it is requested that the aforesaid sum, when paid, and the interest thereon from time to time received, together with the whole disposition and distribution of the same be fairly entered in a book of record, for this purpose provided, and ever open to the inspection and perusal of all men.

" In witness of all which I have hereunto set my hand and seal, this twelfth day of December, in the year of our Lord one thousand eight hundred and one.

" Signed, sealed, and delivered, in presence of — SAMUEL PHILLIPS.

" FRANCIS L. LEE,
" AMOS BLANCHARD, JR."

" Being desirous, in addition to the appropriation made in an instrument, bearing date December twelfth, in the year of our Lord one thousand eight hundred and one, of contributing still farther of the substance wherewith God hath blessed me, to the *pious education* of young children in my native town; and also to a more extensive diffusion of *religious knowledge* and *Evangelical piety*, I, Samuel Phillips of

Andover, in the County of Essex, and Commonwealth of Massachusetts, Esquire, do now make another donation for the purposes hereinafter mentioned; and I do hereby direct my heirs, executors, and administrators, within one year after my decease, to pay to the Trustees of Phillips Academy in Andover, or their successors in office, the sum of four thousand dollars in money or in private notes of hand, with such securities as the said Trustees shall fully approve, in trust for the purposes hereinafter mentioned; to the payment of which, well and truly to be made, I bind my heirs, executors, and administrators firmly by these presents.

"The said sum to be by the Trustees aforesaid and their successors always kept out at interest on good security, and the interest thence arising to be disposed of in the manner following; to wit: one sixth part to be ever hereafter annually added to the principal for an increasing capital sum; and the other five sixth parts of the interest of the said capital sum to be laid out in the manner following; that is to say, the five sixth parts of the interest arising from one fourth part of the aforesaid capital sum, to be appropriated and applied, according to the best judgment of the said Trustees, partly for rendering those females who may be employed as instructors in the several District Schools, within the aforesaid Town of Andover, better qualified for the discharge of their delicate and important trust; and partly for extending the term of their instruction in such districts within the said town, as, notwithstanding the provision therefor annually made by said town, may stand in most need of additional aid; provided always, that this additional aid shall in no one year be given to more than one third part of the whole number of districts within the present boundaries of the aforesaid town of Andover; and the five-sixth parts of the interest, arising from the other three-fourth parts of the aforesaid capital sum, to be appropriated and applied in the following manner, to wit: for procuring the following books, namely, Bibles, Testaments, and Psalters; the Westminster Assembly's Shorter Catechism, Dr. Watts's Divine Songs for Children, Dr. Hemmenway's Discourse to Children, Dr. Doddridge's Address to the Master of a Family on Family Religion, his Sermons on the Religious Education of Children, his Rise and Progress of Religion in the Soul, Law's Serious Call to a Devoted and Holy Life, Mason's Treatise on Self-Knowledge, Henry's Discourse concerning Meekness, and Orton's Discourse to the Aged, together with other like pious books, as the income of the said capital sum, agreeably to the aforementioned apportionment may permit; to be distributed by the said Trustees and their successors, or by a committee or agents of their appointment, among poor and pious Christians not belonging to the aforesaid town, to whom such writings may be peculiarly grateful, and also among the inhabitants of new towns and plantations or other places, where the means of religious knowledge and instruction are but sparingly enjoyed, in such manner as the Trustees in their wisdom and prudence may think best calculated to promote the object of this donation.

"And to enable the said Trustees and their successors in office to form the most correct opinion of the proper object of this donation, they are respectfully desired to request the necessary information of pious ministers of religion in different parts of the country. It is also requested, that the said sum first above mentioned, when paid, and the interest thereon from time to time received, together with the whole disposition and distribution of the same, be fairly entered in a book of record, for this purpose provided, and ever open to the inspection and perusal of all men.

"And it is farther requested, that the said Trustees and their successors, as aforesaid, in all future time, may ever bear in mind that the principal object of this donation, is the preservation of the essential and distinguishing doctrines of the Gospel, as professed by our pious ancestors, the first settlers of New England, and of such writings as are consentaneous thereto; above all, it is ardently hoped and expected, that in their selection of books for the distribution aforesaid, all possible care will be taken by the Trustees aforesaid, to guard against the dissemination of the least particle of Infidelity, or Modern Philosophy; and also against the dispersion of such Theological treatises, or speculations, as tend to undermine the fundamental principles of the Gospel plan of salvation, or to reduce the Christian religion to a system of mere morality; without which guard there will be great reason to fear that the object of this donation will be totally frustrated.

"Confiding, however, in the wisdom and fidelity of the said Trustees, I cheerfully commit the execution of the design of this donation, as herein expressed, to their pious care, and the success of it to the blessing of Almighty God, whose gracious smiles are, through the Mediator, humbly implored on it and them.

"In witness of all which, I have hereunto set my hand and seal, this twenty-seventh day of January, in the year of our Lord one thousand eight hundred and two.

"Signed, sealed, and delivered in presence of

SAMUEL PHILLIPS.

"SAMUEL FARRAR,

"AMOS BLANCHARD, JR."

In these unpretending donations, we have the whole system of our modern tract societies and systems of colportage for the circulation of religious volumes in miniature, long before such organizations were thought of. Nor has this pioneer enterprise of his sagacious mind done of itself a trivial work, although in some measure overshadowed by these associations.

The trust has been most religiously discharged. The schools of Andover are every year materially aided from the income of his fund. Valuable books have been often distributed to every family in the town, at as short intervals as the fund would allow, and over large sections of New England, and of the territory westward, the work of scattering a great variety of religious volumes has been and continues to be prosecuted, sometimes by private agency, sometimes through the channel of other religious associations, while the fund itself has been steadily augmenting for a similar mission in the future.

We speak of these donations, so carefully directed with a view to the attainment of such a variety of objects, present or remote, as eminently *characteristic* of him. So in fact was every project in which we find him engaged. Few men would have struck the golden veins which he so assiduously worked, — fewer still would have pursued his method, or have breathed the spirit which stirred him, in his chosen life-work. For, although he was one of the most symmetrical of men, having nothing in excess and no glaring defect, his individuality was remarkable in many particulars; and, in all, it was but the many-sided bodying forth of his deep religious principle.

We have not been able to discover a trait or an incident in his career, which has not seemed to us the product of his religion more than of any thing else. He was not the great and good man whom we revere by the force mainly of rare circumstances, or of genial impulses, or of a mechanical conformity with models before him; but, with the help of God, "by patient continuance in well doing." Frail in childhood, amid the graves of all his brothers and sisters, and an invalid ever afterwards, he seemed daily to hear the admonition, "*whatsoever thy hand findeth to do, do it with thy might:*" and it is in the light of his religious faith, or as the forms in which his religious principle clothed itself, that we must weigh his peculiarities.

Thus, *he was intensely methodical and careful.* Men who attempt to do so much are usually negligent of minutiæ; but if he had measured all the ground he ever went over, inch by inch, he could not have been more particular. Any one of his hundreds of manuscripts now extant, taken up at random, would be an illustration of this trait. He erased, he interlined, he changed the collocation of words or paragraphs, he put in afterthoughts and side-thoughts, in a common family letter, with as much painstaking as in the draft of a State paper. In writing the most familiar communications to his son or his wife, he would copy, or give an apology for not copying, as if he would not consent to do any thing which he was not anxious to do well; and the same scrupulous exactness was shown by him through the whole circuit of his labors, not more as a habit, than as a purpose.

So, too, *he was a prodigy of activity:* not of haste and bustle, but of rapid, effective labor, in a quiet, unruffled spirit. His equilibrium was one secret of his momentum. Serene and sunny in temperament, he sang with the morning and the evening birds. Men everywhere said, "he is too busy," "he will soon be spent," but he heard them not; work had a charm for him — any work, all work, if so be it were only good.

And, then, *he had a most vivid sense of the value of time:* in this respect he has made a stronger impression on us, than any man of whom we ever heard. He is perpetually recurring to the subject in his letters, and no less constantly acting as he writes. Take, for example, the following sentences, from a succession of letters to his son in college: —

"Remember that *time* is a most invaluable talent; be covetous of every parcel of it;" — "bar your doors, and secure your eyes, your ears, and your heart against all who would rob you of your treasure; I mean, your time;" — "you can hardly have a better security against vice, next to the grace of God, than *uniform diligence* in the pursuit of useful knowledge; be, therefore, more covetous of your hours, than misers are of gold;" — "a more favorable opportunity for improvement it is not probable you will ever see — perhaps never another equally so — and the motto of our Academy seal still applies, as you are beginning a new year, new studies, and in a new situation, 'Finis origine pendet;'" — "I cannot persuade myself to omit any opportunity of expressing my solicitude that you should participate of my feelings, respecting the *importance of time*, especially of *holy time;* next to this the importance of governing the passions;" — "let no day be barren of improvement, but even at those seasons when close application to study is not expected, recollect the past and make some useful reflections on whatever you see and hear, that 'you may give for every day some good account at last;'" — "realize more and more the worth of time — of the present moment in particular — and make it your invariable rule, not to defer any duty till the next hour or moment which can be performed in the present; a religious observation of this rule will be of immense advantage to you through life; advice of more importance is not in the power of Your affectionate parent,

"S. PHILLIPS."

"A *religious* observation of this rule:" — how exactly does this describe his own habit!

And as his religion thus exalted his estimate of time, so it made him, in the words of one of his admirers, "*an enthusiast for virtue.*" Whenever he touched upon "virtue" in its abstract oneness, or upon "the virtues" as a sisterhood of graces, his spirit always kindled. Like the "aliquid immensum infinitumque" of the old Roman sage, toward which he was ever struggling, his ideal of virtue fascinated him. She stood before him, you would think, in the grace of a living, personal beauty; she breathed into him the spirit of her own serenity; he sat at her feet to learn, to admire, to love; she thrilled him with thoughts of what he might be and do as her votary. It was not a poetic fancy of virtue, as above God or apart from God, but a moral perception of virtue in and from God, that was such a sunbeam in his soul. And, therefore, with persistent devotion, he gravitated toward her as the needle does to the polar star, and the charm of her presence irradiated his whole character and life.

But even this characteristic was, if possible, less prominent in him, than *his intensely ethical vein.* Had he lived in the age of Seneca or of Socrates, he would have rivalled them. But in a better day he was a wiser moralist. The strong tendency in his nature to that clear, concentrated method of reflection which is apt to express itself pithily in the form of maxims, was so wedded to his vital religious experience, that, with their advantages, he would have written as a Christian philosopher better than Paley or Butler; less coldly, with less intellectual force, perhaps, but not less clearly, and far more evangelically. He cannot allude in a letter to a slight trouble with a domestic, without dignifying the occasion by the exclamation,—"how dependent the highest upon the lower classes! and all upon each other!" If he writes upon some matter of business, he must enforce discretion in it, by the broad precept,—"let *caution* be your motto." When he commends a friend for kindnesses to the poor, in sickness, he makes it a deed of heaven rather than earth by the saying,—"to pour the balm of comfort into the bosom of the afflicted is a *Godlike* employment." As he expounds to a jury their duty, the law becomes suddenly personified and present, providing them "as the eye and the ear of the public." When he elaborates the constitution of an academy, its entire preamble is a cluster of ethical utterances, and its delineation of a teacher's duties is in the richest strain of ethical suggestion. Everywhere, amid the memorials which he has left, we encounter such gems of thought, and of diction fitly clothing it.

With this ethical mind he united *an impressive sedateness.* Sallies of wit in others he could appreciate and enjoy richly. His wife and his cousin, Miss Sally Phillips, were especially gladdening to him in their exuberant vivacity at their fireside; but though he was habitually cheerful, he could not be drawn into the mirthful vein. It was a study, as well as an instinct, with him to be serious, yet not sombre. "He was the gravest man I ever saw," says one; "he had a most *benignant* countenance," says another, "and *such a smile!*" The gravity which so awed, and yet won both old and young, was doubtless the more characteristic, because of his attenuated figure and the pallor of disease, which at fifty gave him the air of a man of seventy years. But it was, after all, a mental more than a physical peculiarity. It was the deep inner habit of the man, intensely reflecting, constructive, utilitarian, and devout, — impressing its image and superscription upon his tall form and pale face.

And the more noticeably so, as to this was added *a profound humility.*

"Should it not," he writes to Madam Phillips when a new chapter in their experience was opening, "give us *complete satisfaction* and *the highest joy*, that this, as well as every other change, is in the hand of that *perfect Being*, to whom the future is as clear as the present or past; who thoroughly comprehending the whole chain of events at one glance, can with *complete certainty* order *every* occurrence as shall be best on the whole, and *most assuredly will do it;* should not we consider ourselves as little atoms, moving in that part of the scene which he has assigned us; and when events appear at hand which are contrary to our wishes, should we not remember how entirely ignorant we are of what is behind the curtain? and that when events appear most against us, they are oftentimes followed with consequences highly beneficial."

Ever appreciative of others' excellence, concerning himself he often speaks in a desponding tone: —

"I feel, more than ever, my barrenness and insufficiency to discharge that mighty debt of gratitude, which I owe to Heaven and those benefactors, granted me by Divine bounty, at the head of whom stands the dear partner of my life, ever ready to bless me with her tender care and kindness." "In the early part of life, I fondly pleased myself with the expectation that I should do some good and communicate some happiness to others; — how strangely have I been disappointed! . . . if I have been so useless in the prime of life, what can be expected when declining, and that so fast! . . . when you are nearest the throne of grace, be entreated earnestly to supplicate the inexhaustible source of all good, in behalf of your unworthy partner, — that his multiplied offences may be forgiven him, — that he may be enabled to discharge all duty far better, in time to come, than in the days that are past; and next to those he owes his Maker, those which are due to his nearest friend and their offspring." —

"Forty and five years of my pilgrimage are now completed, and to very little purpose, either for the honor of my Maker or the benefit of mankind; consequently I have hardly learned the true end of living. The time that is past seems but a span! and although a very poor account can be rendered of it, the best part of life is gone irrecoverably; upon the most favorable calculation much cannot be expected from the remainder, and *no dependence* can be placed on any thing future ; were it not for the hope of Divine mercy how wretched would be my lot! But what ground for hope in this mercy without a life of *repentance, faith, and new obedience!* Let us daily, whether together or apart, unite our supplications at the throne of grace, that we may be disposed to live *that life;* that the remaining part of our life may be more fruitful of service to others, and comfort to ourselves."

Such, year after year, are his pensive words, until we are ready to say, "he must have been a sad man;" no! he was a self-tasking man; and his standard was so high that he seemed, to himself, immeasurably below it. His was not the humility of indifference, nor of dejection, but of greatness in thought and deed, as Newton compared all his researches to the gathering of a few pebbles on the shore of the wide ocean of truth. He thought so much less of himself than other men do, because he saw so much more than others do in virtue, in duty, in every thing good.

In apparent contrast with these characteristics, yet in admirable proportion to them, there was one which adds a charm to his memory; *he cherished a special fondness for the young.* His sensibilities were attuned to this affection; his whole character was touched by its magnetism. Companion of statesmen as he was, and a proverb for his gravity, he was never more in his element than when conversing with a little child, or dropping his goodly maxims, like the gentle dew, into the heart of some listening youth. It was not a patronizing, but a parental interest, which he exhibited, especially when through his prolonged efforts the Academy brought him into such contact with the sons of his friends and countrymen from all points of the compass.

But all these traits would not have completed his type of Christian symmetry, without his *rare estimate of the uses of wealth, as the handmaid of learning and religion.* There was a disinterestedness, a loftiness of virtue, in the strength with which he grasped the idea of consecrating large estates to such ends, which commands our reverence. And the form which this idea took, is especially to be admired. It sought an embodiment in far-reaching plans, — in works for the great future, — in permanent institutions. It concentrated and accumulated in one focus, the best efforts of a lifetime. It did not refuse daily bread to the poor, nor any other transient charity; neither did it scatter all its stores in such infinitesimal subdivisions. It pursued the golden *via media*, proposing to itself prominently ONE GREAT WORK to be accomplished, while not neglecting such others as were consistent with it; and therefore it "took root downward and bore fruit upward;" it gave to his own spirit breadth and versatility; it linked to itself, as with a chain of gold, all his other schemes: it subsidized a family of kindred spirits, and unlocked their hoards and hearts; it reached out, first in the faith, and then in the vision of its fruits, to the very ends of the earth; and "by it, he being dead yet speaketh."

# CHAPTER XII.

## HIS DECEASE.

The best life must end; often the very virtues of the good are presages of their early translation to a brighter world. As his years glided swiftly away, with increasing debility Judge Phillips redoubled his activity, until he completed his self-immolation in mid-life. For some years prior to his death, he distinctly foresaw it approaching. His chronic asthma began to be ominous of fatal consumption. Often, for weeks in succession, it prevented his enjoying an hour's invigorating sleep, and oppressed him with an insatiable thirst. With unflagging persistency, therefore, he "redeemed the time," not thinking how to relieve his over-tasked system, but how to fill out the measure of his life-work in every relation. Had he consented at a much earlier date to relax the tension of his zeal, the shadow on his dial might have returned ten degrees backward, as it did for a sign to the good king Hezekiah.

But his election was made; of the two, he preferred to live fast rather than long; to do his utmost to-day and not count upon to-morrow; to do as many things as possible, and all as well as possible, though the fire of such a devotion might soon consume him. This seems to most minds an error — a morbid zeal; and for ordinary men it would be so, but there is little hazard of their being infected with it. In any case, it is "a fault that leans to virtue's side." But in his case, we shrink on the whole from pronouncing it a fault, or even a mistake. To live a single year as he did, is more than ten years of ordinary activity; and, in the words of Burke, "we must pardon something to the spirit of liberty," with which such a soul is fired in its work. It cannot be mechanically moderate; it cannot gauge every thing by the canons of mere reason, uninfluenced by its ruling passion. Trim it and tame it by such processes and you extinguish it. The extraordinary man is made "altogether such an one as ourselves." What makes him so remarkable; what has given him such power, and made him accomplish so much, until you feel what a pigmy you are by his side, is the very peculiarity out of which you must see his life-springs flowing so fast and full, that they cannot flow long. Let us see him, then, at fifty "setting his house in order." In the summer of 1801, he makes a last effort to recruit his strength, by journeying in company with Madam Phillips and his friend Dr. Pearson, who exclaims, in reporting their progress: "may gracious Heaven still smile on the undertaking, and preserve a life so dear to his friends, so important to the public." Their tour extends through the western counties of the Commonwealth as far as Albany; but no skill or assiduity can avail, and he returns to his home, resigned to the will of God in the blighting of their hopes.

The postscript in that long New Year's letter to his son, added when his own hand has become too feeble to copy it, completes his work for him; so in every direction, and to all classes of friends, he sends now his final words of counsel or of adieu; he gathers the Trustees about him, and "particularly requests that a select committee be chosen to meet once in a quarter or oftener, to inquire into the state of the Academy, the proficiency of the scholars, and the conduct of the instructors, that the *core* of the Institution may be attended to;" thus, with his latest breath, planning for its welfare;[1] he remembers the church of his choice in his prayers and gifts, directing that a massive silver flagon be presented to them, "as a memorial of his sincere affection and esteem, and his earnest request that the laudable practice of reading in the house of public worship between services on Lord's Day may be continued, so long as even a small number shall be disposed to attend the exercise;"[2] and then, amid the tenderest endearments of his be-

[1] Records of Phillips Academy, p. 155.

[2] Records, South Church.

loved family, he calmly expires; meeting death, as he had ever met his duty, in the serenity of Christian hope and faith. The friends who know him, and feel his death, now lead us again over the circuit of his life, and pay such tributes to his character as nothing but the heartiest homage could ever call forth; we accept their words, and repress our own.

In the Centinel, February 13, 1802, we read: —

"Died, at his seat in Andover, at 2 o'clock on Wednesday afternoon, his Honor SAMUEL PHILLIPS, Esquire, Æt. 50, Lieutenant-Governor of the Commonwealth of Massachusetts.

"A loss deeply to be deplored by every friend of his State and country. It is the lot of few to acquire a reputation so bright and unspotted as that which he possessed, and of fewer still to take an active and decided part in all political events, and yet preserve integrity unimpeached, and talents uncontroverted. He graduated at Harvard College in 1771. While yet a youth, the qualities which made eminent his riper years, rendered him beloved and conspicuous. At this early period of his life, he was distinguished for that solidity of judgment, deep penetration, strict moral principle, active virtue, and stable Christian piety, which constituted the striking features of his character, and attained for him the notice of his instructors, and the attachment of his equals. He had scarcely reached manhood, when his fellow-townsmen, with a readiness which does honor to their sagacity, elected him their Representative; and, by their suffrages and that of his district, he was raised to a seat in the House and Senate of the State for twenty-five years successively, until the public voice elevated him to the high station in which he died. . . . The Academy which bears his family name, and which is indebted principally to his patronage for its existence and celebrity, witnesses his love of literature and his ardent exertions in its cause. An enthusiast in his attachment to virtue, a Christian in sentiment and the strictest profession, eminent for piety, private friendship, and zeal for the public, what good breast which knew his worth, is not wrung at his loss; what lover of his country does not lament one of the firmest pillars of the State, and of private worth one of the brightest examples?"

In the Journal of the Legislature, we read: —

"House, Thursday, February 11.

"The Secretary delivered the following Message from the Governor: —

"Gentlemen of the Senate, and Gentlemen of the House of Representatives, — The Commonwealth has lost one of its best and ablest friends by the death of the Lieutenant-Governor. He died yesterday about two in the afternoon; and his family propose that his funeral shall be attended on Monday next at two o'clock. A long and intimate acquaintance with him, enables some of us to bear testimony to his distinguished merit. He was solicitous to preserve the good order of society, and to exhibit to his fellow-citizens a pattern of every civil and moral virtue. Without any solicitation on his part, he was many years elected a member of the Senate, and presided in their deliberations with candor and dignity. In the office of Lieutenant-Governor, he secured respect by mild deportment, resulting from the testimony of a good conscience. He was firm and inflexble whenever the interests of the Commonwealth were concerned; and he acquitted himself with honor in all the offices confided to him by the public, and in all the relations of private life. I shall be ready to join with you, gentlemen, in any tribute of esteem and respect, which you may think due to the merit of his public services.

"CALEB STRONG.

"COUNCIL CHAMBER, February 11, 1802.

The Centinel of February 17, continues the narration: —

"In conformity to the Resolutions of the Legislature, the tribute of esteem and respect so justly due the deceased, was paid on Monday last, in this town and at Andover. In this town the members of the Legislature moved in procession to the old brick meeting-house, where the Rev. Mr. Baldwin, Chaplain of the House, delivered a very pertinent and pathetic discourse from John i. 47, 'Behold an Israelite indeed, in whom is no guile.' The Rev. Dr. Thatcher, Chaplain of the Senate, concluded the solemnity with prayer. At two o'clock, all the bells in town commenced tolling, and continued until four o'clock, during which time minute guns were discharged by Captain Johonnot's company.

"At Andover the remains of the deceased were entombed with those demonstrations of esteem, respect, and affection, which his singular worth demanded. The procession moved from the late mansion-house of the deceased, in the following order to the meeting-house: —

The present pupils of the Academy,
Those who have heretofore received instruction in that Institution,
The Trustees of the Academy,
Trustees of Phillips Exeter Academy,
The Corpse,
The pall was borne by His Excellency the Governor, three of the Council, the President of the Senate, and Speaker of the House of Representatives,
The Relatives, and a very long train of mourning fellow citizens followed the Corpse.

"At the meeting-house, a select choir of singers performed an anthem. The throne of grace was pertinently and fervently addressed by the Rev. Mr. French, whose fast flowing tears testified his sincere grief for the loss of his most excellent parishioner and beloved friend. The Rev. Dr. Tappan delivered an affecting discourse from the words, — 'help, Lord, for the godly man ceaseth, for the faithful fail from among the children of men;' in which he delineated in just and glowing colors the character of the illustrious deceased Christian, Patron of Science, and Patriot. An anthem suitable to the solemn occasion closed the service. His Excellency Governor Gilman, and other eminent characters from New Hampshire, paid a just tribute to departed worth, piety, and patriotism, by attending the funeral rites of this highly venerated and esteemed magistrate.

"The Committee of the Legislature omitted to recommend any military escort on the occasion, in consequence of the earnest request of the deceased expressed a few days before his death, he being apprehensive that the health of his fellow-citizens at this season of the year might be affected by the service."

A mourning sheet, on which one of the anthems here referred to was printed for the occasion, lies before us, the only copy we have seen: and it is easy to imagine ourselves listening to the pathos with which the choir sings, —

"Th' enlightened FRIEND of human kind,
The MAN of uncorrupted mind,
Whose only fault was too much zeal
And ardor for the public weal;

"Whose spotless life has ever stood,
A living monument of good;
Best model for a virtuous age,
And glory of the historic page;

"Though lost to earth, is blest above,
Arrayed in robes of peace and love,
Convened amid the choir divine,
In realms of endless day to shine.

"PARENT OF ALL! whose sovereign will
Obedient cherubim fulfil,
Oh, teach us, in the hour of death,
With tranquil hope to yield our breath;

"On wings of faith with transport rise,
To meet thy welcome to the skies;
Enjoy thy rest, receive thy crown,
And at THY SON'S right hand sit down."

While Dr. Baldwin, in his sermon at Boston, gives a

rapid sketch of the deceased, in which every paragraph is a eulogy, and of which one sentence is a summary, — "he was the accurate scholar, the enlightened statesman, the accomplished gentleman, and the exemplary Christian," — Dr. Tappan, before his vast auditory at Andover, pays a more elaborate and lofty tribute to his worth. In addition to what has been already quoted from this discourse, we would gladly cite whole pages here, but must confine ourselves to mere sentences. Portraying him as "a distinguished ornament and pillar both of the church and the Commonwealth," he says: —

"The Author of nature had bestowed on him many eminent gifts," which "were early and constantly devoted to the best ends by a sublime spirit of benevolence and godliness;" "the piety of our illustrious citizen was equal to his patriotism; his religion supported and exalted both his private virtues and public energies;" "he was a distinguished pattern of virtuous *diligence* and *resolution;*" "both his solitary and social hours were *intensely devoted to some object of utility;*" "his cordial and extensive hospitality, his tender and zealous patronage of friendless or indigent merit, his eager sacrifices of private business and interest to public exigencies, his efforts to rouse, direct, and encourage the charity and public spirit of others, his distinguished contributions of time, influence, and property to seminaries of learning and religion, loudly attest his PURE AND EXALTED PHILANTHROPY;" "the history of man does not often furnish a character so full of various, well directed, and useful energies. It does not often illustrate the art of living so much in so small a compass of years;" "his soul was on the stretch to do good almost to his latest breath."

The immense concourse, the presence of so many distinguished civilians, the universal sensibility, and the impressive exercises, with which her favorite son was thus laid in his tomb, made this a most memorable day to Andover; such as she had never seen before, and will never see again. Even her own town records, where deaths are not usually noted, appear to throb in sympathy with the scene; on one of the pages, a deep mourning border is drawn, enclosing this entry:—

"The Honorable Samuel Phillips, Esquire, was elected Lieutenant-Governor, qualified for that office agreeable to the Constitution, and continued therein, until Wednesday, the tenth day of February, 1802, about two o'clock, P. M., when he departed this life, aged fifty years and five days, universally lamented."

To these garlands, showered upon his tomb at the hour, and which a whole Commonwealth laid, with the insignia of her seal, upon his coffin, we add some passages from a later encomium — the more remarkable, because they show how little a score of years could do to efface his image from the memory of one who had fully known him. It is from the pen of Dr. Dwight[1] in 1821, in these words:—

[1] Dwight's Travels, Vol. I. p. 399, 400.

"To the memory of Lieutenant-Governor Phillips, I would willingly pay that tribute of respect, which would be challenged as due to him by all his countrymen, acquainted either with his private or public character. In the year 1782 and 1783, I lodged in the same house with him in Boston, for three months; and being occupied in the same concerns, had every opportunity of learning his character which I could wish; particularly as he treated me with the most entire frankness and intimacy.

"The mind of this gentleman, by nature vigorous and discerning, was early strengthened by habits of industry, and expanded by a liberal education." . . . "The learning and science to which he chiefly addicted himself, was that which most usefully affects the great interests of man. Of a character eminently practical, knowledge merely speculative, presented few allurements to his eye; action, he considered the end of thinking. He thought, therefore, and read, not merely that he might know more, but that he might become better; not that he might display his knowledge to his fellow men, but that he might do them good. A species of ethical cast marked his conversation and life, and distinguished him from all other men whom I have known." . . .

"He who is able and willing to do much business, will have much to do. Accordingly, he had a primary agency in all the measures of the State in which he lived, for near thirty years. Without exaggeration it may, I believe, be said, that the man is not remembered, who, in the same offices, was more able, industrious, faithful, or useful." . . . "In his mind Christianity flourished. In his life its fruits were genuine, fair, and abundant. Whether Mr. Phillips was a Christian, in the evangelical sense, is a question which, I suspect, has never been asked by any man acquainted with his character.

"His person was tall and slender, and his manners were a happy combination of simplicity with refinement, of modesty with dignity. His countenance was grave, mild, and commanding; his features were fixed in the sedateness of thought, and gentle with the amenity of virtue."

The character which, after the lapse of twenty years, could be painted so vividly and with such nice discrimination, is yet again portrayed for us, from memory, with graphic distinctness, at the close of half a century, by one from whom it is our good fortune to have elicited the tribute in the following letter:—

"Rev. J. L. Taylor:—

"Dear Sir,—Your favor of the 10th ultimo has lain by me without reply; but when you approximate your eighty-fourth year, you will find that, though the spirit is willing, the flesh is weak; and that *time*, when he sees gray hairs on the head, will often amuse himself with rubbing out impressions on the brain, so that they become feeble and at times obliterated. Though I have omitted to reply, I have at no moment lost my sense of gratification at the information your letter contains, that, at this late day, you have undertaken to do such justice to the memory of Lieutenant-Governor Samuel Phillips, as the lapse of time and the scanty documents at your command permit. It would give me great pleasure to contribute to your design, as you request, but I fear I can do little justice even to my own impressions concerning his character, and far less than his merits and his efficient influence on the period in which he lived, deserve. I have already, in reply to letters addressed to me by President Woods and Dr. Sprague of Albany, probably exhausted all the few reminiscences at my command. I will not, however, on that account, refuse briefly to contribute to your purpose, though at the danger of repeating myself.

"Samuel Phillips, known the greater part of his life, in consequence of the life of his father, by the addition of *Junior*, was an extraordinary man; but it is very difficult to give, at this day, a just impression of his character. The religious and moral element in it was mixed so intimately, and yet so unaffectedly, with the business of the world and the habits of active life, that he seemed to be a perfect embodiment of the Christian statesman, scholar, and philanthropist. I had opportunities of observing him from the year 1778, when I joined the Academy, being then but six years of age, and occasionally, until the time of his death in 1802. I was a frequent visitor in his family, though never a member of it. My mother was daughter of his father's brother, and always stayed in his house when she visited Andover, which brought me to be almost a daily inmate. I have heard his addresses to the school as a Trustee, to the College as an Overseer, and, as a boy and a man, my opportunities for personal intercourse with him have been many; and I can truly say that I have never met, through my whole life, with an individual in whom the spirit of Christianity and of good-will to mankind were so naturally and beautifully blended with an indomitable energy and enterprise in active life. He was a leader in the church, a leader in the State; the young loved and listened to him, the old consulted and deferred to his advice.

"I have travelled with him from Boston to Andover alone, then a journey of the chief part of a day; his discourse, adapted to a boy as I then was, full of sweetness and instruction.

"His love of the young was intense. He delighted in the poetry of Watts, which he seemed to have, all of it, by heart; so readily and appositely he introduced it in conversation, accompanied by a never ceasing flow of wise maxims, given not with an air of authority, but as the natural outpouring of a good and kind heart.

"I cannot, in language, do justice to the interest and affection with which, on these occasions, he excited the young mind.

"In his capacity for business, there was, as it were, an universality or ubiquity. In the town, in the Senate, in the courts of justice, in committees of the legislature, as a referee in cases of great importance, in all other associations on affairs of business, his influence was, as far as was possible in respect of any one man, paramount. For twenty years he was a member, and for fifteen President of the Senate of the State, at a period when statesmen were not made out of every sort of wood. He was judge of the Essex Court of Common Pleas, a member of every important committee, on like occasions a referee, and, at the same time, owned and took a general superintendence of two stores, one at Andover, another at Methuen, of a saw-mill, a grist-mill, a paper-mill, and a powder-mill, on the Shawshine, giving to each a sufficient and appropriate share of his oversight; with a spirit subdued by the predominancy of the religious sentiment, he was as earnest, active, and indefatigable in this multitude of his engagements, as though this world was every thing.

"In fulfilling business duties, difficulty did not repress his ardor, nor dangers deter. Boston and Andover were the chief seats of his labors. The business of one sometimes interfered with that of the other. In such cases, to him no obstacle was formidable. It was not uncommon for him to leave Boston at sunset and travel to Andover, a distance of twenty-two miles, on horseback, and sometimes not reaching home until midnight. On one occasion falling asleep, his horse took a wrong path in passing through woods, and he became lost in them, and reached home not until nearly morning. At another time his horse fell in the dark; a broken leg, and three weeks' detention at a friend's house, in Medford, was the consequence. His friends remonstrated, on these occasions, at his imprudence. But it was his nature to be unmindful of every thing but his duty. He undoubtedly, by thus exposing himself, laid the foundation of the asthma and of other disorders, which brought him to his grave when but little past the meridian of life.

"Samuel Phillips (junior) was, probably, in the general opinion of the period, the efficient founder of Phillips Academy.[1] He was, indeed, a young man, not yet thirty years

[1] In addition to our own statements, on this point, in a previous chapter, of the same tenor with Mr. Quincy's, we here insert the formal and explicit testimony of Dr. Tappan and Dr. Pearson to the same effect. Dr. Tappan, who was his class mate and a Trustee of the Academy, speaks of him in the discourse at his funeral as "its earliest projector;" Dr. Pearson, his confident, a resident in the place, with whom he conferred often while writing the Constitution, and the first Preceptor, in his historic sketch delivered at the opening of the Theological Institution, says of the Academy, "the tribute of justice has not been paid to the prime mover, as well as active

old, but there was a maturity of mind, an impressive gravity in his demeanor, to which the old as well as the young bowed down. He was equally the favorite of the three brothers; while they found the means, he selected the locality, wrote the Constitution, and appointed the Instructor.

"I have thus, Sir, with a rapid hand, endeavored, as well as I could, to come in aid of your purpose. Its success lies near my heart; and I shall be happy to reply to any questions in relation to him or the Academy you may submit. With respect, I am your servant,

"JOSIAH QUINCY.

"BOSTON, December 13, 1855."

In the freshness and fragrance of such reminiscences, lingering longer in the minds of his survivors than the whole term of his life, we see with what force his character projected itself into the future, for which he lived. And as we thus gather up evidence of the impressions which he had made, in the spontaneous homage of all classes of minds, uttered at his death and afterwards, we look upon it all as prophetic of his destiny here.

patron, of that Seminary. Let it then for once be publicly announced, and this without diminishing the merit of the generous Founders, that to the sagacious, originating, and disinterested mind of the late patriotic Lieutenant-Governor PHILLIPS, is the world indebted for the conception of an Institution, from which so many blessings have already flowed to the community;" and, at the close of his testimony, he crowns the eulogy, by the deep utterance of "regret, that this paragon of public spirit so early took his upward flight!"

It cannot be that such a character will ever be forgotten. It was formed to live on, like the works it produced, in such perpetuity as earth can give, as well as in the immortality of Heaven. The gratitude of men, and the providence of God, must conspire to bear along its image, parallel with the history of his favorite Institution, and beaming forth, at intervals, in new lustre, as its great career expands. Yet, aside from the brief obituary, or the discourse of an hour, or some scanty page in a biographical dictionary, or a passing tribute in a journal of travels, such as have here been cited, *there has been no written memorial of him!*

The surviving members of his immediate family, we are assured, had so profound a reverence for his character, that they always shrank from the proposal to sketch it, as an impossible achievement; and so they passed away, with other admiring friends, who longed to see his biography written, but had not the courage to undertake it, lest it should prove unworthy of him. And with them have glided into oblivion countless incidents, and memories, and impressions, which, at an early day, might have helped to daguerreotype him more perfectly than is now possible.

But if we must acquiesce in this long delay, and in all that it has detracted from the fulness of his portraiture, it was at least our duty to have done what we could now to commemorate the grand distinguishing outlines of a character and life so extraordinary, both as a monument to his own memory, as well as to the name and fame of his family, and for the honor of the Institution in which he is held in deep gratitude and veneration by all.

In one important respect the delay, which we lament, has not been an evil. It has given time to see, on a broad scale, the real magnitude of his good deeds by their fruits. It has shown us in history, what an earlier memoir could only have prophesied in hope. And having spared no labor in the collection or use of our materials, sustained in the effort by an interest which has made it all a pastime, yet the more we have toiled growing only the more conscious that no memorial can equal his desert, but with devout gratitude for the opportunity to study him so intimately, and to contribute any thing toward holding him up as an example to the young, the enterprising, the educated, the wealthy, the honored, — who, with special advantages, may be stimulated by his influence to special activity in fostering our institutions of learning, with every other good work, — we now make this offering to his memory, in the hope that, as successive generations shall continue to reap their golden harvests from seed sown by him in love to God and man, yet other tongues and pens will join to honor him with ampler tributes, while time shall last.

We are not uninfluenced by the further hope, that inaugurating the organic era of our Andover institutions as he did, such a memorial of him may give him now his fitting position in the historic era to which the lapse of years has brought us. Whoever may be moved to write of the gifts, or the doctrines, or the names, which a grateful world shall associate with Andover in the work of education, must, in his measure, touch upon some aspect or feature of this rare character. From the beginning, Andover, in all this work, has drawn to itself the devoted zeal of men worthy to second the plans of so disinterested and sagacious a projector: the names of *Abbot,* and *Bartlet,* and *Brown,* and *Norris,* and *Pearson,* and *Spring,* with their elect compeers and successors, will be immortal here amid the circle of the PHILLIPSES; but among them all he must ever stand conspicuous, our admiration, as he was theirs; to be copied, if he cannot be equalled; to be commemorated, if not reproduced: to be honored, loved, revered, wherever learning shall find a friend, or religion a votary.

# APPENDIX.

---

## A.

Rev. George Phillips was the son of Christopher Phillips, of Rainham, St. Martin, Norfolk county, England, " mediocris fortunæ." He entered Gonville and Caius College, Cambridge, April 20, 1610, aged seventeen years; graduated B. A. 1613, and M. A. 1617; giving there indications of deep piety, uncommon talents and love of learning, and distinguishing himself by his remarkable proficiency:[1] the name was written by him with one L, " George Philips," but by all his descendants with the two L's.

The original name of the Arbella was the Eagle, " a ship of 350 tons."

1630. — On Wednesday, the 7th of April, before the company had taken their final leave of the country, although they had been several days on shipboard, their remarkable letter was addressed " to the rest of their brethren in the Church of England," subscribed by Winthrop, Dudley, Johnson, Saltonstall, Fiennes, Coddington, and Phillips.

" Tuesday, the 27th. — We appointed Tuesdays and Wednesdays to catekise our people, and this day Mr. Phillips began it."

" Lord's day, May 2. — Through God's mercy, we were

[1] Genealogies, and History of Watertown, by Henry Bond, M. D. Vol. II. p. 872.

very comfortable, and few or none sick, but had opportunity to keep the Sabbath, and Mr. Phillips preached twice that day."[1]

"August 23. — The first court of assistants, held at Charlestown. Present, Governor Winthrop, Deputy-Governor Dudley, Sir Richard Saltonstall, Mr. Ludlow, Rossiter, Nowell, T. Sharp, Pynchon, and Bradstreet; wherein the first thing propounded is, how the ministers shall be maintained? Mr. Wilson and Phillips only proposed; and ordered, that houses be built for them with convenient speed at the publick charge. Sir R. Saltonstall undertook to see it done at his plantation for Mr. Phillips; and the Governor at the other plantation for Mr. Wilson."[1]

'Ordered, that Mr. Phillips should have allowed him 3 hogsheads of meale, 1 hogshead of malte, 4 bushells of Indean corne, 1 bushell of oatemeale, half an hundred of salte fishe; for apparell and other provisions, XX£, or els to have XL£ given him in money per annum, to make his owne provisions, if hee chuse it the rather, the yeare to begin the first of September nexte.'[2]

"September, 30. — Mr. Phillips, the minister of Watertown, and others, had their hay burnt."[1]

"November 30, 1630. — 'It is ordered, that there shall be 60£ collected out of the severall plantacions following, for the maintenance of Mr. Wilson and Mr. Phillips, namely: out of Boston, 20£; Waterton, 20£; Charlton, 10£; Rocksbury, 6£; Medford, 3£; Winett-semett, 1£.'"[2]

1631. "July 21. — The Governor and deputy, and Mr. Nowell, the elder of the congregation at Boston, went to Watertown to confer with Mr. Phillips, the pastor, and Mr. Brown, the elder of the congregation there, about an opinion which they had published, that the chh$^s$ of Rome were true chh$^s$."[3]

[1] Winthrop's Journal, Vol. I. p. 1, 5, 14, 15, 30, 36.

[2] Records of Massachusetts, Vol. I. p. 73, 82.

[3] Winthrop's Journal, Vol. I. p. 58; see also p. 67, 68, 81, 95.

"February 17.—The Governor and assistants called before them, at Boston, divers of Watertown; the pastor and elder by letter, and the others by warrant. The occasion was, for that a warrant being sent to Watertown for levying of £8, part of a rate of £60, ordered for fortifying of the new town, the pastor and elder, etc., assembled the people and delivered their opinions, that it was not safe to pay moneys after that sort, for fear of bringing themselves and posterity into bondage."[1] Commenting on this transaction, Dr. Bond says, "it is not now easy to estimate the extent and importance of the influence of Mr. Phillips in giving form and character to the civil and ecclesiastical institutions of New England;" and he refers, besides Winthrop's Journal, to Hubbard's History, p. 186; Richard Brown, p. 117; John Oldham, p. 863; Francis's History, p. 13–38, etc.; see Bond's Genealogies and History of Watertown, p. 873. . . .

1644. "5 . . 2.—Mr. George Phillips was buried. [He died the day previous, July 1st.] He was the first pastor of the church of Watertown, a godly man, specially gifted, and very peaceful in his place, much lamented of his own people and others."[2]

Referring to the estimation in which he was held in England, Cotton Mather says,—"He found much acceptance with good men, as being a man mighty in the Scriptures. But his acquaintance with the writings and persons of some old *Non-Conformists*, had instilled into him such principles of *Church Government* as were like to make him unacceptablė unto some who then drove the world before them. . . . And as for Mr. Phillips, the more he was put upon the study of the *Truth* in the matter controverted, the more he was confirmed in his own opinion of it. . . . When the *spirit of persecution* did at length with the extremest violence urge a conformity to *Ways* and *Parts* of Divine worship, conscientiously scrupled by such persons as our Mr. Phillips, he with

[1] Winthrop's Journal. Vol. I. p. 70. [2] Ibid. Vol. II. p. 171.

many more of his neighbors, entertained thoughts of transporting themselves and their families into the Deserts of America; . . . here quickly after his landing he lost the desire of his eyes, in the death of his desirable consort, who, though an only child, had cheerfully left her parents to serve the Lord Jesus Christ, in a terrible wilderness. At *Salem* she died, entering into the *Everlasting Peace*. . . . Mr. Phillips, being better acquainted with the true church discipline than most of the ministers that came with him into the country, their proceedings about the gathering and ordering of their church were *methodical* enough, though not in all things a *pattern* for all the rest. Upon a day set apart for solemn fasting and prayer, the very next month after they came ashore they entered into this *Holy Covenant:*—

"July 30, 1630.—We whose names are hereto subscribed, having through God's mercy, escaped out of the *pollutions* of the world, and been taken into the *society* of his people, with all thankfulness do hereby with *heart* and *hand* acknowledge, *That*, his gracious goodness and fatherly care towards us: and for further and more full declaration thereof, to the present and future ages, have undertaken (for the promoting of his *glory* and the churches *good*, and the honor of our blessed *Jesus*, in our more full and free subjecting of ourselves and ours, under his gracious *government*, in the practice of, and obedience unto all his holy ordinances and orders, which he hath pleased to prescribe and impose upon us) a long and hazardous voyage from *East* to *West*, from *Old England* in *Europe*, to *New England* in *America:* that we may walk before him, and *serve him without fear in holiness and righteousness all the days of our lives;* and being safely arrived here, and thus far onwards peaceably preserved by his special *Providence*, that we may bring forth our *Intentions* into *Actions*, and perfect our *Resolutions* in the beginnings of some just and meet *Executions:* We have *separated* the *day* above written from all other services, and *dedicated* it wholly to the Lord in divine employments for a day of *afflicting our souls*, and humbling ourselves before the Lord, to seek *him*, and at his hands, a way to walk in, by *fasting* and *prayer*, that we *might know what was good in his sight;* and the Lord was intreated of us.

" For in the end of that day, after the finishing of our public duties, we do all, before we depart, solemnly, and with all our hearts, *personally*, man by man, for ourselves and ours, (charging *them* before Christ and his elect angels, even *them* that are not here with us this day, or are yet unborn, that they keep the promise unblameably and faithfully unto the coming of our Lord Jesus,) promise, and *enter into a sure covenant* with the Lord our God, and before him with one another, by *Oath* and serious *Protestation* made, to renounce all *idolatry*, and *superstition*, and *will-worship*, all human *traditions* and *inventions* whatsoever, in the *worship* of God; and forsaking all *evil ways*, do give ourselves wholly unto the Lord Jesus, to do him faithful service, observing and keeping all his statutes, commands, and ordinances, in all matters concerning our *Reformation;* his worship, administrations, ministry, and government, and in the carriage of ourselves among ourselves, and one towards another, as he has prescribed in his *Holy Word;* further swearing to cleave unto *that* alone, and the true sense and meaning thereof, to the utmost of our power, as unto us the most clear *Light* and infallible *Rule*, and all-sufficient *Canon*, in all things that concern us in this our way.

" In witness of all we do *ex animo*, and in the presence of God hereto set our *names* or *marks*, in the day and year above written. About forty men, whereof the first was that excellent knight, Sir Richard Saltonstall, then subscribed this instrument, in order, unto their coalescence into a *Church estate*. . . .

" A *church* of believers being thus gathered at *Watertown*, this reverend man continued for divers years among them, faithfully discharging the duties of his ministry to the *flock whereof he was made* the overseer; and as a *faithful steward*

29

*giving to every one their meat in due season.* Herein he demonstrated himself to be a *real divine ;* but not in any thing more than in his most intimate acquaintance with the *Divine Oracles* of the Scripture. . . . He had so thoroughly perused and pondered them, that he was able on the sudden to turn to any *text*, without the help of *concordances ;* and they were so much his *delight*, that as it has been by some of his family affirmed, he *read* over the whole Bible six times every year; *nevertheless he did use to say that every time he read the Bible, he observed or collected something, which he never did before.* . . . He was indeed — among the first saints of New England — a *good man and full of faith and of the Holy Ghost;* and for that cause he was not only in public, but in private also, very full of *holy discourse* on all occasions; especially on the *Lord's day*, at noon, the time intervening between the two exercises he would spend in conferring with such of his good people as resorted unto his house, at such a rate as *marvellously ministered grace unto the hearers.*" . . .

The preceding extracts from Mather's enthusiastic and discriminating tribute to the memory of Mr. Phillips, fill us with surprise that, by any sudden freak of his unique genius, he could have penned the following whimsical and ambiguous

*Epitaphium.*

Hic jacet GEORGIUS PHILLIPPI.
Vir Incomparabilis, nisi SAMUELEM genuisset.[1]

---

## B.

Rev. Samuel Phillips, of Rowley, had a numerous family; his third child, Samuel, who was his eldest surviving son, born March 23, 1657–8, engaged in business as a goldsmith in Salem, married, in 1687, Mary Emerson, daughter of Rev.

[1] Magnalia, Book III. p. 82, 83, 84.

John Emerson, of Gloucester, and died October 13, 1722, aged sixty-five. It is through this son that we connect his ancestry with most of the Phillipses named in this memoir.

Another son, George, his seventh child, named after the family patriarch at Watertown, was born in 1664; graduated at Harvard University, 1686, and labored in the ministry, first in Jamaica, L. I., until 1697, and afterwards in Brookhaven, until his death in 1739. "His character and qualifications were of a high order."[1] Thus the family connection with the ministry and with liberal learning was continued. One of his sisters was also married to Rev. Edward Payson, of Rowley, the colleague of his father. At the decease of the father, he was greatly lamented. "In 1839," says Dr. Bond, "a chaste and handsome marble monument was placed over the remains of Mr. Phillips and his wife, in the burial-ground of Rowley, by Hon. Jonathan Phillips of Boston, their great-great-great-grandson. Upon it is an inscription to their memories, and likewise to several of their honorably distinguished descendants."[2] Various manuscripts of this venerated man are still preserved in the family, especially his sermons and lectures. The handwriting is extremely minute, so as to be deciphered with difficulty, — more so than that of any of the family, which we have had occasion to examine; yet there is a characteristic neatness and symmetry, which one would not fail to admire.

---

## C.

Mr. Phillips began to preach in this precinct April 30, 1710; and after gathering about him, in the true spirit of a

[1] See Winthrop's Journal, Vol. II. p. 171.

[2] Bond's Gen. and Hist., p. 875, etc.; the inscription in full, as referred to above, may be seen in Gage's History of Rowley, p. 73, 74; together with other interesting statements respecting Rev. Mr. Phillips and his descendants.

pioneer missionary, a little band, he united with them in the formation of the Church, his name being the first subscribed to their covenant, followed by thirty-four others. This covenant as recorded, and doubtless drawn up by his own hand, is as follows: —

"*A Covenant for the Gathering and Settling of a Church in the South Precinct of Andover.*

"We, whose names are hereunto subscribed, apprehending ourselves called of God to join together in Christian communion (acknowledging our unworthiness of such a privilege, and our inability to keep covenant with God unless Christ shall enable us thereunto), in humble dependence on free grace for Divine assistance and acceptance, we do, in the name of Christ Jesus our Lord, freely covenant and bind ourselves, solemnly, in the presence of God himself, his holy angels, and all his servants here present, to serve the only living and true God, Father, Son, and Holy Ghost, whose name alone is Jehovah, cleaving to him as our chief good, and unto our Lord Jesus Christ as our only Saviour, the Prophet, Priest, and King of our souls, in a way of Gospel obedience: Avouching the Lord to be our God, and the God of our children, whom we give unto him; and resolve that we and our houses will serve the Lord, counting it as an high favor, that the Lord will accept of us, and our children with us, to be his people.

"We do also give ourselves one to another in the Lord, covenanting to walk together as a Church of Christ in all the ways of his worship, according to the Holy Rules of his Word; promising, in brotherly love, faithfully to watch over one another's souls, and to submit ourselves to the discipline and power of Christ in his Church; and duly to attend the seals and censures, or whatever ordinances Christ has commanded to be observed by his people, so far as the Lord by his word and spirit has or shall reveal unto us to be our duty, adorning the doctrine of God our Saviour in all things, avoiding even the very appearance of evil.

" And that we may keep our covenants with God, we desire to deny ourselves, and to depend wholly on the free mercy of God, and upon the merits of Jesus Christ; and, wherein we shall fail, to wait on him for pardon, through his name, beseeching the Lord to own us as a Church of Christ, and to delight to dwell in the midst of us."

It is now nearly a century and a half since this Church was thus in due form constituted; and few churches in any community have been more prosperous or useful; or have with more hearty unanimity continued to cherish the memory of their first pastor. To this day the Church reminds itself of Covenant obligations, and of its early spiritual guide, by printing in its catalogues his comprehensive answer to the question, —

" *What shall we do that we may keep in mind our Covenant?*

"1. Very diligently and devoutly attend to the Covenant, whensoever it is publicly propounded to any person; and yield your assent and consent to every article and tittle of it.

"2. Not only wait upon Christ at his table on all opportunities, but always eye the Lord's Supper as the SEAL of the Covenant. And every time you partake, realize that you have bound yourselves afresh to keep Covenant with God; for, to take the Sacrament, is to take the oath of obedience and loyalty.

"3. Look upon the Holy Scriptures, in your daily reading of them, as the book of the Covenant; for so it is, inasmuch as it exhibiteth our duty towards God and man; and also what we may hope and expect to receive from the hand of God if we keep his statutes. Exod. xxiv. 7.

"4. Labor to have it impressed and fixed upon your minds, that heaven and earth are witnesses of your covenanting with the great God; and that God, angels, and men will certainly appear as such, either for or against you, in the day of reckoning.

"5. Discourse frequently together of the things pertaining to the kingdom of God, and particularly of the Covenant; namely, the precepts, prohibitions, promises, and threatenings; of the vows which you have made, and the comfortable experience which you and others have had of God's gracious presence, etc. This practice will be of eminent service to help the memory, as also to quicken unto obedience.

"6. Frequently renew your Covenant with the Lord in secret, as becomes those who resolve to stand to what they have said; this is not only the duty, but I should think will be also very much the delight of a sincere soul; and a choice help it is, to revive our remembrance of the Covenant, and to excite our affections, and to quicken us to mend our pace.

"7. Keep your Covenant by you as a memorial of the solemn transactions which have passed between God and you, and frequently review the same.

"8. And, lastly, *prayer* must be always one direction. And this duty must be attended and performed not only in public, and in and with the families which you respectively belong unto, but also in secret. *Thou, when thou prayest, enter into thy closet, and when thou hast shut thy door, pray to thy Father, which is in secret.*— Matth. vi. 6. This duty of secret prayer I hope you do not dare to neglect; you cannot, I think, ordinarily omit it, if you have a living, holy, principle within you. Well, and you must pray especially for spiritual blessings; and in particular, that the Lord would please to put his *law in your inward parts, and write it in your hearts;* 'that He would make it ready and familiar to you, at hand when you have occasion to use it, as that which is written in the heart; that He would work in you a strong disposition to obedience, and an exact conformity of thought and affection to the rules of the Divine law, as that of the copy to the original.' You have a disposition this way already; pray that it may abide and grow, and plead that precious promise in Jer. xxxi. 33; and the more you are disposed this way, the less danger will there be of your forgetting the Covenant of the Lord your God.

"USE. — From what has been said, let professors be exhorted *to put one another in mind of their Covenant duties and obligations.* It is true, we may not watch over others and neglect ourselves, as some to their great reproach are said to do; neither may our charity end at home; for the law of God obliges us to love our neighbor as ourselves. And again it is written, *Exhort one another daily.* And it is remarked concerning those that fear the Lord, that *they spake often one to another.* — Mal. iii. 16. And have we not expressly bound ourselves by Covenant to watch over one another? Yes, verily. How then shall we dare to neglect it; especially considering that a great deal of sin and sorrow might probably be prevented, if professors would in this way be kind and faithful to one another? Thus, for instance, when a neighbor or brother is observed to be going into temptation, or in present danger of falling into some transgression, it is not improbable that these words, spoken in a suitable manner, in his hearing, *remember your Covenant,* would prevent his fall; or, if he has already fallen, it may be those words would be the means of recovering him out of the snare of the devil; and of bringing him unto unfeigned repentance. And so, if you see a brother backward to any good work, respecting either God or man, perhaps this memento would shame and quicken. Now we are undoubtedly obliged to do this, and much more, to prevent each other's hurt, and to promote each other's good. O let us not be negligent."

Under what influences Mr. Phillips was led to devote himself to the ministry we are not informed; but his mother was the daughter of a clergyman, Rev. John Emerson, of Gloucester; his uncle George was then a useful pastor; his venerable grandfather, at Rowley, lived to be quite distinctly remembered by him, as a vision of his childhood, and the names of both the grandfather at Rowley, and the great-grandfather at Watertown, were cherished with affectionate veneration in the family. . . . Such influences, united with his own self-relying character, and his decisive religious convictions and experience, were adapted to make him cling with ardor to the profession of his choice, and with somewhat of the spirit of a champion, in defence of his tenets. "Being sincerely attached," says Allen, "to those views of religious truth, which were embraced by the first fathers of New England, he could not quietly see the efforts that were made to pervert the faith, which he was persuaded was once delivered to the saints. He exerted himself both by his preaching and his writings, to guard his people against the intrusion of error."[1] "His anxiety on the subject," says the compiler of the History of Andover, "may be easily seen in some of his last publications,"[2] his zeal growing more intense with his years. It may be a matter of interest to some of the readers of this Memoir, to state that among his manuscript sermons which we have examined, are two preached by him upon which he wrote the following memoranda:—

"'Andover, May 12th, 1734: Being the last Sabb: of our meeting in our old meeting-house; which had been improved 24 years and almost 4 mo: John 14, ult;—Arise: let us go hence.'

"'Andover, May 19th, 1734: Being ye First Sabb: of our meeting in our new meeting-house. I Chron: 29, 13, 14: Now yrf; our God, we thank thee and praise thy glor: N. But wo am I, and wt is my pp, &c.'"

The language of his will in the bequests to charitable objects, referred to in the text, and which illustrates his great discrimination and carefulness, is as follows:—"I give the just sum of £100 L. M'y, as an abiding fund for ye relief of indigent Persons in the South Parish of Andover, aforesaid; namely, proper objects of charity, and such as receive no help

[1] Allen's Biog. Dict. p. 477.

[2] History of Andover, by Abiel Abbot, A. M. 1829, p. 106.

from the town, more especially those of y$^{e}$ ch$^{h}$, in the said Parish, standing in need of relief; the said sum of money to be paid by my executors to y$^{e}$ ministers and deacons of said society or parish after my decease; namely, at the resettlement of a pastor of y$^{e}$ congregational persuasion; the principal always to be kept out upon interest on good security, never to be disposed of, and only y$^{e}$ interest thereof to be given away; and when there is not occasion for y$^{e}$ whole of y$^{e}$ interest, then y$^{e}$ remainder to be added to y$^{e}$ principal, and to be put out upon interest also; and the whole to be conducted as y$^{e}$ said ministers and deacons of y$^{e}$ said Parish, for y$^{e}$ time being, to y$^{e}$ end of time, shall, in their wisdom, judge best: and a fair and just account to be taken and preserved by y$^{m}$ in a book for that purpose, of their disposal of the same from year to year, to be produced for y$^{e}$ information of any who may desire it. I give the like sum of £100 L. M'$^{y}$, for y$^{e}$ pious and charitable use of propagating Christian knowledge among y$^{e}$ Indians of North America; and to be disposed of for that intent, at such times, and to such person or persons, as my exec$^{trs}$ shall think best." These executors were his three sons.

The children of Rev. Samuel Phillips, were: —

1. *Mary*, born November 30, 1712, O. S.; baptized the next Lord's day; admitted to the church, July 8, 1734; married to Samuel Appleton, of Haverhill, October 12, 1736, and died in 1737.

2. *Samuel*, born February 13, 1715; baptized the same day; admitted to the church on the same day with his sister Mary, July 8, 1734; dismissed to the North Church in Andover, April 1, 1739, where he resided till his death, August 21, 1790.

3. *Lydia*, born June 10, 1717; baptized the next Lord's day; married Dr. Parker Clark, May 18, 1742; died November 4, 1749.

4. *John*, born December 27, 1719; baptized the same day;

recognized his baptismal covenant, April 27, 1735; graduated at Harvard College, 1735; died August 21, 1795.

5. *William*, born June 25, 1722; baptized July 1; recognized his baptismal covenant, December 5, 1736; died January 15, 1804. See Bond's Gen. & Hist.; Records of the South Church, Andover, etc. The date of William's birth, as here given, differs from Dr. Bond's, perhaps from an error in connection with the change of style; as the addition of eleven or twelve days would bring our date forward to his, July 6th.

---

## D.

Mr. Phillips and Miss Barnard were married July 11, 1738; their children were: —

1. Theodore, born May 2, 1739; baptized May 6; died January 25, 1740.

2. Hannah, born January 20, 1742; baptized January —; died June 15, 1764.

3. Samuel, born November 6, 1743; baptized November 6; died December 24, 1744.

4. Theodore, born September 6, 1745; baptized September —; died December 1, 1758.

5. Elizabeth, born October 31, 1747; baptized October —; died June 24, 1748.

6. Samuel, born February 5, 1752; baptized February —; died February 10, 1802.

7. Elizabeth, born October 18, 1755; baptized October —; died April 19, 1757.

See Bond's Gen. & Hist. of Watertown, p. 881. Records of First Church in Andover; Abbot's History of Andover, etc. etc.; in the date of the last Samuel's birth, as here given, according to the various records in Andover, which we consider decisive, there is a slight variance from Dr. Bond, and also from other notices of him; the *day* of the baptism of these children is not usually entered in the records of the church, but only the *month*. It will be noticed from these dates, that three of the children died subsequent to his birth, and that but one, except Samuel, lived beyond early childhood, and that one many years his elder, rather than a child with him in age and sympathy.

---

## E.

Under date of August 19, 1769, he writes in his Journal, — "Came to Cambridge Wednesday, and found I was put with Osgood in chamber No. 26, Hollis Hall; very good chamber. This afternoon I received a copy of a vote wherein I was ordered to sit between Vassal and Murray; it occasions considerable talk. Some say I bought it, others, I have tried for it; but promotion always breeds enemies, and envious ones are the most spiteful; let me be interested in the Lord, and no matter who is against me."

The remonstrance of his father to the College government upon the subject, is referred to in the Records of the Faculty, as follows, — "At a meeting of the Tutors of Harvard College, August 18, 1769, present Mr. Eliot, Mr. Scales, Mr. Hillyard, Mr. Willard; Samuel Phillips, of Andover, Esquire, having some time ago entered a complaint to the President and Tutors, that his son, Samuel Phillips, a student at the College, had not his proper place in the class; particularly, that he did not rank with the sons of those gentlemen who were Justices of the Quorum, when he himself had been in the Commissions of the Peace and Quorum unus, a longer time than any of them, — and having had, from the late President Holyoke and others in the government of the College, a promise, that the records at the Secretary's office should be consulted, and if it did appear that there was a mistake, it should be rectified:—the Secretary's book having been accordingly consulted, it appeared, that Mr. Phillips was put into the Commission of the Peace in the year 1752, and that he was made Justice of the Quorum, November 19, 1761; that John Murray, Esquire, (whose son is placed at the head of the sons of the Justices,) was put into the Commission of the Peace January, 1754, and was made Justice of the Quorum in 1762.

"Therefore, Voted, That Phillips, son to the above-mentioned Samuel Phillips, Esquire, do for the future take his place between Vassal and Murray—and ordered, that Mr. Eliot, tutor to the class in which Phillips is thus placed, do deliver a copy of the above vote to him."

---

## F.

In connection with the termination of the siege of Boston, we here insert some of the congratulations with which Washington was honored, as a fit contrast to his own and others' long-continued discontents while it was in progress.

"The selectmen of Boston waited upon the General and presented the following address:—

"May it please your Excellency,—The selectmen of Boston, in behalf of themselves and fellow-citizens, with all grateful respect, congratulate your excellency on the success of your military operations, in the recovery of this town from an enemy, collected from the once respected Britons, who, in this instance, are characterized by malice and fraud, rapine and plunder, in every trace left behind them.

"Happy are we that this acquisition has been made with

so little effusion of human blood, which, next to the Divine favor, permit us to ascribe to your excellency's wisdom, evidenced in every part of this long besiegement.

"If it be possible to enhance the noble feelings of that person, who from the most affluent enjoyments, could throw himself into the hardships of a camp, to save his country, uncertain of success, 't is then possible this victory will heighten your excellency's happiness, when you consider you have not only saved a large, elegant, and once populous city, from total destruction, but relieved the few wretched inhabitants from all the horrors of a besieged town, from the insults and abuses of a disgraced and chagrined army, and restored many inhabitants to their quiet habitations, who had fled for safety to the bosom of their country. May your excellency live to see the just rights of America settled on a firm basis, which felicity we sincerely wish you; and at a late period, may that felicity be changed into happiness eternal!

"To his Excellency, GEORGE WASHINGTON, Esq.,

"General of the United Forces in America."

On the 29th of March, the Provincial Congress sent in from Watertown, a joint committee of the Council and Representatives, with a long and flattering testimonial. It alluded to the early resistance of this Colony to the tyrannical policy "impelled by self-preservation and the love of freedom:" to the satisfaction at the appointment of Washington to be commander-in-chief; to the wisdom, and prudence, and success of his measures; and it concluded as follows: — "May you still go on, approved by Heaven, revered by all good men, and dreaded by those tyrants who claim their fellow men as their property. May the United Colonies be defended from slavery by your victorious arms. May they still see their enemies flying before you; and (the deliverance of your country being effected) may you, in retirement, enjoy that peace and satisfaction of mind which always attend the good and great; and may future generations, in the peaceable enjoyment of that freedom the exercise of which your sword shall have established, raise the richest and most lasting monuments to the name of Washington."

The Continental Congress heard of the evacuation of Boston on the 25th, and "immediately, on the motion of John Adams, passed a vote of thanks to Washington, and the officers and soldiers under his command, for their wise and spirited conduct, and ordered a gold medal to be struck and presented to the General;—also appointed a committee, consisting of John Adams, John Jay, and Stephen Hopkins, to prepare a letter of thanks. This letter was reported to Congress and adopted April 2, namely:—

"PHILADELPHIA, April 2, 1776.

"SIR,—It gives me the most sensible pleasure to convey to you, by order of Congress, the only tribute which a free people will ever consent to pay,—the tribute of thanks and gratitude to their friends and benefactors.

"The disinterested and patriotic principles which led you to the field, have also led you to glory; and it affords no little consolation to your countrymen to reflect, that as a peculiar greatness of mind induced you to decline any compensation for serving them, except the pleasure of promoting their happiness, they may, without your permission, bestow upon you the largest share of their affection and esteem.

"Those pages in the annals of America will record your title to a conspicuous place in the temple of fame, which shall inform posterity that, under your directions, an undisciplined band of husbandmen, in the course of a few months, became soldiers; and that the desolation meditated against the country by a brave army of veterans, commanded by the most experienced generals, but employed by bad men, in the worst of causes, was, by the fortitude of your troops, and the address of their officers, next to the kind interposition of Providence, confined for near a year within such narrow limits as scarcely to admit more room than was necessary for the encampments and fortifications they lately abandoned.

"Accept, therefore, Sir, the thanks of the United Colonies, unanimously declared by their delegates to be due to you, and the brave officers and troops under your command; and be pleased to communicate to them this distinguished mark of the approbation of their country.

"The Congress have ordered a gold medal, adapted to the occasion, to be struck, and, when finished, to be presented to you.

"I have the honor to be, with every sentiment of esteem, Sir, your most obedient and very humble servant,

"JOHN HANCOCK, President.

"To His Excellency, GEORGE WASHINGTON."

The medal, which was struck in Paris, from a die cut by Duvivier, contains on the obverse a head of Washington in profile, exhibiting an excellent likeness, and around it the inscription,

"GEORGIO WASHINGTON, SUPREMO DUCI EXERCITUUM ADSERTORI LIBERTATIS COMITIA AMERICANA."

On the reverse is the town of Boston in the distance, with a fleet in view under sail. Washington and his officers are on horseback in the foreground, and he is pointing to the ships as they depart from the harbor. The inscription is: —

"HOSTIBUS PRIMO FUGATIS BOSTONIUM RECUPERATUM, XVII. MARTII, MDCCLXXVI."[1]

Among other testimonials which he received at this time, the Corporation and Overseers of Harvard University conferred upon Washington the Honorary degree of Doctor of Laws, "as an expression of the gratitude of this College for his eminent services in the cause of his country, and to this society." He was the first person on whom the College con-

[1] Spark's Works of Washington, Vol. I. p. 175; Vol. III. p. 533, 534; also Frothingham's History of the Siege of Boston, p. 316–320.

ferred this degree. The diploma "was signed by all the members of the Corporation, except John Hancock, who was then in Philadelphia, and it was immediately published in the newspapers of the period, with an English translation."[1]

The diploma is as follows: —

"Senatus Academiæ Cantabrigiensis in Nov. Angliâ omnibus in Christo fidelibus, ad quos literæ præsentes pervenerint, salutem in Domino sempiternam.

"Cum eum in finem Gradus Academici instituti fuerint, ut Viri Scientiâ, sapientiâ, et virtute insignes, qui de Re literariâ et de Re Publicâ optime meruerint, honoribus hisce laureatis remunerarenter; maxime decet ut honore tali afficiatur Vir illustrissimus Georgius Washington, Armiger Exercitûs Coloniarum in Americâ Foederatarum Imperator prœclarus. cujus scientia et amor patriæ undique patent; qui propter eximias virtutes tam civiles quam militares, primùm, a civibus suis Legatus electus, in Consessu celeberrimo Americano de Libertate ad extremum periclitatâ, et de Salute publicâ, fideliter et peritissime consuluit; deinde, postulante Patriâ, sedem in Virginiâ amoenissimam et res proprias perlubenter reliquit, ut per omnes castrorum labores et pericula, nulla mercede acceptâ, Nov-Angliam ab armis Britannorum iniquis et crudelibus liberaret, et Colonias cæteras tuereter; et qui, sub Auspiciis Divinis maxime Spectandis, ab Urbe Bostoniâ per undecim menses clausâ, munitâ, et plusquam septem millium militum præsidio firmatâ, naves et copias hostium in fugam præcipitem et probrosam deturbavit; adeo ut cives, plurimis duritiis et sævitiis oppressi, tandem salvi lætentur, villæ vicinæ quiescant, atque sedibus suis Academia nostra restituatur.

"Sciatis igitur, quod nos Præses et socii Collegii Harvardini in Cantabridgiâ Nov-Anglorum (consentientibus honorandis admodum et reverendis Academiæ nostra Inspectoribus) Dominum supradictum, summo honore dignum, Geor-

[1] Quincy's History of Harvard University, Vol. II. p. 167.

gium Washington, Doctorem Utriusque Juris, tum Naturæ et Gentium, tum Civilis, statuimus et creavimus, eique simul dedimus et concessimus omnia jura, privilegia, et honores ad istum gradum pertinentia.

"In cujus rei testimonium nos, communi sigillo Universitatis hisce literis affixo, chirographa apposuimus die tertio Aprilis, anno salutis millesimo septingentesimo septuagesimo sexto."[1]

---

## G.

To assist any who may feel an interest in tracing out the localities of so early a period here, we insert brief memoranda of the deeds, not only of the territory first purchased by the Founders of the Academy, but of various later purchases, covering together the entire tract on "Andover Hill." The references are to the Treasurer's files in Phillips Academy: —

I. January 24, 1777: Deed *A*, copy.

*Solomon Wardwell to Samuel Phillips, Esq.*

This deed covers two tracts; the first, of about twenty-two acres, on which was an old house and a joiner's shop, lying on the west side of our Main street, and extending along the line of the old road, as the large elms now stand, from the corner of Phillips street, southwardly, nearly to the old well on the common, south-east of the Printing-house; and westwardly on Phillips street, to a point nearly opposite the old house, west of the Latin Dormitories: — the second, of about seventeen acres, lying on the east side of the old road, and including the whole space from a point by the road nearly opposite the President's House, so-called, north-

[1] Quincy's History of Harvard University, Vol. II. Appendix, No. XIX. p. 506, 507.

westerly down to the double-brick house, thence easterly by the Stone Academy, around to a point near Bartlett Hall; and thence, by an irregular line westerly, across the Seminary Lawn to the road again.

II. March 1, 1777: Deed *B*, copy.

*Joshua Holt, Administrator on Estate of George Abbott, to Samuel Phillips, Esq.*

This deed conveys three parcels; the first, of twelve acres, lying north of Phillips street, and west of Main and School streets, extending northerly toward the Village nearly to the English Dormitories, and westerly a short distance beyond the old house, by the Latin Dormitories. This old house was the dwelling of George Abbott, and was occupied as mentioned in the text, for some years, by Judge Phillips, after its purchase for the school: — the second, of twenty-eight acres, lying across the road from this old house, and west of the first piece obtained from Solomon Wardwell: — the third, of thirty acres, lying beyond the Hill on the south, and extending from a point near Mrs. Flagg's east, about forty rods, then south to the old cross road, then westerly along this road to a point near Samuel Abbott's, then northerly to the road near Moses Abbott's, and then northeasterly by this road to the point of beginning.

III. October 9, 1784: Deed No. 9.

*Isaac Blunt to the Trustees of Phillips Academy.*

This deed describes the common opposite the Mansion House, called the "Old Training Field," twenty-two rods southerly from the corner by the old road, eighteen and three-quarter rods easterly on the Salem road. The deed in this case is to the Trustees, but an entry in the Academy journal shows that the land was bought by the three brothers, Samuel, John, and William Phillips, in connection with the building of the "New Academy" about this date, and was *given* by them, with the building, to the Trustees. See Old Academy Journal, p. 6, where the language is "the Academy *and land south of the same*, etc."

IV. September 1, 1792: Deed No. 11.

*Samuel Phillips to the Trustees of Phillips Academy.*

This deed of Judge Phillips, covers three and one-quarter acres in the southwesterly portion of the present Seminary lawn, being the lot on which the second Academy building, above referred to, was erected by his father and uncles in 1785. Mr. Phillips had obtained this land, with a section east of it, from William Foster, January 15, 1782, as referred to in the text (see Deed C, copy). The portion conveyed by him to the Trustees, extended from the corner northwesterly about twenty rods, and east twenty rods; an entry in the Academy Journal, p. 1, shows that he deeded this lot to the Trustees *in exchange* for the site of his mansion-house, one and a half acres.

V. January 10, 1801: Deed No. 16.

*Asa Towne to the Trustees of Phillips Academy.*

This deed describes the site of the Adams House, so-called, etc., an acre and a half, on which a small dwelling-house was standing, which is now the L of the Adams House, bounding on the Common twenty rods, and on the Salem road twelve rods. The Adams House, as now standing, was erected here in 1805, and was first occupied by Dr. Pearson in the spring of 1806.—*Academy Records*, p. 198.

VI. April 15, 1809: Deed No. 21.

*Isaac Blunt to the Trustees of Phillips Academy.*

This deed conveys the site of the Brick Academy and the lot south, about two and one fifth acres, bounded on the Salem road eleven and a half rods.

VII. June 9, 1812: Deed No. 24.

*Phœbe Phillips to the Trustees of Phillips Academy.*

This deed conveys the mansion-house of Judge Phillips with about nine acres of land adjoining the same, extending on the street southerly to the premises occupied by the late Professor Stuart; also the Blanchard Lot and House, so-called, now in the Seminary lawn, containing about three acres, extending northward to include the present site of Bartlett Hall, being the remainder of the tract obtained by Mr. Phillips of William Foster (Deed C, copy). All the land now common between the Mansion-house, Printing-house, etc., and the row of large elms in front, then within the fence, was thrown out by Mr. Farrar at a later date, in connection with the building of the houses for Dr. Griffin and Dr. Woods.

VIII. July 8, 1814: Deed No. 26.

*The Trustees of the Ministerial Fund in the South Parish in Andover to the Trustees of Phillips Academy.*

This is a deed of a piece of land, sixty square rods, lying between our Main and School streets, north-west of the Stone Academy; in the change of the old road now School street, a portion of this tract was cut off; the deed bounds it fourteen rods on the turnpike now Main street.

IX. April 1, 1815: Deed No. 29.

*Samuel Farrar to the Trustees of Phillips Academy.*

This is a deed of "the Chandler Pasture," as it was long termed; a tract of seven and a half acres, north and east of the Stone Academy, bounded on Main street northerly nine rods, and on the private way easterly about thirty-six rods, including the sites of the Samaritan House and Professor Stowe's residence. Mr. Farrar had purchased this lot a year or two previous on his own account, but with a view to its passing finally to the Trustees.

X. August 30, 1815: Deed No. 27.

*Benjamin Gleason to the Trustees of Phillips Academy.*

This deed conveys the Gleason House, so called, now occupied by Dr. S. C. Jackson, with the land, bounded on Main street northerly from the corner of the Chandler Pasture, 23 rods. This was Lot No. 1 of the Parish lands, sold at auction April 18, 1810.

XI. April 20, 1818: Deed No. 30.

*Hannah Poor and Daniel A. Poor to the Trustees of Phillips Academy.*

This deed conveys a tract of a little more than eight acres, westward of the original Phillips purchase from the estate of George Abbott, and on the northerly side of Phillips street, bounded on Academy street forty-two rods: this section includes the present site of the West House, so called, and the three adjoining lots north and west of the same.

XII. April 29, 1818: Deed No. 31.

*Mark Newman to the Trustees of Phillips Academy.*

This deed covers the Brown Professor's house and lot, and the site of the book bindery and store beyond; containing about two acres, being the same lot of land obtained by Mr. Newman of Isaac Blunt, March 13, 1805, on which Mr. Newman had erected the dwelling-house and store as now standing. The dwelling-house was assigned to the Brown Professor, by vote of the Trustees in 1843, in connection with a donation by Miss Banister of $4,000, as an equivalent for the same. — *Seminary Records*, Vol. II. p. 22.

XIII. May 8, 1818: Deed No. 39.

*William Bartlett to the Trustees of Phillips Academy.*

This deed, conveys, (1st) the President's House, so called, with the land adjoining, which Mr. Bartlett had bought of the Trustees in order to build on it: (2d) the Stuart House, and twelve and a half acres of land which he had bought of Madam Phillips, May 8, 1810, in order to build on it also; bounded on the street in front fourteen and three fourths rods. This land was part of a purchase by Judge Phillips of Ebenezer Jones and wife, heirs of Samuel Abbott, made March 19, 1782, as he was arranging to erect the mansion-house (see Deed *D*, copy); (3d) a small piece back of the Seminary, which Mr. Bartlett bought of Isaac Blunt, August 29, 1809; and (4th) the Chapel.

XIV. August 16, 1820: Deed No. 36.

*Isaac Blunt to the Trustees of Phillips Academy.*

This is a deed of a small lot of two and a half acres back of the Seminary, now included in the Garden and Cemetery.

XV. September 6, 1823: Deed 38.

*Isaac Blunt to the Trustees of Phillips Academy.*

This is a deed of about two and a half acres northerly of the Seminary.

XVI. March 23, 1824: Deed No. 37.

*Amos Holt to the Trustees of Phillips Academy.*

This deed covers the narrow strip of land between the two streets beyond the Printing-house, which is to be kept as a common, upon which Mr. Holt was preparing to erect a cooper's shop: and also a small section nearly in front of the double brick house, between the turnpike and the line of the old road, on which Levi Davis attempted at one time to build a three story house with brick ends, but a violent wind prostrated the building, when Mr. Davis sold the lot to Mr. Holt.

XVII. December 1, 1829: Deed No. 44.

*Jonathan Clement to the Trustees of Phillips Academy.*

This deed conveys the Clement House, so called, and land

adjoining, about three and a half acres, on which the English Dormitories now stand, including the avenue in front of them to the road, and the lot north and west.

XVIII. March 25, 1831: Deed No. 46.

*Isaac Blunt to the Trustees of Phillips Academy.*

This deed conveys fifteen and a half acres east and north-east of the Seminary, adjoining lots previously sold by Mr. Blunt to the Trustees.

XIX. December 24, 1825: Deed No. 68.

*Leonard Woods to the Trustees of Phillips Academy.*

This is a deed of two and a third acres, north-east of the Seminary, which Dr. Woods had bought of Mr. Blunt, September 7, 1819.

XX. October 12, 1830: Deed No. 51.

*Isaac Blunt to the Trustees of Phillips Academy.*

This is a deed of "the gravel pit," being the tract directly south of the Cemetery and Garden, about an acre and one third.

XXI. March 15, 1833: Deed No. 55.

*David Hidden to the Trustees of Phillips Academy.*

This is a deed of a pasture, upwards of nine acres, back of the premises occupied by the late Professor Stuart, and is appropriated to the Brown Professorship.

XXII. September 22, 1853: Deed No. 71.

*Henry J. Gray to the Trustees of Phillips Academy.*

This deed conveys the Gray House, so called, on the point between Main and School streets, opposite the Gleason House; and completes the title of the Trustees to all lands adjoining the highways across the hill in every direction.

The remaining portions of the tract of pasturage north and north-east of the Seminary along the line of Pike street including the woodland, in that region, came to the Trustees, through the estate of Henry Abbot, under a mortgage of Samuel Abbott, Esquire, which had been foreclosed.

---

## H.

One peculiarity of the Act, incorporating the Academy, is the summary rehearsal of its Constitution which it embodies, while the whole is made to conform so exactly to Judge Phillips's style as well as to his views, that no other evidence of its authorship is needed. We insert the Act with the various signatures.

1780 — Oct. 4.

STATE OF MASSACHUSETTS BAY — AN ACT TO INCORPORATE AN ACADEMY IN THE TOWN OF ANDOVER, BY THE NAME OF PHILLIPS ACADEMY.

Preamble.

WHEREAS the education of youth has ever been considered by the wise and good, as an object of the highest consequence to the safety and happiness of a people; as at that period the mind easily receives and retains impressions, is formed with peculiar advantage to piety and virtue, and directed to the pursuit of the most useful knowledge: and, whereas the Honorable Samuel Phillips of Andover, in the County of Essex, Esq., and the Honorable John Phillips of Exeter, in the County of Rockingham, and State of New Hampshire, Esq., on the first day of April, in the year of our Lord, one thousand seven hundred and seventy-eight, by a legal Instrument of that date, gave, granted, and assigned to the Honorable William Phillips, Esquire, and others, therein named, and to their heirs, divers lots and parcels of land, in said Instrument described, as well as certain other estate, to the use and upon the trust following, namely, that the rents, profits, and interest thereof, be forever laid out and expended by the Trustees in the said Instrument named, for the support of a Public Free School or Academy, in the town of Andover: — and, whereas the execution of the generous and important design of the grantors aforesaid will be attended with very great embarrassments, unless by an act of incorporation, the Trustees, mentioned in the said Instrument, and their successors, shall be authorized to commence and prosecute actions at law, and transact such other matters in their corporate capacity, as the interest of the said Academy shall require: —

### Academy Established.

I. Be it therefore enacted by the Council and House of Representatives in General Court assembled, and by the authority of the same; that there be and hereby is established in the Town of Andover, and County of Essex, an Academy, by the name of *Phillips Academy*, for the purpose of promoting true piety and virtue, and for the education of youth, in the English, Latin, and Greek languages, together with Writing, Arithmetic, Music, and the Art of Speaking; also practical Geometry, Logic, and Geography, and such other of the liberal Arts and Sciences, or Languages, as opportunity may hereafter permit, and as the Trustees, hereinafter provided, shall direct.

### Trustees Appointed and Incorporated.

II. Be it further enacted by the authority aforesaid, that the Hon. Samuel Phillips of Andover aforesaid, Esq., the Hon. John Phillips of Exeter aforesaid, Esq., the Hon. William Phillips and Oliver Wendell, Esqs., and John Lowell, Esq., of Boston, in the County of Suffolk, and State of Massachusetts Bay, the Rev. Josiah Stearns of Epping, in the County of Rockingham aforesaid, the Reverend William Symmes of said Andover, the Reverend Elias Smith of Middleton, in the said County of Essex, the Reverend Jonathan French, Samuel Phillips, Jun'r, Esq., Mr. Eliphalet Pearson, gentlemen, and Mr. Nehemiah Abbot, yeoman, all of Andover aforesaid, be, and they hereby are nominated and appointed Trustees of said Academy; and they are hereby incorporated into a body politic, by the name of the *Trustees of Phillips Academy;* and that they, and their successors, shall be and continue a body politic and corporate, by the same name forever.

Lands Confirmed to the Trustees.

III. And be it further enacted by the authority aforesaid, that all the lands and monies, which, by a legal Instrument, bearing date the first day of April, in the year of our Lord, one thousand seven hundred and seventy-eight, were given, granted, and assigned, by the afore-mentioned Samuel Phillips and John Phillips, unto the said William Phillips, Oliver Wendell, John Lowell, Josiah Stearns, William Symmes, Elias Smith, Jonathan French, Samuel Phillips, Jun'r, Eliphalet Pearson, and Nehemiah Abbot, and to their heirs, be, and they hereby are confirmed to the said William Phillips and others, last named, and to their successors, as Trustees of Phillips Academy forever, for the uses and purposes, and upon the Trust, which in said Instrument are expressed: and the Trustees aforesaid, their successors, and the officers of the said Academy, are hereby required in conducting the concerns thereof, and in all matters relating thereto, to regulate themselves conformably to the true design and intention of the said grantors, as expressed in their instrument above mentioned.

Trustees to have one common Seal.—May Sue and be Sued.

IV. And be it further enacted by the authority aforesaid,

that the said Trustees and their successors, shall have one common Seal, which they may make use of in any cause or business that relates to the said office of Trustees of the said Academy; and they shall have power and authority to break, change, and renew the said Seal, from time to time, as they shall see fit; and that they may Sue and be Sued in all actions real, personal, and mixed, and prosecute and defend the same unto final judgment and execution, by the name of the *Trustees of Phillips Academy.*

Empowered to Elect their Officers, and Ordain Rules, etc.

V. And be it further enacted by the authority aforesaid, that the said Samuel Phillips and others, the Trustees aforesaid, and their successors, the longest livers and survivors of them, be the true and sole Visitors, Trustees, and Governors of the said Phillips Academy, in perpetual succession forever; to be continued in the way and manner hereafter specified, with full power and authority to elect such officers of the said Academy, as to them, the said Trustees, Governors, and Visitors aforesaid, and their successors, shall from time to time, according to the various occasions and circumstances seem most fit and requisite; all which shall be observed by the officers, scholars, and servants of the said Academy, upon the penalties therein contained: provided notwithstanding, that the said rules, laws, and orders be no ways contrary to the laws of this State.

Number of Trustees not to exceed thirteen.

VI. And be it further enacted by the authority aforesaid, that the number of the Trustees aforesaid, and their successors, shall not at any one time be more than *thirteen* nor less than *seven;* seven of whom shall constitute a quorum for transacting business, and the major part of the members present at any legal meeting, shall decide all questions that shall come before them, except in the instances hereinafter excepted.

The principal Instructor to be one.

That the principal Instructor for the time being, shall ever be one of them; that a major part shall be laymen and respectable freeholders; also, that a major part shall consist of men who are not inhabitants of the town where the Seminary is situate. And to perpetuate the succession of said Trustees.

Vacancies of Trustees, how supplied.

VII. Be it further enacted by the authority aforesaid, that as often as one or more of the Trustees of said Phillips Academy shall die or resign, or in the judgment of a major part of the other Trustees be rendered by age or otherwise, incapable of discharging the duties of his office, then, and so often, the Trustees then surviving and remaining, or the major part of them, shall elect one or more persons to supply the vacancy or vacancies.

The Trustees to be deemed capable in the law to take and receive by gift, grant, etc.

VIII. And be it further enacted by the authority aforesaid, that the Trustees aforesaid, and their successors, be and they hereby are rendered capable in law to take and receive by gift, grant, devise, bequest, or otherwise, any lands, tenements, or other estate, real and personal; provided that the annual income of the said real estate shall not exceed the sum of five hundred pounds, and the annual income of the said personal estate shall not exceed the sum of two thousand pounds, both sums to be valued in silver at the rate of six shillings and eight pence by the ounce; to have and to hold the same to them, the said Trustees and their successors, on such terms and under such provisions and limitations, as may be expressed in any deed or instrument of conveyance to them made; provided always, that neither the said Trustees, nor their successors, shall ever hereafter receive any grant or donation, the condition whereof shall require them or any others concerned, to act in any respect counter to the design of the first grantors, or of any prior donation. And all deeds and instruments, which the said Trustees may lawfully make, shall, when made in the name of the said Trustees, and signed and delivered by their Treasurer, and sealed with the common seal, bind the said Trustees and their successors, and be valid in law.

Two thirds of said Trustees empowered to remove the Seminary.

IX. And be it further enacted by the authority aforesaid, that if it shall hereafter be judged, upon mature and impartial consideration of all circumstances, by two thirds of all the Trustees, that, for good and substantial reasons, which at this time do not exist, the true design of this Institution will be better promoted by removing the Seminary from the place where it is founded, in that case it shall be in the power of the said Trustees, to remove it accordingly, and to establish it in such place within this State as they shall judge to be best calculated for carrying into effectual execution the intention of the founders.[1]

In the House of Representatives, October 4, 1780.

This Bill having been read several times, passed to be enacted. JOHN HANCOCK, *Speaker.*

In Council, October 4, 1780.

This Bill having had two several readings, passed to be enacted. JOHN AVERY, *D. Secretary.*

We consent to the enacting of this bill.

| | | |
|---|---|---|
| S. CUSHING, | T. DANIELSON, | SAMUEL NILES, |
| J. FISHER, | BENJ. AUSTIN, | A. FULLER, |
| MOSES GILL, | N. CUSHING, | JNO. PITTS, |
| H. GARDNER, | WM. WHITING, | STEPHEN CHOATE. |

[1] Acts and Laws of Massachusetts, 1780, p. 327–329.

The above subscription, and also the caption to the Act Incorporating the Academy, is copied from the original document on file in the office of the Secretary of State in Boston. The Preamble there stands in the handwriting of Judge Phillips, and also the first enacting clause in part. The remainder of the manuscript is partly in his hand, and partly in that of two others.

---

## I.

The following letter from the present Principal of the Exeter Academy, in reply to inquiries recently addressed to him, will be read with interest for the information it summarily presents, in regard to the history and the present condition of this Institution.

"PHILLIPS EXETER ACADEMY, Exeter, June 22, 1856.

"DEAR SIR,—I have been prevented from attending sooner to the inquiries contained in your letter; I must now be brief in my answers.

"1. The Act of Incorporation of the Phillips Exeter Academy is dated April 3, 1781.

"2. A meeting of the Trustees was held on the 31st of April, 1783; and Benjamin Thurston was 'appointed to address the Preceptor on his induction to his academical function,' and the meeting was adjourned till the next day, when, May 1st, 1783, I suppose the Preceptor, William Woodbridge, entered upon the duties of his office. There is a tradition that the school had been in operation some weeks before, conducted by one of the Trustees, but no record of it.

"3. I am not able to say what was the cost of the original Academy buildings. The first building was sold; and the present must have cost from seven to ten thousand dollars.

In 1821, wings were added to this building at a cost of about twenty-five hundred dollars. 'Abbot Hall,' a substantial and exceedingly convenient building, has been erected within the last year. This building is for the accommodation of the poorer class of students. It is a boarding-house, accommodating fifty students with very good rooms without rent. The cost of this building was about eighteen thousand dollars. The amount expended for buildings, up to the present time, must be nearly thirty thousand dollars, including the house occupied by the Principal.

"4. Nothing has been received, in addition to the original endowment, for the general purposes of the Institution. One thousand dollars was left by the late Nicholas Gilman for instruction in sacred music; and one hundred dollars by the late Leverett Saltonstall of Salem, Massachusetts, for the Library.

"The present amount of productive funds may be stated, in round numbers, at one hundred thousand dollars, perhaps a little less.

"5. Whole number of pupils, twenty-nine hundred.

"6. A marble slab, with an appropriate inscription, covers the grave of the Founder. There is no written memorial of him. Neither the Act of Incorporation, nor the Constitution of the Academy, has ever been printed.

"In great haste, very respectfully,

"GIDEON L. SOULE."

---

## J.

The record of the action of the Trustees on this occasion, dated March 29, 1788, is as follows: —

"Understanding it is proposed that the meeting-house in this place should be taken down, —

"*Voted*, That the inhabitants of the South Parish be informed, that they shall be welcome to the use of the Academy chamber for the purpose of public worship, after the present meeting-house shall be taken down, until the meeting-house, that shall be erected in its place, can be fit for use, if agreeable to the parish.

"*Voted*, That the Honorable Samuel Phillips, Jr., be a committee to communicate the above vote to the parish."[1]

The old meeting-house, as appears from the church records, was occupied for the last time April 20, 1788, when Rev. Mr. French preached from Haggai i. 7 and 8: "Thus saith the Lord of hosts, consider your ways; go up to the mountain and bring wood, and build the house; and I will take pleasure in it, and I will be glorified, saith the Lord." The new house was raised on the 26th and 27th of May; and, after occupying the Academy Hall thirty-two Sabbaths, the pastor preached a discourse at the opening of this new church, on the Lord's day, December 7th, from the text John x. 22, 23: "And it was at Jerusalem the feast of the dedication, and it was winter; *And Jesus walked in the Temple.*"

---

## K.

In the Chronicle of June 19, 1788, and in succeeding issues of that paper, the following advertisement was printed, and is here inserted as an illustration of the care and thoroughness of Judge Phillips in such services: —

"Commonwealth of Massachusetts.

"The subscribers, appointed a committee to sell unappropriated lands belonging to the Commonwealth, and lying within the counties of York, Cumberland, and Lincoln, do hereby notify the public: —

[1] Academy Records, p. 69.

"That there are for sale large and valuable tracts of land, situated between the Highlands and the Atlantic Ocean, from north to south; and between the river St. Croix and the State of New Hampshire, from east to west. The many fine rivers which have their sources in that tract, among which are the rivers Kennebec and Penobscot, running nearly parallel, at about forty miles distance, above one hundred and fifty miles within the country above described, and navigable for vessels of almost any burden for fifty miles; the great number of excellent harbors on the sea-coast, *their* neighborhood to the fishing-banks of Newfoundland; the large quantities of salmon, shad, and alewives in the rivers, and the great plenty of valuable pine and other timber, give the fairest prospect that this country will, in a very few years, become the principal source from whence the West India Islands will draw their supplies. No country is better calculated for grazing, and the great improvements made in agriculture within the last ten years, evidence that the soil is exceeding good, and capable of producing wheat, rye, Indian corn, flax, peas, potatoes, and every species of vegetables which grow in any of the New England States. Besides lumber, fish, and potashes, beef, butter, peas, and flax-seed have already become articles of exportation, and in a few years will be added thereto cheese, barley, hemp, and flax. The above lands will be laid out in townships of six miles square, and will be sold by the township, half township, or mile square, as may best suit the purchaser, and the consolidated notes of this Commonwealth received in payment.

"When it is considered that a township of six miles square between the Kennebec and Penobscot, is ordered by Government to be laid out and appropriated for the building and supporting a public Seminary of Learning; that in each town there are reserved four lots of three hundred and twenty acres each for public uses, and that *the lands are exempted from all State taxes for ten years;* the committee flatter themselves that the most valuable tracts will find a ready sale.

"Every application will be duly attended to, and every person inclined to purchase, as far as possible, accommodated by applying to

"SAMUEL PHILLIPS, Jun., at Andover, County of Essex.

"NATHANIEL WELLS, at Wells, County of York.

"LEONARD JARVIS, at Boston, County of Suffolk.

"JOHN REED, at Roxbury, County of Suffolk.

"DANIEL CONY, at Hallowell, County of Lincoln.

"N. B. Any of the above lands will be sold to any foreigner who shall contract to settle thereon, in three years from the purchase, one or more families to every mile square.

"BOSTON, June 18, 1788."

---

## L.

The Resolve of the General Court, making the grants of land to the several Institutions, was as follows: —

"February 27, 1797.

"*Resolved*, That in pursuance of a report of a joint special Committee, which has been accepted by both branches of the Legislature, there be, and hereby is granted to the Trustees of *Dummer Academy*, to the Trustees of *Phillips Academy*, to the Trustees of *Groton Academy*, and to the Trustees of *Westford Academy*, respectively, and to their respective successors, one half township of six miles square, for each of their Academies, to be laid out or assigned by the committee for the sale of Eastern lands, in some of the unappropriated lands in the district of *Maine*, belonging to this Commonwealth, excepting all lands within six miles of *Penobscot River*, with the reservations and conditions of settlement which have usually been made in cases of similar grants; which tracts the said Trustees, respectively, are hereby empowered to use, sell, or dispose of as they may think most for the benefit of their respective Institutions.

"SAMUEL ADAMS, *Governor.*
"SAMUEL PHILLIPS, *President of the Senate.*
"EDWARD H. ROBBINS, *Speaker.*
"JOHN AVERY, *Secretary.*"

---

## M.

As this Memoir may, in some cases, fall into the hands of those who are not familiar with the character and history of the Theological Seminary, we here insert the Instrument by which it was founded, and which connects it so closely with the origin and progress of the Academy. It would be digressing too far from our proper work in this Memoir, to give other documents and statistics of great interest pertaining to the Seminary; nor have we sought to trace in so very minute detail as may be desired by some, the forecastings of such an Institution, in the life-long projects of Judge Phillips or his associates, lest we should, in so doing, possibly appear to incumber our narrative too much, or to appropriate ground, which it is expected will be carefully covered by another work — Dr. Woods's History of the Seminary. Some interesting documents, relating to the historical and doctrinal connection of the two Institutions, we have not had opportunity to use, as they were previously tendered to Dr. Woods, and many incidents which have come to our knowledge, we have refrained from using, that our work might not in any way supersede the most elaborate treatment of these interesting topics in his, although our field is, at some points, unavoidably the same.

The Instrument by which the Seminary was founded, drafted by the careful hand of Dr. Eliphalet Pearson, the first Principal of the Academy and the intimate friend of Madam

Phillips, in consultation sentence by sentence, not only with her and her son, but with Rev. Mr. French, and Samuel Abbot, and Samuel Farrar, Esquires, is as follows:—

"CONSTITUTION OF THE THEOLOGICAL SEMINARY.

"It having pleased the Father of lights and Author of all good to inspire the late Honorable SAMUEL PHILLIPS of Andover in the County of Essex and Commonwealth of Massachusetts Esquire, and the late Honorable JOHN PHILLIPS of Exeter in the County of Rockingham and State of New Hampshire, Esquire, with the pious determination to make 'a humble dedication to their Heavenly Benefactor of the ability, wherewith He had blessed them,' by laying, in the year 1778, in the South Parish in Andover aforesaid, the foundation of a public Academy, for the instruction of youth, not only in the learned Languages and in various useful Arts and Sciences, but principally for the promotion of true PIETY and VIRTUE;—it having also pleased the INFINITE MIND, at subsequent periods, to excite the said JOHN PHILLIPS, and likewise the late Hon. WILLIAM PHILLIPS of Boston in the County of Suffolk and Commonwealth aforesaid, Esquire, to make liberal provision, not only for 'promoting the virtuous and pious education of indigent youth of genius, and of serious disposition, in said Academy;' but 'more especially for the benefit of charity Scholars of excelling genius, good moral character, hopefully pious, and designed for the great and good work of the gospel ministry, who, having acquired the most useful human literature, may be assisted in the study of Divinity, under the direction of some eminent Calvinistic Minister of the gospel, until such time, as an able, pious, and orthodox Instructor shall be supported in the said Academy, as a Professor of Divinity, by whom they may be taught the important and distinguishing tenets of our HOLY CHRISTIAN RELIGION;'

"In pursuance therefore of the same benevolent and pious

object, and with a desire to devote a part of the substance, with which Heaven has blessed us, to the defence and promotion of the Christian Religion, by making some provision for increasing the number of *learned* and *able* Defenders of the gospel of CHRIST, as well as of *orthodox*, *pious*, and *zealous* Ministers of the New Testament; being moved by the same Spirit, which actuated the Founders and Benefactors aforesaid, and influenced, as we hope, by a principle of gratitude to God and benevolence to man; —

"We, PHŒBE PHILLIPS of said Andover, Relict of SAMUEL PHILLIPS Esq., late Lieutenant-Governor of the Commonwealth aforesaid, and JOHN PHILLIPS, son of the said SAMUEL PHILLIPS and PHŒBE PHILLIPS do hereby jointly and severally obligate ourselves to erect and finish, with all convenient despatch, two separate buildings; one of which to be three stories high, and of such other dimensions as to furnish convenient lodging rooms for fifty Students; and the other building to be two stories high, and of such dimensions as to furnish, in addition to a kitchen and private rooms necessary to a Steward's family, three public rooms, one for a dining Hall, one for a Chapel and Lecture room, (each sufficiently large to accommodate sixty Students) and the third for a Library, the said buildings to be located by direction of the TRUSTEES OF PHILLIPS ACADEMY; — and I, SAMUEL ABBOT of Andover aforesaid, Esquire, with the same views, and in furtherance of the same design, do hereby give, assign, and set over unto the TRUSTEES aforesaid the sum of twenty thousand dollars, in TRUST, as a Fund for the purpose of maintaining a professor of Christian Theology (reserving to myself the right of appointing the first Professor on this Foundation) and for the support and encouragement of Students in Divinity; both the said buildings and the interest or annual income of the said sum of money to be forever appropriated and applied by the TRUSTEES aforesaid for the use and endowment of such a public THEOLOGICAL INSTITUTION in PHILLIPS ACADEMY, as is hereinafter described, and on the following express conditions, namely, that the said INSTITUTION be accepted by the TRUSTEES aforesaid, and that it be forever conducted and governed by them, and their Successors, in conformity to the following general Principles and Regulations, which we unitedly adopt and ratify as the CONSTITUTION of the same, reserving to ourselves, however, during our natural lives the full right, jointly to make any additional Regulations, or to alter any Rule herein prescribed; provided such Regulation or Alteration be not prejudicial to the true design of this Foundation.

" ART. I. This INSTITUTION or SEMINARY shall be equally open to Protestants of every denomination for the admission of young men of requisite qualifications.

" ART. II. Every candidate for admission into this Seminary shall produce satisfactory evidence, that he possesses good natural and acquired talents, has honorably completed a course of liberal education, and sustains a fair moral character. He shall also declare that it is his serious intention to devote himself to the work of the gospel ministry, (unless in certain peculiar cases it appear to the TRUSTEES, or a Committee of their appointment, that the object of this INSTITUTION will be promoted by excusing a pious Applicant from making this declaration) and exhibit proper testimonials of his being in full communion with some Church of CHRIST; in default of which he shall subscribe a declaration of his belief of the Christian Religion.

" ART. III. The Students in this Seminary shall be aided in their preparation for the ministry by able Professors; whose duty it shall be, by *public* and *private* instruction, to unlock the treasures of divine knowledge, to direct the Pupils in their inquiries after sacred truth, to guard them against religious error, and to accelerate their acquisition of heavenly wisdom.

" ART. IV. The *public* instruction shall be given in Lectures on Natural Theology, Sacred Literature, Ecclesiastical History, Christian Theology, and Pulpit Eloquence.

" ART. V. In the Lectures on *Natural Theology*, the existence, attributes, and providence of God, shall be demonstrated; the soul's immortality and a future state, as deducible from the light of nature, discussed; the obligations of man to his Maker, resulting from the divine perfections and his own rational nature, enforced; the great duties of social life, flowing from the mutual relations of man to man, inculcated; and the several personal virtues deduced and delineated; the whole being interspersed with remarks on the coincidence between the dictates of reason and the doctrines of revelation, in these primary points; and notwithstanding such coincidence, the necessity and utility of a divine revelation stated.

"Art. VI. Under the head of *Sacred Literature* shall be included Lectures on the formation, preservation, and transmission of the Sacred Volume; on the languages, in which the Bible was originally written; on the Septuagint version of the old Testament, and on the peculiarities of the language and style of the new Testament, resulting from this version and other causes; on the history, character, use, and authority of the ancient versions and manuscripts of the old and new Testaments; on the canons of biblical criticism; on the authenticity of the several books of the sacred Code; on the apocryphal books of both Testaments; on modern translations of the Bible, more particularly on the history and character of our English version; and also critical Lectures on the various readings and difficult passages in the sacred writings.

"Art. VII. Under the head of *Ecclesiastical History* shall be comprised Lectures on Jewish antiquities; on the origin and extension of the Christian church in the first three centuries; on the various sects and heresies in the early ages of Christianity; on the character and writings of the Fathers; on the establishment of Christianity by Constantine, and its subsequent effects; on the rise and progress of popery and Mohammedanism; on the corruptions of the church of Rome; on the grounds, progress, and doctrines of the reformation;

on the different denominations among Protestants; on the various constitutions, discipline, and rites of worship, which have divided, or may still divide the Christian church; on the state and prevalence of Paganism in our world; and on the effect which idolatry, Mohammedanism, and Christianity have respectively produced on individual and national character.

"ART. VIII. Under the head of *Christian Theology* shall be comprehended Lectures on divine revelation; on the inspiration and truth of the old and new Testaments, as proved by miracles, internal evidence, fulfilment of prophecies, and historic facts; on the great doctrines and duties of our holy Christian Religion, together with the objections made to them by unbelievers, and the refutation of such objections; more particularly on the revealed character of GOD, as Father, Son, and Holy Ghost; on the fall of man and the depravity of human nature; on the covenant of grace; on the character, offices, atonement, and mediation of Jesus Christ; on the character and offices of the Holy Spirit; on the Scripture doctrines of regeneration, justification, and sanctification; on evangelical repentance, faith, and obedience; on the nature and necessity of true virtue or gospel holiness; on the future state, the immortality of soul and body, and the eternity of future rewards and punishments, as revealed in the gospel; on the positive institutions of Christianity; on the nature, interpretation, and use of prophecy; and on personal religion, as a qualification for the ministry; each Lecture under this head to be preceded and followed by prayer.

"ART. IX. Under the head of *Pulpit Eloquence* shall be delivered a competent number of Lectures on the importance of oratory; on the invention and disposition of topics; on the several parts of a regular discourse; on elegance, composition, and dignity in style; on pronunciation, or the proper management of the voice and correct gesture; on the immense importance of a natural manner; on the rules, to be observed in composing a sermon, and on the adaptation of the principles and precepts of ancient rhetoric to this modern species of oration; on the qualities in the speaker, in his style, and in his delivery, necessary to a finished pulpit Orator; on the methods of strengthening the memory, and of improving in sacred eloquence; on the character and style of the most eminent Divines and best models for imitation, their respective beauties and excellences in thought and expression; and above all, on the transcendent simplicity, beauty, and sublimity of the SACRED WRITINGS.

"ART. X. It shall be the duty of the Professors, by *private* instruction and advice, to aid the Students in the acquisition of a radical and adequate knowledge of the sacred Scriptures in their original languages, and of the old Testament in the Septuagint version; to direct their method of studying the Bible and all other writings; to superintend and animate their pursuits by frequent inquiries and examinations, relative to their progress in books and knowledge; to assign proper subjects for their first compositions, and to suggest a natural method of treating them; frequently and critically to examine their early productions, and in a free, but friendly manner, to point out their defects and errors, in grammar, method, reasoning, style, and sentiment; to improve them in the important art of reading, and to give them opportunities of speaking in public, favoring them with their candid remarks on their whole manner; to explain intricate texts of Scripture, referred to them; to solve cases of conscience; to watch over their health and morals with paternal solicitude; and by every prudent and christian method, to promote the growth of true piety in their hearts; to give them friendly advice with relation to their necessary intercourse among men in the various walks of life, and especially with respect to the manner, in which it becomes a minister of the meek and lowly JESUS to address both GOD and man, whether in the assembly of his saints, or in the chamber of sickness and of death.

"Art. XI. Every Professor in this Seminary shall be a Master of Arts, of the Protestant reformed religion, in communion with some Christian Church of the Congregational or Presbyterian denomination, and sustain the character of a sober, honest, learned, and pious man; he shall moreover be a man of sound and orthodox principles in Divinity, according to that form of sound words or system of evangelical doctrines, drawn from the Scriptures, and denominated the Westminster Assembly's shorter Catechism, and more concisely delineated in the Constitution of Phillips Academy.

"Art. XII. Every person, therefore, appointed or elected a Professor in this Seminary, shall on the day of his inauguration into office, and in the presence of the said Trustees, publicly make and subscribe a solemn Declaration of his faith in divine revelation, and in the fundamental and distinguishing doctrines of the gospel of Christ, as summarily expressed in the Westminster Assembly's shorter Catechism; and he shall furthermore solemnly promise, that he will open and explain the Scriptures to his Pupils with integrity and faithfulness; that he will maintain and inculcate the Christian faith, as above expressed, together with all the other doctrines and duties of our holy religion, so far as may appertain to his office, according to the best light God shall give him; and in opposition, not only to Atheists and Infidels, but to Jews, Mohammedans, Arians, Pelagians, Antinomians, Arminians, Socinians, Unitarians, and Universalists, and to all other heresies and errors, ancient or modern, which may be opposed to the gospel of Christ, or hazardous to the souls of men; — that by his instructions, counsels, and example, he will endeavor to promote true Piety and Godliness; that he will consult the good of this Institution and the peace of the churches of our Lord Jesus Christ on all occasions; and that he will religiously observe the Statutes of this Institution, relative to his official duties and deportment, and all such other Statutes and Laws, as shall be constitutionally made by the Trustees of Phillips Academy, not repugnant thereto.

"ART. XIII. The preceding Declaration shall be repeated by every Professor in this Seminary, in the presence of the said TRUSTEES, at the expiration of every successive period of five years; and no man shall be continued a Professor in this INSTITUTION, who shall not continue to approve himself, to the satisfaction of the said TRUSTEES, a man of *sound* and *orthodox* principles in *Divinity*, agreeably to the system of evangelical doctrines contained in the aforesaid Catechism. Accordingly, if at any meeting regularly appointed, it should be proved to the satisfaction of a majority of the whole number of the said TRUSTEES, that any Professor in this INSTITUTION has taught or embraced any of the heresies or errors, alluded to in the Declaration aforesaid; or, should he refuse to repeat the same, as herein required, he shall be forthwith removed from office.

"ART. XIV. Every Professor in this INSTITUTION shall be under the immediate inspection of the said TRUSTEES; and by them removed, agreeably to the will of his Founder, for gross neglect of duty, scandalous immorality, mental incapacity, or any just and sufficient cause.

"ART. XV. Whenever a Professor in this Seminary shall be removed by death or otherwise; the said TRUSTEES shall elect a Successor within twelve months.

"ART. XVI. The TRUSTEES aforesaid, in conformity to the Statutes of every Founder, shall assign to the Professors in this Seminary their respective departments of instruction, the times for reading their lectures, and their several public and private duties, in such manner, as, after consultation with the said Professors, shall to the said TRUSTEES appear most convenient and useful; provided, however, that the course of lectures in each department be always completed within the space of three years.

"ART. XVII. The necessary expenses of indigent Students at this Seminary, for board, lodging, washing, fuel, and light, will be defrayed out of funds, appropriated to this purpose, agreeably to the Regulations, in such case provided, and as said funds may permit.

" Art. XVIII. No person shall be admitted a Student on the charitable Foundation who is not distinguished by natural abilities, literary acquirements, unblemished morals, and hopeful piety; a certificate of which qualities will be required from known and respectable characters in order to the enjoyment of this charity.

" Art. XIX. To be entitled to the maintenance aforesaid, each Student on the charitable Foundation, unless prevented by sickness, must reside at this Seminary eight months at least in each year, regularly attending the exercises aforesaid, as well as diligently prosecuting the studies prescribed, and in all respects conforming to the Rules of this Constitution, and to the Laws and Orders of the said Trustees.

" Art. XX. Whatever may be the number of vacations, the aggregate thereof shall not exceed twelve weeks in any one year; and the constant presence of the Professors and Students will be expected in term time.

" Art. XXI. Every Student in this Seminary shall constantly, punctually, and seriously attend the religious exercises of the chapel morning and evening, and all the public lectures of the several Professors; and, to increase the reverence, due to religious institutions, as well as to give weight to public instruction, it is expected, that the Professors not only frequent the chapel at morning and evening prayers, but that they constantly attend each other's public lectures.

" Art. XXII. Every Student in this Seminary is required to devote so much time to the study of the learned languages, as shall increase his knowledge of them, especially of the Greek and Hebrew languages; to pay due attention to Philology, Rhetoric, and Oratory; to read the best treatises on natural and revealed Religion, and on the fundamental doctrines of the Gospel; to make himself master of the principal arguments and evidences of the truth of Christianity; to pay due attention to ecclesiastical History, and to the canons of biblical Criticism. But above all, it is required, that he make the BIBLE the object of his most attentive, diligent, and prayerful study.

"ART. XXIII. It will be the duty of the Professors in this Seminary to prepare a list of such books, and to point out such a course of study, as in their opinion may be the most congenial to the true design of this Institution, and most beneficial to the Students in it; which list of books and course of study, being approved by said TRUSTEES, said Students shall pursue; they shall also frequently ask the advice and assistance of the Professors with reference to their studies; and often submit their theological compositions, especially their first essays, to the friendly inspection and faithful remarks of one or more of the said Professors.

"ART. XXIV. Each Student, once at least in every year, shall acquaint the Professors with the books he has read, and with his course of study during said year; and shall also be examined in the original languages of the Old and New Testament, and in the Septuagint version of the former; also with reference to the leading sentiments and arguments of the principal authors he has perused; but especially with respect to the style, character, and design of those sacred writers, which agreeably to direction he has particularly studied.

"ART. XXV. If upon due and impartial examination it be found, that any Student on the charitable Foundation aforesaid, has not made reasonable proficiency in the studies prescribed him, he shall be continued thereon no longer; and, if any Student whatever in this Seminary shall be guilty of any gross immorality, or of any insult or oppugnation to the said TRUSTEES, or to any Professor or Officer of this Seminary, he shall be cut off from all the advantages and benefits of this INSTITUTION, unless he make reasonable and immediate satisfaction for his offence.

"ART. XXVI. Whenever a Student shall have honorably finished his term and course of study under the direction of the Professors, and such Student shall request it; a Certificate, signed by the Professors, specifying how long such Student has studied under the direction, and attended the lectures of the Professors, that he has prosecuted his studies with diligence, and sustained a good moral character, shall be given him; provided always, that his conduct, and proficiency in theological knowledge be such, as to merit the same.

"ART. XXVII. After the expiration of the first three years from the opening of this INSTITUTION, it will be required of all persons, who may wish to enjoy the advantages of the same, that they statedly reside at the Seminary three full years, vacations excepted; a period scarcely sufficient for acquiring that fund of knowledge, which is necessary for a minister of the gospel. No Student, therefore, after the expiration of the first three years of the INSTITUTION, shall be entitled to the Certificate aforesaid; nor can any one leave the Seminary in an honorable manner, within the term of three years of such residence, except by permission, specially obtained of the TRUSTEES, in case of necessity.

"ART. XXVIII. Every morning and evening, during the term time, religious exercises shall be performed in the chapel, and these exercises shall usually be, as follows. The divine assistance and blessing shall be first implored in a short prayer; a devotional chapter or psalm shall then be read, accompanied with pious and practical reflections; or, instead of this, once at least in every week, an exposition shall be given upon some deeply interesting passage of scripture; to this shall succeed a piece of genuine psalmody; and the services be concluded by an appropriate prayer. In these exercises the Professors shall preside, and ordinarily officiate; but Students of two years standing may occasionally perform them in whole or in part, according to the desire and direction of the Professors. Moreover as soon as circumstances will permit, a regular Church will be formed in this Seminary, consisting chiefly of the Professors, Students, and families, connected with this Seminary and PHILLIPS Academy; after which, if not before, divine services will be publicly celebrated in the chapel of the Seminary, in the forenoon and afternoon of every Lord's day during term time. These services shall be usually performed by the Professors; but sometimes by such senior Students as may have obtained permission of the Professors to preach occasionally; and they shall be attended by all the Students of this INSTITUTION, and by as many of the families of the Professors and Officers, connected with it, or with PHILLIPS Academy, as may wish for this privilege, and by as many pupils of said Academy as may be deemed expedient by the TRUSTEES aforesaid.

"ART. XXIX. The senior Students will be required, not only to prepare sermons, but occasionally to deliver them in public, both in the Seminary and in neighboring congregations, as may be judged expedient by the said Professors. No Student, however, shall presume to preach, before, upon thorough examination of his qualifications and motives for preaching, he shall have obtained a written permission therefor, subscribed by the Professors, or a major part of them. This permission, however, is never to supersede the customary approbation or license of some regular Association or Presbytery.

"ART. XXX. Sacred Music, and especially Psalmody, being an important part of public, social worship; and as it is proper for those, who are to preside in the assemblies of God's people, to possess themselves of so much skill and taste in this sublime art, as at least to distinguish between those solemn movements, which are congenial to pious minds, and those unhallowed, trifling, medley pieces which chill devotion; it is expected that serious attention will be paid to the culture of a true taste for genuine Church Music in this Seminary; and that all Students therein, who have tolerable voices, will be duly instructed in the theory and practice of this celestial art; and whenever it shall be in the power of either of the said Professors, it shall accordingly be his duty to afford this necessary instruction; and whenever this shall not be the case, it is expected that an Instructor will be procured for this purpose.

"ART. XXXI. All Professors, Officers, and Students in this Seminary, and all other persons employed in its service, together with the Lands, Buildings, Library, Funds, and all other Property, thereto belonging, shall be under the immediate inspection and government of the TRUSTEES aforesaid; and be regulated and managed by them in strict conformity to this Constitution, and to the *Statutes* and *Will* of every FOUNDER of a *Professorship* or *Benefactor* of this INSTITUTION. And the said TRUSTEES are hereby authorized and empowered to make such additional Regulations (not inconsistent with the Regulations established in this *Constitution*, nor with the *Statutes* or *Will* of any *Founder* or *Donor*, nor with the object of this Institution, nor in any degree avoiding them, or either of them), as they in their wisdom shall deem necessary to give the fullest efficacy to these provisions, or to the consistent provisions of future BENEFACTORS; whether such Regulations may relate to the conduct of the Professors, the government of the Students, their various duties and exercises, their lodgings and diet, the prevention and punishment of offences, the preservation of health, the promotion of order, peace, and harmony, to the safety of the Buildings, or to the security of the Funds, which last are to be effectually guarded against all loss and diminution; in a word, to do every thing, under the foregoing limitations, which, upon serious and mature deliberation, may appear to them necessary to secure and promote the true object of this INSTITUTION.

"ART. XXXII. Notwithstanding this Seminary is placed by this Constitution under the immediate care and government of the TRUSTEES of PHILLIPS ACADEMY; it is always to be understood, and it is hereby expressly declared, that every FOUNDER of a Professorship, Scholarship, or any other Living whatever in this INSTITUTION, will have the exclusive right of prescribing the Regulations and Statutes, to be observed by the said TRUSTEES in conducting the concerns of the same, said Regulations and Statutes being always consistent with the principles and object of this INSTITUTION; and also the right, for the term of his life, of appointing in the original deed or grant, such local VISITOR or VISITORS, as he may think proper, and to endow him or them with all visitatorial powers and authorities, necessary to secure and enforce due observance and execution of his said Regulations and Statutes.

"ART. XXXIII. Whereas the necessary business of this Seminary will be sufficient to employ the said TRUSTEES one day at least in every year; they are requested to hold an annual meeting for transacting the same, on such day in each year, as they may appoint; and likewise to meet as much oftener as the good of said Seminary may require; and at each annual meeting to read this Constitution. The rules and modes of doing business at all such meetings shall be the same, *mutatis mutandis*, which are prescribed in the Constitution of PHILLIPS ACADEMY. Decent, not extravagant entertainment shall be made for the TRUSTEES, while attending such meetings; reasonable compensation made to the Treasurer of said Academy for his services; and other necessary expenses of this INSTITUTION defrayed out of the income of its Funds. It is also particularly requested, that all the transactions of the said TRUSTEES, relative to the said THEOLOGICAL INSTITUTION, be recorded in a distinct book; and likewise that all property given, devised, or bequeathed for the support of this Seminary, be separated and for ever kept distinct from all other property, to the TRUSTEES aforesaid in any way or for any other purpose intrusted, being never blended therewith, in any part or degree, by loan or purchase; and that the said Treasurer accordingly keep all his accounts and entries, relative to these Funds, in distinct books; and all moneys, evidences of property, receipts, papers, and books of account, appertaining to this INSTITUTION, in a separate trunk or chest, prepared for prompt removal on any emergence; and that the accounts of said Treasurer be annually audited by a Committee, for this purpose appointed, who shall report to the said TRUSTEES in writing.

"ART. XXXIV. Confiding in the wisdom and fidelity of

the said TRUSTEES and their Successors in office, and with the pleasing hope and expectation, that they will religiously appropriate the aforesaid Buildings, and the income of the aforesaid Fund, and of all future Donations for the same pious purpose, to the great object of supporting a Theological Seminary, such as herein contemplated and described, agreeably to the Principles and Regulations contained in this Constitution; we do now under GOD cheerfully commit this our Foundation to their pious and watchful care; trusting that no exertion on their part will be wanting to the success of an INSTITUTION, so intimately connected with the glory of GOD, the advancement of the Redeemer's kingdom, and the salvation of their fellow-men.

"But, while we thus express our conviction of the necessity and utility of this INSTITUTION, it is our earnest prayer, that our own minds, and the minds of the TRUSTEES, Professors, Students, and all connected therewith, may be ever penetrated by a deep sense of the necessity of the DIVINE direction, influence, and blessing, to render even the wisest provisions and the best human instructions ultimately successful.

"To the SPIRIT of truth, to the Divine AUTHOR of our faith, to the only Wise GOD, we desire in sincerity to present this our humble offering; devoutly imploring the FATHER of lights, richly to endue with wisdom from above all his servants, the TRUSTEES of this SEMINARY; and with spiritual understanding the Professors therein; that, being illuminated by the HOLY SPIRIT, their doctrine may drop as the rain, and their speech distil, as the dew; and that their Pupils may become trees of renown in the courts of our GOD, whereby HE may be glorified.

"In witness whereof we, the Subscribers, have hereunto set our hands and seals this thirty-first day of August in the year of our LORD one thousand eight hundred and seven.

"Signed, sealed, and delivered in presence of

"SAMUEL STEARNS,
"JOSEPH PHELPS,
"AMOS BLANCHARD.

PHŒBE PHILLIPS, (S.)
JOHN PHILLIPS, Jun. (S.)
SAMUEL ABBOT. (S.)"

The Foundation of the Theological Seminary originating in the Phillips family, in connection with the Academy, as set forth in the preceding Constitution, was, after the lapse of a few months, enlarged by a union with the Associate Founders, Messrs. Bartlet, Brown, and Norris, on the basis of the Associate Statutes, and of additional Statutes by Madam Phillips and son, and Mr. Abbot; in both of which, provision was made for a Board of Visitors to act with the Board of Trustees, and a more full and elaborate Creed was prescribed. This Creed we here give, as adjusted to the original Constitution in these additional Statutes. After a brief preamble, the Founders say: —

"Having provided in the twelfth Article of our said Constitution, that 'every person, appointed or elected a Professor in the said Seminary, shall, on the day of his inauguration into office, publicly make and subscribe a Declaration of his faith in Divine Revelation, and in the fundamental and distinguishing doctrines of the Gospel of Christ, as summarily expressed in the Westminster Assembly's Shorter Catechism:' We now ordain the following addition, to be inserted in said Article, in connection with the said clause, namely, 'and as more particularly expressed in the following Creed, to wit,

"'I believe that there is one and but one living and true God; that the word of God, contained in the Scriptures of the Old and New Testament, is the only perfect rule of faith and practice; that agreeably to those Scriptures GOD is a Spirit infinite, eternal, and unchangeable in his being, wisdom, power, holiness, justice, goodness, and truth; that in the Godhead are three Persons, the FATHER, the SON, and the HOLY GHOST; and that these THREE are ONE GOD, the same in substance, equal in power and glory; that GOD created man after his own image, in knowledge, righteousness, and holiness; that the glory of GOD is man's chief end, and the enjoyment of GOD his supreme happiness; that this enjoyment is derived solely from conformity of heart to the moral character and will of GOD; that ADAM, the federal head and representative of the human race, was placed in a state of probation, and that, in consequence of his disobedience, all his descendants were constituted sinners; that by nature every man is personally depraved, destitute of holiness, unlike and opposed to GOD; and that, previously to the renewing agency of the DIVINE SPIRIT, all his moral actions are adverse to the character and glory of GOD; that, being morally incapable of recovering the image of his CREATOR, which was lost in ADAM, every man is justly exposed to eternal damnation; so that, except a man be born again, he cannot see the kingdom of GOD; that GOD, of his mere good pleasure, from all eternity, elected some to everlasting life, and that he entered into a covenant of grace, to deliver them out of this state of sin and misery by a REDEEMER; that the only REDEEMER of the elect is the eternal SON of GOD, who for this purpose became man, and continues to be GOD and man in two distinct natures and one person forever; that CHRIST, as our Redeemer, executeth the office of a Prophet, Priest, and King; that, agreeably to the covenant of redemption, the SON of GOD, and he alone, by his sufferings and death, has made atonement for the sins of all men; that repentance, faith, and holiness are the personal requisites in the Gospel scheme of salvation; that the righteousness of CHRIST is the only ground of a sinner's justification; that this righteousness is received through faith; and that this faith is the gift of GOD; so that our salvation is wholly of grace; that no means whatever can change the heart of a sinner and make it holy; that regeneration and sanctification are effects of the creating and renewing agency of the HOLY SPIRIT, and that supreme love to GOD constitutes the essential difference between saints and sinners; that by convincing us of our sin and misery, enlightening our minds, working faith in us, and renewing our wills, the HOLY SPIRIT makes us partakers of the benefits of redemption; and that the ordinary means, by which these benefits are communicated to us, are the word, sacraments, and prayer; that repentence unto life, faith to feed upon Christ, love to God, and new obedience, are the appropriate qualifications for the Lord's Supper; and that a Christian Church ought to admit no person to its holy communion, before he exhibit credible evidence of his godly sincerity; that perseverance in holiness is the only method of making our calling and election sure; and that the final perseverance of saints, though it is the effect of the special open operation of God on their hearts, yet necessarily implies their own watchful diligence; that they, who are effectually called, do in this life partake of justification, adoption, and sanctification, and the several benefits, which do either accompany or flow from them; that the souls of believers are at their death made perfect in holiness, and do immediately pass into glory; that their bodies, being still united to Christ, will at the resurrection be raised up to glory, and that the saints will be made perfectly blessed in the full enjoyment of God to all eternity; but that the wicked will awake to shame and everlasting contempt, and with devils be plunged into the lake that burneth with fire and brimstone forever and ever. I moreover believe that God, according to the counsel of his own will, and for his own glory, hath foreordained whatsoever comes to pass, and that all beings, actions, and events, both in the natural and moral world, are under his providential direction; that God's decrees perfectly consist with human liberty; God's universal agency with the agency of man; and man's dependence with his accountability; that man has understanding and corporeal strength to do all that God requires of him; so that nothing but the sinner's aversion to holiness, prevents his salvation; that it is the prerogative of God to bring good out of evil, and that he will cause the wrath and rage of wicked men and devils to praise Him; and that all the evil which has existed, and will forever exist in the moral system, will eventually be made to promote a most important purpose under the wise and perfect administration of that Almighty Being, who will cause all things to work for his own glory, and thus fulfil all his pleasure.' "

In pursuance of the stipulations embodied in this Constitution, buildings were promptly erected, larger even than was contemplated at first, and in September, 1808, the Institution was in due form opened for the reception of students. After the sale of the mansion-house to the Trustees, Madam Phillips removed to the house of Samuel Farrar, Esquire, then recently erected; where in full view of the noble work upon which she had concentrated her gifts and prayers, she passed the evening of her life, and finally rested from her labors, October 31, 1812, in the seventieth year of her age.

It deserves to be here added, as a fact of special interest, that the family tie of blood and sympathy which through her and her son linked the later as well as the earlier Institution with the name of Phillips as *one* ever more in their aims and destiny, has been still further strengthened by the congenial efforts of other distinguished donors of the same genealogy.

Lieutenant-Governor William Phillips, of Boston, who was the honored President of the Board of Trustees for many years, added to his earnest counsels and prayers for the Seminary, as mentioned in the text, his frequent gifts while he lived, and his legacy for the library and for the aid of indigent students at his death.

Samuel Abbot, Esquire, of Andover, who united with Madam Phillips and her son, in the founding of the Seminary, by endowing the Abbot Professorship of Christian Theology, was a *grandson* of Samuel Phillips, Esquire, the goldsmith at Salem.[1]

The wife of Moses Brown, Esquire, of Newburyport, the founder of the Brown Professorship of Ecclesiastical History, was a great-grand-daughter of the Salem goldsmith also,[2] and the Seminary is not only largely indebted to her munificent husband, but to her own benefactions, and especially to the liberality of her granddaughter, Mrs. Sarah W. Hale, widow of Ebenezer Hale, M. D., who a few years since

[1] Bond, Gen. and Hist. of Watertown, 902. [2] Ibid.

added to the original endowment of the Brown Professorship a donation of four thousand dollars to provide a house for the Professor.

Mrs. Sarah Abbot, also, (widow of Mr. Nehemiah Abbot,) who was the chief founder of our Abbot Female Academy, as well as a zealous friend of the Seminary, was a great-great-granddaughter of the same Mr. Phillips at Salem.[1]

[1] Bond, Gen. and Hist. of Watertown, 888.

www.ingramcontent.com/pod-product-compliance
Lightning Source LLC
LaVergne TN
LVHW020108110826
845151LV00001B/93
* 9 7 8 1 4 2 5 5 4 5 0 9 3 *